THE INCARNATIONAL *ART* OF

FLANNERY O'CONNOR

THE INCARNATIONAL *ART* OF FLANNERY O'CONNOR

Christina Bieber Lake

Mercer University Press
Macon, Georgia
25th Anniversary

ISBN 0-86554-943-5
MUP/H680

First Edition.

Library of Congress Cataloging-in-Publication Data

Lake, Christina Bieber.
The incarnational art of Flannery O'Connor / Christina Bieber Lake.--
1st ed.
p. cm.
Includes bibliographical references and index.
ISBN 0-86554-943-5 (alk. paper)
1. O'Connor, Flannery—Criticism and interpretation. 2. Christianity
and literature--United States--History—20th century. 3. Art and
literature—United States—History—20th century. 4. Body, Human,
in literature. 5. Artists in literature. I. Title.
PS3565.C57Z74 2004
813'.54—dc22
2004025895

To Lisa and Steve

CONTENTS

ACKNOWLEDGMENTS

It is impossible to imagine completing a project like this one without help. My deepest gratitude goes to my friend and mentor Elizabeth Fox-Genovese, whose insights made the book stronger and whose encouragement helped me resist the temptation to despair that eventually comes to anyone who cares to do this kind of work.

I would also like to thank Nancy Bray and the staff at the Ina Dillard Russell library at Georgia College, where I spent many an afternoon, and Bill Sessions, who generously shared with me his memories of a woman I never had the chance to meet. I am especially grateful to Marc Jolley and the staff at Mercer University Press for helping me prepare and publish this book.

Many faculty members and students at Wheaton College have provided assistance and encouragement along the way, particularly Jill Baumgaertner, Jeffry Davis, Daniel and Adriel Driver, and Sara Knox. I am blessed with many friends who have proven to be invaluable readers and sounding boards, including Michelle Brady, Jason and Kristin Constantine, Stephen and Tina Master, and Tim McIntosh.

Finally, it is clear to me that I would not have been able to start this work without the support of my friend Lisa Phillips, nor enjoy its completion without the love of my husband Steve. Thank you both for keeping me balanced and whole.

ABBREVIATIONS

Abbreviations of works frequently cited in the text refer to the following editions:

CW *Collected Works*. Edited by Sally Fitzgerald. New York: Library of America, 1988.

HB *The Habit of Being: Letters of Flannery O'Connor*. Edited by Sally Fitzgerald. New York: Farrar, Straus and Giroux, 1979.

MM *Mystery and Manners: Occasional Prose*. Edited by Sally Fitzgerald and Robert Fitzgerald. New York: Farrar, Straus and Giroux, 1969.

RB *Flannery O'Connor's Library: Resources of Being*. Arthur F. Kinney. Athens: University of Georgia Press, 1985.

All Bible references are from the Douay-Rheims version unless otherwise indicated.

Prologue

The Incarnational Art of Fiction

> When people have told me that because I am a Catholic, I cannot be
> an artist, I have had to reply, ruefully, that because I am a Catholic I
> cannot afford to be less than an artist.
>
> —*CW*, 808–809

> The hint half guessed, the gift half understood, is Incarnation.
> —T. S. Eliot, *The Four Quartets*

A month before turning twenty-four, Flannery O'Connor was well on
her way to earning a permanent place in American literature. Seeking
to publish her first novel *Wise Blood*, she wrote a letter to John Selby
of Rinehart & Company to tell him she would not implement the
changes to the novel that he demanded. She even claimed that what
he most wanted to change was precisely what she most wanted to
keep.

> I feel that whatever virtues the novel may have are very much
> connected with the limitations you mention. I am not writing a
> conventional novel, and I think that the quality of the novel I write will
> derive precisely from the peculiarity or aloneness, if you will, of the
> experience I write from…in short, I am amenable to criticism but only
> within the sphere of what I am trying to do; I will not be persuaded to
> do otherwise. The finished book, though I hope less angular, will be just

as odd if not odder than the nine chapters you have now. The question is: is Rinehart interested in publishing this kind of novel? (*CW*, 881)

Peculiar. Alone. Odd. These are the self-descriptions of the prophet who will speak her vision without fear because she already knows she will be misunderstood. She will speak because she feels she must. And to be heard at all—since this particular prophet happens to be an artist—she must create something of unarguably high quality. It must be enduring, it must follow its own logic, and it must stand-alone. At age twenty-four, Flannery O'Connor was already completely committed to the task. Because she was a devout Catholic writing for a non-Catholic audience, she expected that audience to be hostile. "The Catholic who does not write for a limited circle of fellow Catholics will in all probability consider that, since this is his vision, he is writing for a hostile audience, and he will be more than ever concerned to have his work stand on its own feet and be complete and self-sufficient and impregnable in its own right" (*CW*, 808).

By describing the work of art as one might describe a fortress, O'Connor revealed that she both desired and expected to produce work that would offend. She did not want anyone to be able to dilute the difference between her vision and the pseudo-religious convictions of most Americans. Her vision was that of a believing Christian, where "belief" could not be interchanged with "taste," as if one could accept or reject Jesus Christ as one might accept or reject a chocolate dessert. O'Connor was clear on the point: genuine Christian belief has largely vaporized in America, even inside the church. While many religious Americans profess Christ, few genuinely inhabit that belief. Instead of standing with the historical church as a radically distinct community, Christians have lost their character as a group who actually believe in the physical birth, death, and resurrection of Christ. O'Connor would have agreed with the thesis of Harold Bloom's *The American Religion*: "There are indeed millions of Christians in the United States, but most Americans who think that they are Christians are truly something else, intensely religious but devout in the American Religion, a faith that is old among us, and that comes in many guises and disguises, and that overdetermines much of our national life."[1] The American Religion is not historical Christianity but an ancient Gnosticism that American religious genius continuously reinvents. Characterized by a dualism that elevates the spirit and distrusts the body, this religion consists of individuals who seek freedom from "society, temporality, and the other." Its adherents have full confidence that they possess the Absolute Truth. None feel any real need for the authority or the tradition of the church.

Unlike O'Connor, Bloom believes that however adverse the social and political consequences of the American Religion may be, in its fullest formulation it is an "imaginative triumph."[2] A self-proclaimed Gnostic Jew, Bloom is best known for promoting a neo-romantic theory of the imagination wherein the young poet, the ephebe, anxiously works to escape the influence of the older generation of poets to carve out a place for his own original work.[3] The poet is the perfect prophet of the American Religion; he is an energetic Prometheus who struggles to free his imagination to make new worlds, to steal fire from the gods, and to escape their attempt to imprison his soul in a determined hell. In so doing, he becomes a god himself. Ralph Waldo Emerson is America's finest Promethean priest. He snatched the flame when he championed self-reliance and defined poets as "liberating gods" who are "free, and make free."[4] The same flame burned in the work of Wallace Stevens, who declared that poetry had replaced belief and that the poet is a "happy creature—It is he that invented the Gods. It is he that put into their mouths the only words they have ever spoken."[5] Bloom celebrates the spirit of the modern age, man's imaginative spirit, which is

[1] Harold Bloom, *The American Religion: The Emergence of the Post-Christian Nation* (New York: Simon & Schuster, 1992) 37.

[2] Ibid., 22.

[3] Harold Bloom, *The Anxiety of Influence; a Theory of Poetry* (New York: Oxford University Press, 1973).

[4] Ralph Waldo Emerson, *Selected Essays*, ed. Larzer Ziff (New York: Penguin, 1982) 277.

[5] Wallace Stevens, *Opus Posthumous*, ed. Milton J. Bates (New York: Vintage, 1990) 193. Stevens also wrote that "the poet is a god or The young poet is a god. The old poet is a tramp" (198). This is a pithy statement of Bloom's theory of the anxiety of influence.

destined to escape its prisons, hover over the world's chaos, and speak itself into being.

What excites Bloom dismayed O'Connor. The Gnostic belief that an individual's soul existed before time, "fell" into matter, and now struggles to transcend it is the problem with twentieth-century American Christianity, intellectual life, and art—it is not a triumph. O'Connor blamed part of the problem on the excesses of the Protestant reformation, which, in its American manifestations, tended to substitute words for presence, text for body. The "Protestant temper," she wrote, is to approach "the spiritual directly instead of through matter" (*HB*, 304). As Protestantism degenerated into modern liberal Protestantism, it moved to "turn religion into poetry and therapy, to make truth vaguer and vaguer and more and more relative, to banish intellectual distinctions, to depend on feeling instead of thought, and gradually to come to believe that God has no power, that he cannot communicate with us, cannot reveal himself to us, indeed has not done so, and that religion is our own sweet invention" (*HB*, 479).

But Protestantism itself is not solely to blame, nor is it the only place where these beliefs are manifest. O'Connor identified the Gnostic strain in Catholicism, although she preferred to call it Manichaeism—an ancient heresy that proposed matter was degraded and needed to be made separate from spirit.[6] "If the average Catholic reader could be tracked down through the swamps of letters-to-the-editor and other places where he momentarily reveals himself, he would be found to be more of a Manichean than the Church permits," she wrote. "By separating nature and grace as much as possible, he has reduced his conception of the supernatural to pious cliché and has become able to recognize nature in literature in only two forms, the sentimental and the obscene" (*CW*, 809).

---

[6] O'Connor probably preferred this term because it represented Gnostic thinking in its most severe and insidious form. The Manichees believed that each human birth created a further dispersal of the original unity of "good" into matter that is "evil." This doctrine is the obverse of the Catholic doctrine of creation.

O'Connor's concerted effort to defy the Gnostic tendencies in American thought defines her both as a religious thinker and as an artist. To that battle O'Connor consistently brought the one fact she believed could change everything: the Incarnation of Christ. Because Gnosticism believes matter to be evil, it spiritualizes the Incarnation so that its meaning for humanity trumps the event as part of actual human history. For example, Emerson in his divinity school address argued that historical Christianity was "defective" because it failed to understand that Jesus merely represents the capacity of man's spirit. Historical Christianity, Emerson held, "dwells with noxious exaggeration about the *person* of Jesus. The soul knows no persons."[7] Emerson insisted that Christ as a historical figure only gets in the way of spiritual growth and that Americans should follow his example of genius, not worship his person. Because Christ as a historical figure is not the issue, Emerson decreed, we should also discard all primitive remnants of his remembrance—the physical elements in the Eucharist. Thus Emerson refused to use them. One could say Emerson's response is Protestantism *in extremis*: Christ cannot be found in the elements, and the elements serve only to limit the power of the human religious imagination.

While Bloom interprets Emerson's move as a triumph, O'Connor saw it as anathema. By now her response to Emerson's idea is legendary. In "Novelist and Believer" she wrote that "when Emerson decided, in 1832, that he could no longer celebrate the Lord's Supper unless the bread and wine were removed, an important step in the vaporization of religion in America was taken, and the spirit of that step has continued apace. When the physical fact is separated from the spiritual reality, the dissolution of belief is eventually inevitable" (*MM*, 161–62). O'Connor held to the doctrine of transubstantiation because she saw its loss as a step down the slippery slope toward the dissolution of belief in the Incarnation, the Resurrection, and the Ascension as historical facts. In another legendary letter she wrote to Elizabeth Hester ("A"), O'Connor described a dinner she had with Mary McCarthy five or six years

[7] Emerson, *Selected Essays,* 114.

prior. She labeled McCarthy as "a Big Intellectual" who told the dinner party that she had come to think of the Eucharist as a "pretty good" symbol. O'Connor reported, "I then said, in a very shaky voice, 'Well, if it's a symbol, to hell with it.' That was all the defense I was capable of but I realize now that this is all I will ever be able to say about it, outside of a story, except that it is the center of existence for me; all the rest of life is expendable" (*HB*, 125).

O'Connor believed the country at mid-century to be completely lost in what Roger Lundin has called a "culture of interpretation," where shared belief in an external reality—seen in tradition, community, and the notion of authority—had been completely supplanted by individual, internal conviction.[8] Emerson's argument was a definitive step in the erosion of the conditions necessary for Americans to come to genuinely redemptive faith in a God that is not the self. With churches weakened into Gnostic spiritual centers, the public naturally becomes less inclined to consider the Incarnation as a historical reality that has any claims on them beyond what the triumphant self desires, or to think of the church as an authority given by God instead of invented by human minds.

O'Connor established herself and her fiction against this erosion. She defined herself as a Christian realist who stood in defiance of all fantasies, whether secular or religious, about the nature of God. In another letter to Hester, O'Connor wrote that "one of the awful things about writing when you are a Christian is that for you the

---

[8] Roger Lundin, *The Culture of Interpretation: Christian Faith and the Postmodern World* (Grand Rapids MI: W. B. Eerdmans, 1993). Lundin's book effectively establishes the continuity between Enlightenment rationality, romanticism, and postmodernism on this issue. He writes, "The romantics had little quarrel with the premises and goals of the Enlightenment project. Like their forebears, the romantic poets and philosophers assumed the validity of the Cartesian and Baconian understanding of the self and its relationship to nature, authority, and tradition. They also took it for granted that the fundamental problems of human life were problems of epistemology, rather than problems of the will. They assumed that truth was the product of the unimpeded interaction of the human subject with nature or of the complex play of the human mind or spirit within itself" (74). When it comes to the description of the nature of the self and God, O'Connor clearly thought of it all as part of the fabric of modernity.

ultimate reality is the Incarnation, the present reality is the Incarnation, and nobody believes in the Incarnation; that is, nobody in your audience. My audience is the people who think God is dead. At least these are the people I am conscious of writing for" (*HB*, 92). Nietzsche pronounced the death of God in the modern world, and O'Connor has his spiritual landscape in mind when she writes, "if you live today, you breathe in nihilism" (*CW*, 949). But we cannot understand the nature of O'Connor's attack on nihilism without understanding which God Nietzsche killed. As Brian Ingraffia argues, because Nietzsche's philosophy assumes Cartesian dualisms that are essentially Gnostic, the God he kills is the one man created—the god of "ontotheology."[9] Nietzsche's virulent attacks on Christianity depend upon his definition of it as "Platonism for the people," or as a religion that devalues the actual world in favor of the spiritual world. This is not the God of historical Christianity, but the God of Feuerbach and Emerson. As Ingraffia explains, "the murder of God means the unmasking of the belief in God as an illusion, the unmasking of religious values as nihilistic. This unmasking is based upon the original presupposition that God is a projection of man."[10] God must be successfully argued into a construction of the human imagination before he can be killed by that same imagination—and all in the name of "reality."

While the philosophers of O'Connor's era worked with Nietzsche's project of trumpeting the death of the God of ontotheology, she built her stories around the God of history. When O'Connor says the "whole reality is the Incarnation," she stands on an event she viewed both as a historical fact with metaphysical implications and as spiritual news that demands personal answerability. Gnosticism hollows out Christianity because it replaces revelation from an outside God with an abstract and interior groping; that is, it replaces God with the self. Christianity amounts to nothing unless the Incarnation actually occurred in space and time. In a letter to Hester in 1955,

---

[9] Brian D. Ingraffia, *Postmodern Theory and Biblical Theology: Vanquishing God's Shadow* (Cambridge & New York: Cambridge University Press, 1995).
[10] Ibid., 48.

O'Connor insisted that the Incarnation does not have to "satisfy emotionally" to be right. "Leaving the Incarnation aside, the very notion of God's existence is not emotionally satisfactory anymore for great numbers of people, which does not mean that God ceases to exist. …the truth does not change according to our ability to stomach it emotionally. A higher paradox confounds emotion as well as reason and there are long periods in the lives of all of us, and of the saints, when the truth as revealed by faith is hideous, emotionally disturbing, downright repulsive" (CW, 952).

While O'Connor was no polemicist, she clearly defined her fiction as a violent attack on the religion of the self, the American Religion.[11] She leveled that attack by always insisting on the Incarnation as a factual reality that lies not *in* the stories, as if inserted artificially, but as a fixed point *outside* of them, upon which everything turns. As she wrote in a letter to Cecil Dawkins:

> I don't really think the standard of judgment, the missing link, you spoke of that you find in my stories emerges from any religion but Christianity, because it concerns specifically Christ and the Incarnation, the fact that there has been a unique intervention in history. It's not a matter in these stories of Do Unto Others. That can be found in any ethical culture series. It is the fact of the Word made flesh. As the Misfit said, "He thrown everything off balance and it's nothing for you to do but follow Him or find some meanness." That is the fulcrum that lifts my particular stories. I'm a Catholic but this is in orthodox Protestantism also, though out of context—which makes it grow into grotesque forms. (HB, 226–27)

To explain how the Incarnation can be a fulcrum to the stories as well as provide their underlying logic is the purpose of this book. Only O'Connor's insistence upon the unique character of the Incarnation can adequately explain the drama of the stories, her aesthetic

---

[11] Ralph Wood explains that O'Connor "deliberately chose, I believe, to concentrate her art on what to her was the prime modern problem: the unprecedented apostasy whereby contemporary man has abandoned faith in anything transcending himself" ("From Fashionable Tolerance to Unfashionable Redemption," in *Modern Critical Views: Flannery O'Connor,* ed. Harold Bloom [New York: Chelsea House Publishers, 1986] 56).

philosophy, and her unique employment of the grotesque.[12] For the Incarnation as fulcrum is not a balancing fulcrum but a *displacing* one, and the displacement is always by means of an actual body. Bodies in O'Connor stories serve always to remind characters and readers of what the Incarnation validates—the inescapable reality of human embodiment. Our bodies' limitations prove that we need a redeemer; Christ's agreement to become flesh proves that the body is redeemable. For unlike Christ, we are created and fallen beings. We share physical embodiment with the animals, and it makes us weak and dependent. If we believe otherwise, we lie to ourselves. And we often do so in order to make the Incarnation irrelevant, to enable us to invent the gods we worship and eventually abandon.

This issue is more than a matter of Christian faith for O'Connor. A dualistic view not only prevents belief in Christ; it also makes the writing of fiction impossible. "The Manicheans separated spirit and matter," O'Connor writes. "To them all material things were evil. They sought pure spirit and tried to approach the infinite directly without any mediation of matter. This is also pretty much the modern spirit, and for the sensibility infected with it, fiction is hard if not impossible to write because fiction is so very much an incarnational art" (*MM*, 68). Taken out of the context of this sentence, the term "incarnational" has been largely misunderstood. O'Connor uses the term in direct opposition to the Gnostic notion of the spirit as good and the flesh as evil. Thus, to mystify the term "incarnational" when we discuss her art is to get it exactly wrong. She did not use the term to argue that fiction somehow competes with Scripture or the sacraments. Fiction, though it should deepen our sense of mystery, is not in and of itself mysterious. Though it follows the definition of sacrament as an outward manifestation of God's grace, it is not in and of itself sacred. It does not work by incantation, mesmerize its readers, touch on eternal verities by way of its own

---

[12] Like the medieval saints she admired, O'Connor not only believed in the historicity of the Incarnation, but she also shared their beliefs in the realities of hell, sin, and the existence of demons. For an excellent treatment of how these realities entered her work, see Richard Giannone, *Flannery O'Connor: Hermit Novelist* (Urbana: University of Illinois Press, 2000).

elegance, or stand in competition to the creation as some kind of second creation. O'Connor was no romantic. Her insistence on the historical reality of the Incarnation separates her aesthetic views even from those of some of the New Critics.[13] The artist does not imitate God in the act of creation; instead, she shows the God of creation through the beauty of the made. This is art as *techne*—that which is made. The distinction was absolutely crucial to O'Connor.

My title for this book, *The Incarnational Art of Flannery O'Connor*, risks the possibility that some readers will dismiss my argument out of hand. The risk is all the greater—and the response understandable—because of the way in which many O'Connor scholars have portrayed the critical landscape. Thus, Sarah Gordon, with good reason, presents the readings of O'Connor as a debate between two distinct perspectives. The more common is the "theological," which is favored by scholars who view O'Connor's style as a strategy for shocking her readers with her message. The other might be called the "aesthetic," and it emphasizes, in Gordon's words, that "O'Connor's art is indeed art, not homiletic."[14] These critics "rescue" O'Connor's fiction from didactic interpreters by treating the fiction as fiction, without regard to her theological concerns. In my judgment, however, to view these two aspects of O'Connor's work as mutually exclusive is to miss its originality and to mistake her purpose.

O'Connor staked everything on her conviction that art as art, story as story, is necessarily theological. She did not consider

---

[13] O'Connor would depart with any New Critic who viewed the idea of myth as a mere ordering principle for art. For O'Connor, the Incarnation as fact provided the theological basis for the whole enterprise of art. Along these lines, Thomas F. Haddox describes the efforts of Allen Tate and Caroline Gordon to steer the agrarian movement toward a more specifically Catholic (and less New Critical) form. While Haddox does not adequately acknowledge the role of the body in his formulation of "incarnational," he is correct to note that "she more properly belongs in Tate and Gordon's paradigm of southern and Catholic literature rather than among the anti-intentionalist and myth-oriented ranks of the New Critics" (Haddox, "Contextualizing Flannery O'Connor: Allen Tate, Caroline Gordon, and the Catholic Turn in Southern Literature," *The Southern Quarterly* 38/1 [1999]: 187).

[14] Sarah Gordon, *Flannery O'Connor: The Obedient Imagination* (Athens: University of Georgia Press, 2000) 34.

art—especially her own—as theological for its purportedly didactic role as justification or explanation of the faith, but because, like life and like God, it is embodied. In this respect the quality of O'Connor's vision that we perceive as harsh more likely results from her desire to be taken seriously as an artist—not as a preacher. We may assuredly disagree with her conception of art, but we should fail as critics if we do not at least acknowledge that conception as something we have never quite seen.

To illustrate O'Connor's vision of fiction as a response to the prevailing Gnosticism in American culture, I rely extensively on her own library—the philosophers and aestheticians she read. These writers, most of them neo-Thomist philosophers from the 1940s and '50s, highlight the importance of our essential embodiment, dependency, and limitations. From them O'Connor learned her narrative of the vaporization of Christianity in the modern world; she also received tools to help her forge (and articulate) an incarnational aesthetic. The argumentation of these mid-century philosophers resembles what we find in their counterparts today, including some feminists. Consequently it will become clear that O'Connor's fiction has a good deal of contemporary purchase. Alasdair MacIntyre would have appealed to O'Connor. MacIntyre builds upon pre-modern sources to argue that Western philosophy, particularly since Descartes, has underestimated the "importance that our bodies are animal bodies" and has "failed to recognize adequately that in this present life it is true of us that we do not merely have, but are our bodies."[15] O'Connor would have encountered this same idea in 1950 in Gabriel Marcel's book *The Mystery of Being*: "My body is *my* body just in so far as I do *not* consider it in this detached fashion, do not put a gap between myself and it. ...my body is mine in so far as for me my body is not an object but, rather, I *am* my body."[16] For MacIntyre, most of the philosophers O'Connor read, true self-

---

[15] Alasdair C. MacIntyre, *Dependent Rational Animals: Why Human Beings Need the Virtues* (Chicago: Open Court, 1999) 6.

[16] Gabriel Marcel, *The Mystery of Being*, vol. 1 (London: Harvill Press, 1950) 100.

discovery depends upon our willingness to tell the truth to ourselves: we are not independent, autonomous minds. We are fallible, limited, and dependent rational animals.[17]

Incarnational art insists on the broken and limited human body as its starting point—the acknowledgment of which is the only means to spiritual growth. O'Connor believed that the only way to give that body a real presence is to make it grotesque. The grotesque for O'Connor, as for Bakhtin, humbles us by reminding us that we are not angels. O'Connor renders the body doubly inescapable—gigantic, deformed, imposing—to illustrate that we cannot escape the body without self-delusion. Bodies function more primally than they do realistically (in the conventional sense of realism). Thus, as we will see, Hazel Motes, Joy/Hulga, and Asbury Fox each have to learn the "primitive" truth that what they do with their bodies does matter. Our embodiment also means that we are dependent upon others both to prosper in community and to see ourselves truthfully.[18] O'Connor's fiction reveals that she believed human beings confronted with the severe limitations of others might be brought, finally, to see their own limitations, disabilities, and dependencies and thereby be opened to revelation. Thus characters such as Francis Tarwater, Tom T.

---

[17] In the opening sections of *Dependent Rational Animals*, MacIntyre confesses that he failed to see how much both Aristotle and Aquinas acknowledged the essential "animality" of humans. He explains the failure by arguing that he received no encouragement from the Western philosophical tradition to take that fact into account: "We human beings are vulnerable to many kinds of affliction and most of us are at some time afflicted by serious ills.... These two related sets of facts, those concerning our vulnerabilities and afflictions and those concerning the extent of our dependence on particular others are so evidently of singular importance that it might seem that no account of the human condition whose authors hoped to achieve credibility could avoid giving them a central place. Yet the history of Western moral philosophy suggests otherwise. From Plato to Moore and since there are usually, with some rare exceptions, only passing references to human vulnerability and affliction and to the connections between them and our dependence on others" (1).

[18] MacIntyre argues that a beginning point might be to see what we have in common with "other intelligent animals." He writes that "in transcending some of their limitations we never separate ourselves entirely from what we share with them. Indeed, our ability to transcend those limitations depends in part upon certain of those animal characteristics, among them the nature of our identity" (*Dependent Rational Animals*, 8).

Shiftlet, and Mrs. Shortley have to learn that they must value the
body of the other, however grotesque, in order to see their own
correctly—as equally grotesque. As we shall see from a look at
Bakhtin's early work, the artist succeeds by rendering that grotesque
body and loving it through aesthetic attention.[19] In short, everyone
who encounters O'Connor's fiction is led to contemplate Ruby
Turpin's question: "How am I a hog and me both? How am I saved
and from hell too?" (*CW*, 652). It is the prodigal son's question. It is
every would-be Christian's question. Ultimately O'Connor hoped her
readers, like Ruby Turpin, would be led to see our own dependent and
disabled state—our own grotesquerie—so that we might also be
displaced from our illusions long enough to hear "the voices of the
souls climbing upward into the starry field and shouting hallelujah"
(*CW*, 654).

---

[19] This study thus draws primarily upon Bakhtin's ideas in these published
volumes: M. M. Bakhtin, *Art and Answerability: Early Philosophical Essays,* ed.
Michael Holquist and Vadim Liapunov, trans. Vadim Liapunov (Austin: University
of Texas Press, 1990); and M. M. Bakhtin, *Toward a Philosophy of the Act*, ed.
Michael Holquist and Vadim Liapunov, trans. Kenneth Brostrom (Austin: University
of Texas Press, 1993). For a treatment of O'Connor's fiction with regard to Bakhtin's
notion of dialogism in the novel, see Robert H. Brinkmeyer Jr., *The Art & Vision of
Flannery O'Connor* (Baton Rouge: Louisiana State University Press, 1989).

Chapter 1

"Who will Remain Whole? Who?"

Ideal Christianity doesn't exist, because anything the human being touches, even Christian truth, he deforms slightly in his own image. Even the saints do this. —CW, 1182

Many casual readers of Flannery O'Connor, especially those whose familiarity with her work begins and ends with "A Good Man Is Hard to Find," associate her with a morbid imagination and an uncanny ease in killing off characters. When I was conducting research in the Ina Dillard Russell Library at Georgia College in Milledgeville, I stayed at a lovely bed and breakfast a couple of blocks away called "Mara's Tara." One morning I conversed with another guest, a young woman who had just moved to Georgia from the North. She told me she had recently started to read O'Connor because she wanted to be familiar with local writers. "I was reading the story about the grandmother," she said, "and was so shocked that the family was murdered. I kept thinking about my own children. I just couldn't read it anymore." I confess that I went into English teacher mode. I tried to remind her of what the Misfit said and of how O'Connor once insisted that "in this story you should be on the lookout for such things as the action of grace in the Grandmother's soul, and not for the dead bodies" (*MM*, 113). The woman gave me a hard stare and changed the subject.

Readers have always stumbled over the dead bodies in O'Connor's fiction. Concerned about how violence can be squared with a Catholic worldview, critics justify it, downplay it, or argue that it subverts

O'Connor's ultimate purpose for the stories.[1] Regardless of how we read it, it is clear that *she* viewed the violence as necessary. Her letters reveal someone who did not come to bring peace, but a sword; and while words might be her only weapons, the characters bleed enough on the page to prove it. We of the enlightened twenty-first century feel assaulted. Her explanatory logic reads to us like a justification of the crusades—moralistic, totalizing, intolerant. Most of all, we assume that such a violent characterization of her own goals means she intended to preach dogma, not to create art.

Indeed, O'Connor believed her fiction to be an assault. But it might more accurately be described as a preemptive defensive maneuver. She felt herself—or more to the point, her views—to be under attack from every side in the world she inhabited. She saw all true Christian writers as resident aliens who wrote against the cultural current: "I think more and more of what writers with Christian concerns write against," she wrote in a letter in 1956. "I don't mean in a polemical way, I mean maybe the climate they write in" (*HB*, 169). They write against; they push violently. "More than ever now it seems that the kingdom of heaven has to be taken by violence, or not at all. You have to push as hard as the age that pushes against you" (*HB*, 229).

These fighting words baffle contemporary critics who assume Christianity to be America's dominant religion. What is there to "write against"? The answer is not merely "secular culture"; O'Connor found her opposition in the church, too. "If you live today you breathe in nihilism. In or out of the Church, it's the gas you breathe. If I hadn't had the Church to fight it with or to tell me the necessity of fighting it, I would be the stinkingest logical positivist you ever saw right now. With such a current to write against it (the result) almost has to be negative. It does well just to be" (*CW*, 949).

---

[1] For two divergent views on how O'Connor's fiction squares with her Catholicism, see Richard Giannone, *Flannery O'Connor and the Mystery of Love* (Urbana: University of Illinois Press, 1989), and Joanne Halleran McMullen, *Writing Against God: Language as Message in the Literature of Flannery O'Connor* (Macon GA: Mercer University Press, 1996).

One either yields completely to this nihilistic "current," or one violently fights it. There is no other choice.

The current that O'Connor saw pushing against historical Christianity is the prevailing and essentially unchallenged view that science is fact and religion is mere belief. It is a view that the autonomous individual mind can reinvent itself in complete freedom and independence. Most insidious of all, it is a philosophical legacy that Americans are not even aware that they have inherited. A sentence O'Connor underlined in her copy of Alexis de Tocqueville's *Democracy in America* explains it succinctly: "America is therefore one of the countries where the precepts of Descartes are least studied and are best applied" (*RB*, 83). O'Connor's personal library is full of volumes by philosophers who explain the turn Descartes took as the turn that narrowed the definition of reason to exclude revelation and thereby destroyed access to genuine Christian faith. To read what O'Connor read is to find one articulation after another that de Tocqueville prophesied the end of genuine Christianity in America with his statement. Through Etienne Gilson, Jacques Maritain, William Lynch, Teilhard de Chardin, the writers of *Cross Currents*, Baron von Hügel, Romano Guardini, Claude Tresmontant, and many others, O'Connor read a version of intellectual history in which America's spiritual blindness was definitively linked to the Enlightenment. These thinkers blame Descartes, Rousseau, Kant, and Hegel, and after them, romantic and modern artists for perpetuating two essentially Gnostic ideas Americans have made their own: (1) that the imagination can be made pure and free, unfettered by the body and (2) that the self can birth itself in complete freedom and independence from the authority and determination of others. These are fantasies so deeply embedded in American culture that we dream them in and out of the church, equally in the name of God or in the name of enlightened human reason. Whatever the name in which we dream them, they vanquish God by asserting the human self.

As we begin the twenty-first century, this critique is finding new voices, many of them trained philosophers. But O'Connor was no philosopher, and she believed the art of fiction was inherently already a response. Written according to its own laws—laws O'Connor believed followed the method of the Incarnation—fiction violently displaces readers and opens them up to the real. It is therefore a violence that is also an act of love.

THE CARTESIAN MIND

Etienne Gilson, a respected neo-Thomist, was one of O'Connor's favorite philosophers. She read, reviewed, and often recommended his book *The Unity of Philosophical Experience*. In it, Gilson pointedly blames Descartes for leading modern philosophy to its ruin and to the prevention of true spiritual discovery among those seduced by it. Gilson argues that Descartes ignored the possibilities for a Christian synthesis with Aristotelian logic that Aquinas labored for and progressed instead with a more Platonic view of reason and reality. Plato viewed the world of the senses as less real than the world beyond, putting his confidence in the existence of idealized "forms" that can only be reached by reason. His famous allegory of the cave depicts mankind fumbling along in the dark in a world of shadows—the world as we know it—until the philosopher leads us into the light—the true world of the abstract forms.

Gilson explains that Descartes, in his search for certainty that would answer philosophical skepticism, followed Plato's lead and turned to the innate ideas of the mind for that certainty. He concluded his search with the famous *cogito ergo sum* (I think; therefore, I am). In Cartesian dualism, only the mind that has been purified of all contamination by the body or the outside world could be trusted to reason its way to the truth. According to Gilson, the *cogito* necessarily describes "man as angel, or disembodied thinking substance."[2]

Gilson chose the word "angel" deliberately. Part of Descartes's project was to denigrate medieval philosophy and its representative thinker, St. Thomas Aquinas, known as the "angelic doctor." Aquinas wrote about angels in order to emphasize that only celestial beings can possess purified reason; man, being embodied and unable to know all,

---

[2] Etienne Gilson, *The Unity of Philosophical Experience* (London: Sheed and Ward, 1955) 164.

must rely on a combination of reason and revelation. The work of Aquinas was, for Gilson, both an exemplary use of reason and a check against philosophy that might claim to proceed by reason alone. For Aquinas, we must take our embodied nature into account in the process. Embodied reason makes man a "knower"; disembodied reason makes him merely a "thinker." In her copy of the writings of St. Thomas Aquinas, O'Connor underlined the following section of Anton Pegis's introduction:

> Man as a knower must be partly material in order to be adequately a knower. Of course, such a notion is bound to sound scandalous to modern ears. For we are the heirs of generations of philosophic speculations according to which man is a *thinker* and a *mind*. Now it is a fact that the Thomistic man is a knower rather than a thinker, and he is a composite being rather than a mind. In fact, St. Thomas does not even have in his vocabulary a term corresponding to the term thinker: you cannot translate such a term into Thomistic Latin. If we are to judge matters as St. Thomas has done, we are bound to say that the European man became a thinker after he ruined himself as a knower; and we can now even trace the steps of that ruination—from Augustinian Platonism to the nominalistic isolationism of Ockham to the despairing and desperate methodism of Descartes. For what we call the decline of mediaeval philosophy was really a transition from man as a knower to man as a thinker—from man knowing the world of sensible things to man thinking abstract thoughts in separation from existence. What is thinking but dis-existentialized knowing? (*RB*, 71–72).

For all of the neo-Thomists, this move from knower to thinker was a tremendous loss, and what was lost was the role of experience in knowledge. C. S. Lewis describes how the definition of the word "reason" narrowed in the modern world. Aquinas, following Aristotle, defined reason both as *Intellectus* (that which can be "simply seen") and *Ratio* (the process of proving a truth that is not self-evident). But following the lead of Descartes, philosophers defined reason only by the specific process of *Ratio*, as if thought could be divorced from experience altogether.[3] The concept of "mind" or "consciousness" as

---

[3] C. S. Lewis, *The Discarded Image* (Cambridge: Cambridge University Press, 1964) 159.

we understand it today thus insists upon a mind/body dualism that was completely foreign to the ancient and medieval worlds. Richard Rorty's argument is similar to Lewis's on this point. He argues that the intellect for Aristotle was less distanced from the world than it is for the modern. For Aristotle, "it is both mirror and eye in one. The retinal image is *itself* the model for the 'intellect which becomes all things,' whereas in the Cartesian model, the intellect *inspects* entities modeled on retinal images. The substantial forms of frogness and starness get right into the Aristotelian intellect, and are there in just the same way they are in the frogs and the stars—*not* in the way in which frogs and stars are reflected in mirrors."[4]

An essential result of this shift is that in the Cartesian vision, the "Inner Eye" must always doubt and test its representations. Skepticism becomes a matter of the mind, not of the whole person. In contrast, skepticism for the pre-modern world, explains Rorty, "had been a matter of a moral attitude, a style of life, a reaction to the pretensions of the intellectual fashions of the day."[5] What had been a matter of alignment with external verities becomes a matter of internal conviction. Thus is the problem of subjectivity born, what Lewis describes as the "great movement of internalisation" that leads necessarily to the "aggrandisement of man and desiccation of the outer universe."[6] The outer universe is desiccated because the modern mind believes itself separate from it. To be separate from the body and from the universe is to render it completely other, an object for scientific study and mastery. Thus man sees his own mind as he had once thought of God—separate from creation, maintaining an unlimited "god's eye" view. He sees everything and need not be affected by anything. For the thinkers O'Connor read, there is no difference between the belief that one has achieved this "god's eye" view and the belief that one has become God. Etienne Gilson argues that Immanuel Kant, following Descartes's lead, "was beginning to

---

[4] Richard Rorty, *Philosophy and the Mirror of Nature* (Princeton: Princeton University Press, 1979) 45.

[5] Ibid., 46.

[6] Lewis, *Discarded Image,* 42.

suspect that he himself might be God," and he quotes from Kant's notebooks that "God is not a being outside me, but merely a thought in me. God is the morally practical self-legislative reason. Therefore, only a God in me, about me, and over me."[7] And in the story Gilson tells, philosophy continued to move in this manner, faring worse under Kant's disciples. With J. G. Fichte the Ego finds himself limited by the material world, and to free himself from it "the Ego brings forth the world of sense and understanding as a substitute for an otherwise unintelligible reality."[8] While Hegel claimed to rescue reason from Kant's abuses, his faith in man's mind is the same. According to Gilson, Hegel begins with the conclusion that the "truth is the whole," where the whole is really an Idea "which expresses itself in space and time according to a dialectical law."[9] Reason does the work, making everything intelligible according to the Idea, until all contradiction is subsumed under its synthesizing power. Baron von Hügel, another writer O'Connor admired, argues that Ludwig Feuerbach continued the move in especially devastating ways. "Steeped in Hegel," Feuerbach believed that "man essentially consists of mind alone; that this human mind can penetrate and can be penetrated by, can know at all, nothing but itself; that it never grows by, or gains a real knowledge of, realities other than man himself. Man's mind is thus affected by but one reality—that of the species man, mankind, the human race, as distinct from what is simply selfishly particularist in an individual man."[10]

But the medieval mind refused this view of the self. Medieval philosophers defined "reason" much more broadly, as that which engages a "participating consciousness" that is "structured around a merger with nature rather than detachment from nature."[11] As Lewis explains, even the language medieval writers used to describe the

---

[7] Gilson, *Unity of Philosophical Experience*, 243.

[8] Ibid., 245.

[9] Ibid., 249.

[10] Baron Friedrick von Hügel, *Essays and Addresses on the Philosophy of Religion: First Series* (New York: E. P. Dutton, 1928) 32.

[11] Susan Bordo, *The Flight to Objectivity: Essays on Cartesianism and Culture* (Albany: State University of New York Press, 1987) 53.

universe suggests "sympathies, antipathies, and strivings inherent in matter itself." They used such language not to argue that the universe is sentient, but to insist on a "sort of continuity between merely physical events and our most spiritual aspirations."[12] Participation in the world is not only a genuine mode of knowledge—it is the only mode.[13] Most of the thinkers O'Connor read would agree that the Cartesian shift was destructive of the possibilities for real knowledge because, as Gabriel Marcel explains, it substitutes abstract schema for the "richness of experience."[14] Beyond experience, Marcel writes, "there is nothing."[15] Nothing, that is, but a disembodied mind plagued with uncertainty.

The interest of some feminist writers in this shift will be important to my argument later. Susan Bordo's book *The Flight to Objectivity* emphasizes that the medieval world saw the universe, upon which the mind was humbly dependent, as feminine. Thus the Cartesian move to relegate the study of "mother earth" and the body to the objective eye of science (rendering it irrelevant to epistemology and moral inquiry) represents a change Bordo interprets as a "flight from the feminine."[16] Knowledge becomes a bodiless,

---

[12] Lewis, *Discarded Image*, 94.

[13] Susan Bordo quotes Morris Berman that for the medieval thinker "real knowledge occurred only via the union of subject and object, in a psychic-emotional identification with images rather than a purely intellectual examination of concepts" (*Flight to Objectivity*, 53).

[14] Gabriel Marcel, *The Mystery of Being*, vol. 1 (London: Harvill Press, 1950) 94.

[15] Ibid., 45. Etienne Gilson was another important influence on O'Connor on this point. The medieval world, for all its flaws, had a richer sense that particulars in nature cannot be objectified, abstracted, and dismissed. Gilson writes that according to Aquinas "the physical order was essentially made up of 'natures,' that is to say, of active principles, which were the cause of the motions and various operation of their respective matters. In other words, each nature, or form, was essentially an energy, an act" (Gilson, *Unity of Philosophical Experience*, 205–206).

[16] See also Sandra Harding, "From Feminist Empiricism to Feminist Standpoint Epistemologies," in *From Modernism to Postmodernism: An Anthology*, ed. Lawrence E. Cahoone (Cambridge: Blackwell, 1996). Harding reads several feminist scholars who contribute to this point as it relates to the natural sciences. According to Harding, Hilary Rose argues that the distinctiveness of feminist epistemology "is to be found in the way its concepts of the knower, the world to be known, and processes

masculinized project—leaving the female body as particularly representative of that which can only impede progress toward philosophical certainty. To be free from error, the autonomous mind must create a "contrastingly impure realm" that can "absorb or take responsibility for the messy aspects of experience."[17] In philosophy, Bordo argues, "the role of the unclean and impure has been played, variously, by material reality, practical activity, change, the emotions, 'subjectivity,' and most often—as for Descartes—by the *body*."[18] On his way to philosophical certainty, Descartes dismissed the "participating consciousness" notion of medieval philosophy as childish. For Descartes, childhood is a time of animality, sensuality, and mystification of and immersion in the body. It is an age before reason, when nothing is known clearly and distinctly.[19] The enlightened world, having escaped from this childish immersion, could dismiss the body as that which was, in Gilson's words, "without either a mind or a soul. It was a mere machine."[20]

By making the body the locus of the impure, Descartes effectively removed it from playing any role in epistemological activity, including spiritual discovery. Such a move is inevitably Gnostic, for when the mind is celebrated for its god-like ability to see clearly, the body is denigrated for creating confusion. Bordo explains that "while the body is thus likened to a machine, the mind (having been conceptually purified of all material 'contamination') is defined by precisely and only those qualities which the human being shares with God: freedom, will, consciousness. For Descartes there is no ambiguity or complexity here. The body is excluded from all

---

of coming to know reflect the unification of manual, mental, and emotional ('hand, brain, and heart') activity characteristic of women's work more generally. This epistemology not only stands in opposition to the Cartesian dualisms—intellect vs. body, and both vs. feeling and emotion—that underlie Enlightenment and even Marxist visions of science but also grounds the possibility of a 'more complete materialism, a truer knowledge' than that provided by either paternal discourse" (Harding, 618).

[17] Bordo, *Flight to Objectivity*, 76.
[18] Ibid.
[19] Ibid., 57.
[20] Gilson, *Unity of Philosophical Experience*, 175.

participation, all connection with God; the soul alone represents the godliness and the goodness of the human being."[21] To overcome error one must move it to the body and then conquer it by the will.

The Modern Artist and the Illusion of Freedom

With this reasoning it is easy to see how freedom of the self or the human spirit might become humanity's ultimate goal. Since the body is seen as a prison, "the chief if not sole impediment to see clearly and distinctly,"[22] the goal is to escape these limitations. And so the romantic and modern artists, as inheritors of Cartesian beliefs, began to point the way to the faculty that would most guarantee freedom from the body—the imagination. The epistemological shift from pre-modern to modern views of the self generated a revolutionary change in aesthetics, as literary critics have outlined.[23] O'Connor read the story of this change in a number of books, including the book *Philosophies of Beauty*, a volume in her library that provides excerpts from various philosophers on the subject of art. In his short excerpt, G. W. F. Hegel describes how art, when it becomes free of the concrete, takes a step toward absolute spirit, the goal of his project: "Poetry is the universal art of the mind, no longer of mind confined for its self-realization to external sensuous materials, but free to expatiate in the imaginary space and time of its own ideas and feelings. But it is at this very stage that art transcends itself. It sacrifices the reconciliation and union of sensuous things with mind and passes from the poetry of imagination to the prose of thought."[24] When art "expatiates in the imaginary space and time of its own ideas and feelings," it is on its way to Gnostic freedom from the crude, sensuous world. It can be ultimately free.

---

[21] Bordo, *Flight to Objectivity*, 94.

[22] Ibid., 89.

[23] See especially Abrams, *The Mirror and the Lamp* (New York: Norton, 1958), and Lewis, *Discarded Image*.

[24] E. F. Carritt, ed., *Philosophies of Beauty: From Socrates to Robert Bridges, Being the Sources of Aesthetic Theory* (New York: Oxford University Press, 1931) 175.

For Hegel, philosophy is higher than art because of this freedom; as "progress" is made toward absolute knowledge, cruder forms drop away or are altered in their incorporation with each new synthesis into a new whole—Hegelian "Spirit." But for modern artists, there is no higher project than the recreation of the world through the imperial imagination. When James Joyce speaks through the artist Stephen Daedalus that he wants to escape the "nets" of nationality, language, and religion that have been flung at his soul "to hold it back from flight," he illustrates the modern conviction that only the completely autonomous self can be released into creativity.[25] From that utterly free space he will do the work of God, he will "forge in the smithy of [his] soul the uncreated conscience of [his] race."[26] With the artist as the great artificer of the world, there is no need for God, who proves to be only a construct of humanity's imagination anyway. Everything depends upon the creation of a supreme fiction. Art, the highest achievement of the autonomous self, will bring order out of chaos. As Wallace Stevens confidently proclaims, "poetry replaces belief."[27]

These versions of the self, the artist, and art were anathema to Flannery O'Connor. She chose to do battle with modern Gnosticism by redefining art or, more accurately, by returning it to its ancient definition of *techne*—that which is made. She did not use art for polemic; she proclaimed for art and the artist a complete dependence upon the world's body, its rules and laws. Fiction is inherently an incarnational art, working at all times at cross-purposes with the conclusions of the *cogito*. Fiction "re-existentializes" readers. It insists that we have bodies, that we cannot escape being situated in them, and indeed that we need them in order to understand anything. And because fiction is by definition *story* that depends upon what Bakhtin refers to as "being-as-event," it teaches us we are not pure

---

[25] James Joyce, *A Portrait of the Artist as a Young Man* (New York: Penguin, 1991) 206.

[26] Ibid., 253.

[27] See, for example, Wallace Stevens, *Opus Posthumous*. Ed. Milton J. Bates (New York: Vintage, 1990) 202, where Stevens states "God and the imagination are one."

minds that think our way to the truth intellectually, but embodied souls that learn when we recognize revelation. This is the reason why O'Connor's stories clearly uphold a reality so primal, so horrifying, so earthly, and so deeply psychological that many critics have been unable to locate the familiar world in them.[28] They assault us with grotesques because we will render irrelevant and ignore anything less. Above all, they insist that the body and soul of human life is an ineffable mystery that we have tried by science and philosophy and psychology to explain away.

Put another way, the incarnational art of fiction points to the created world because it views that world as supreme, second only to its Creator. It does not try to create the "supreme fiction" that Wallace Stevens's godless universe mandates. In opposition to Stevens's recipe for art—"It Must Be Abstract," "It Must Change," and "It Must Give Pleasure"—O'Connor proposed an entirely different set of ingredients.[29]

IT MUST BE CONCRETE

Catholic theology of the Incarnation relies heavily upon its theology of the creation. According to Genesis, God both made the world and declared it to be good. Though the world fell because of Adam's disobedience, the Incarnation validates God's original declaration, because if God chose to become a real man with real flesh and blood (and not just a symbol in a story or a supernatural angel), then all real flesh and blood of creation must be good at its core, no matter how corrupted it has become. That original goodness makes the corruption

---

[28] Claire Kahane writes that "O'Connor undermines the reader's sense of security, undermines comic elements by making the familiar world strange, by weakening our sense of reality through the distorting lens of an imagery that evokes archaic fears. ...this is an animistic world, fraught with images of infantile fears—of devouring, of penetration, of castration—in which the distinctions between physical and psychical reality blur. The comic vision has yielded to reveal its fearsome, uncanny origins" (Kahane, "Flannery O'Connor's Rage of Vision," in *Critical Essays on Flannery O'Connor*, ed. Melvin J. Friedman and Beverly Lyon Clark [Boston: G.K. Hall & Co., 1985] 123).

[29] See Wallace Stevens, "Notes Toward a Supreme Fiction," in *The Palm at the End of the Mind,* ed. Holly Stevens (New York: Knopf, 1989).

worthy to be redeemed and redeemable. O'Connor believed an artist (particularly the fiction writer) has *by definition* sacramental instincts that are aligned with this kind of reasoning. Because she is used to "penetrating the concrete" with her senses, the artist knows by instinct what the Western world used to know, that this "physical, sensible world is good because it proceeds from a divine source" (*MM*, 157).[30] O'Connor also believed that with this understanding evil comes into sharper focus; it becomes "intelligible as a destructive force and a necessary result of our freedom" (*MM*, 157). Consequently, any artist who does not follow these instincts or begin with these assumptions (even if unconsciously) will operate at cross-purposes with himself. He will actually eliminate the conditions necessary for fiction, because fiction, regardless of its subject matter, insists that penetrating and presenting the concrete is a worthwhile activity. It is remarkably difficult to argue against O'Connor's logic here because the novel would cease to be the novel without its attention to concrete detail. To accept her description of the novelist's goals is also to see why she felt that her incarnational theology led her to the truest of novelistic instincts: the better her theology was, the better writer she would be. The "real novelist, the one with an instinct for what he is about," she wrote, "knows that he cannot approach the infinite directly, that he must penetrate the natural human world as it is. The more sacramental his theology, the more encouragement he will get from it to do just that" (*MM*, 163).

Without a belief in the goodness of the created world, the artist will follow Descartes's lead and exercise an abstracted or "angelic" imagination whereby he tries to escape or transcend any particulars he wishes to change or "tidy up." O'Connor's attack on the angelic imagination places her within a strong and enduring Southern tradition. Allen Tate and John Crowe Ransom both insist on the

---

[30] It is instructive to note that O'Connor's most characteristic example of an artist who understood this fact is Joseph Conrad, who is not generally considered a Christian writer. "When Conrad said that his aim as an artist was to render the highest possible justice to the visible universe, he was speaking with the novelist's surest instinct. The artist penetrates the concrete world in order to find at its depths the image of its source, the image of ultimate reality" (*MM*, 157).

Southerner's post-"fall" (the Civil War) ability to understand that the real cannot be set aside or remade according to one's wishes. Ransom argues that art, relying upon the world of things instead of pure ideas, stands against Plato's theory of the forms: "now the fine Platonic world of ideas fails to coincide with the original world of perception, which is the world populated by the stubborn and contingent objects, and to which as artists we fly in shame."[31] The artist flies to "stubborn and contingent objects" in shame because in doing so he admits that *they* contain the truth—not his own imagination.

This aspect of O'Connor's view of the imagination can be seen in a book she read that few read today: Father William Lynch's *Christ and Apollo.*[32] Lynch applies the method of the Incarnation to the writing of fiction by standing upon the argumentation in Claude Tresmontant's *Study of Hebrew Thought*. With the Incarnation as his focal point, Tresmontant argues in favor of Hebrew thinking, which insists on the body, over Greek thinking (of which Plato is representative), which sees the body as an impediment. Grounded in the particular, Hebrew thought supports no dichotomy between body and soul. Tresmontant argues that Hebrew thought cherishes the elements and the flesh; its logic is "poetic materialism." Although Hebrew thought compares to Greek idealism in its belief that "the sensible world is intelligible, that the world is essentially porous to intelligence because it is created by the word," it is also "irreconcilably opposed to idealism by its realistic metaphysics of being, its love of the carnal, and its conception of work and action in the elements. It is the thought of shepherds and farmers."[33]

Since Greek thought is committed to the abstract, it has little patience for the contingencies and particularities of a faith built out of an ancient, chosen tribe and the historical Jesus whose lineage can be traced back to it. Tresmontant explains how the Greeks consider

---

[31] John Crowe Ransom, *The World's Body* (New York: Charles Scribner's Sons, 1938) 123.

[32] William F. Lynch, S. J., *Christ and Apollo: The Dimensions of the Literary Imagination* (New York: Sheed and Ward, 1960).

[33] Claude Tresmontant, *A Study of Hebrew Thought*, trans. Michael Francis Gibson (New York: Desclee Co., 1960) 47.

the story of the Bible in contrast to the truth they see in human reason:

> From the Greek point of view there are too many particulars in the books of Israel for their contents to be a metaphysics: too many proper names, too much geography, too many dates, and too much history. Too many contingencies: truth is necessary. Too many sensible things: truth is abstract. Too many real people: truth holds no personal preference. Too much geography: truth is beyond space. Too many historical events: truth is beyond time. Too many particulars: truth is universal. Why, they ask, should such a people rather than another, such a man, such a time, such a day and not another, be favored by a choice? All our most deeply ingrained intellectual habits inherited from Greek philosophy are opposed to the idea that truth is to be reached through the existing particular, opposed to this *nativity* of truth, to this manifestation of truth in some particular concrete reality. This method, which is the "method" of the Incarnation, offends the deep, congenital dualism of our minds, a dualism which establishes an essential distinction between the intelligible which belongs to the order of essence, and the existent, the order of fact, which is contingent and absurd.[34]

Concrete, particular, located, contingent, absurd: fiction's method is incarnational. Its laws are the laws of the flesh; know these laws and you will know the spirit that inhabits them. O'Connor wrote to Hester that "for my part I think that when I know what the laws of the flesh and the physical really are, then I will know what God is. We know them as we see them, not as God sees them. For me it is the virgin birth, the Incarnation, the resurrection which are the true laws of the flesh and the physical. Death, decay and destruction are the suspension of these laws" (*CW*, 953).

This insistence on the laws of the flesh explains how a decidedly anti-Gnostic reading of the Gospel according to John stands behind O'Connor's entire *oeuvre*. "In the beginning was the Word: and the Word was with God: and the Word was God.... And the Word was made flesh and dwelt among us (and we saw his glory, the glory as it were of the only begotten of the Father), full of grace and truth."[35]

---

[34] Ibid., 64.
[35] John 1:1, 14.

God exists as logical word or "logos"—a Greek term that presupposes intelligibility.[36] But that intelligibility is fully available only to the angels, who are spirit. The purpose of the Word becoming flesh is revelation to those who are inexorably spirit *and* flesh. The Incarnation is a continuation of the logic of Hebrew thought: if the Word did not become flesh, he would not truly be known by humanity. O'Connor believed the Incarnation teaches that humanity will discover more if we *start with the flesh*, which is living and personal, and move back to mystery. We should start not just with the flesh of Christ, but also the flesh of creation, even that which man has corrupted. Death and decay, when penetrated, make sense when seen as a suspension of the laws of the Incarnation.

Modernity begins the project of knowledge with confidence in human reason, not in the revelation of the Incarnation. So when Christian writers breathe the air of modernity, they defeat their project by trying to prove abstract truths with Greek logic instead of telling stories with the Hebrew logic of the concrete. In "The Catholic Novelist in the South," O'Connor criticizes the Catholic novelist for this problem. The Catholic novelist thinks he is doing Christianity a favor by writing morality plays or inserting orthodoxy into his novels, but he does a disservice because he thereby treats spirit as separate from matter. Since God reveals himself incarnationally—in the person of Christ and through his people and not in an abstract theorem—fiction should do the same. Writes O'Connor, "Our sense of what is contained in our faith is deepened less by abstractions than by an encounter with mystery in what is human and often perverse. We Catholics are much given to the instant answer. Fiction doesn't have any. Saint Gregory wrote that every time the sacred text describes a fact, it reveals a mystery. And this is what the fiction writer, on his lower level, attempts to do also"

---

[36] In the *Theological Dictionary of the New Testament*, George Kittel writes that in the Greek world *logos* indicates "an existing and significant content which is assumed to be intelligible," and "it is presupposed as self-evident by the Greek that there is in things, in the world and its course, a primary *logos*, an intelligible and recognizable law, which then makes possible knowledge and understanding in the human *logos*" (vol. 4 [Grand Rapids: W. B. Eerdmans, 1967] 80–81).

(*CW*, 863). The word "reveals" cannot be replaced by "explains." The fact described by either Scripture or the novelist does not evaporate so that the reader can absorb the essence, getting what O'Connor called "instant enlightenment." Instead the fact is inexorably part of the revelation, just as Christ *is* God and does not merely describe or symbolize him. The spiritual is an "added dimension," and "what the Catholic writer and reader will have to remember is that the reality of the added dimension will be judged in a work of fiction by the truthfulness and wholeness of the natural events presented. If the Catholic writer hopes to reveal mysteries, he will have to do it by describing truthfully what he sees from where he is" (*CW*, 811).

If a novelist accepts these separations instead of defying them, she will fail. She will write sentimental literature, which delivers emotion severed from reality, or pornography, which treats readers as mere bodies instead of embodied souls. "Positive" religious tracts, though well intentioned, only reinforce the dualisms. O'Connor explains this failure: The religious writer "will try to enshrine the mystery without the fact, and there will follow a further set of separations which are inimical to art. Judgment will be separated from vision; nature from grace; and reason from the imagination. These are separations which are very apparent today in American life and in American writing" (*CW*, 864).

Fiction remains in the realm of the concrete by insisting on the story. O'Connor felt at home with descriptions of herself as a Southern writer because she felt that Southerners understood the importance of narrative. The Catholic novelist from the South has a distinct advantage in becoming a storyteller because Southerners still live in a storied community. They even have a sacred history in common—or at least ghostly remnants of it—because of the enduring presence of the Bible. O'Connor acknowledged as a "deficiency" the fact that some Catholics do not see Christianity biblically, claiming that if Catholicism accommodates to that failure instead of overcoming it "our literature will always be going downhill and ourselves behind it" (*CW*, 858). A biblical revival would be good for Catholic literature not because absolute truth will be systematically handed down in life-changing concepts, but because "to be great storytellers, we need something to measure ourselves against, and this is what we conspicuously lack in this age. Men judge themselves now by what they find themselves doing" (*CW*, 858). Stories affect "our image and judgment of ourselves." O'Connor continues, "Abstractions, formulas, laws will not do here. We have to have stories. It takes a story to make a story. It takes a story of mythic dimensions; one which belongs to everybody; one in which everybody is able to recognize the hand of God and imagine its descent upon himself" (*CW*, 858-859).

While O'Connor criticized liberal Protestantism for contributing to a God-destroying abstraction, she clearly also credited Protestant fundamentalists for the fact that the South still lives in a world steeped in Bible stories that belong to everyone. The crazy backwoods Protestants in her fiction (such as old man Tarwater) who actually believe the Bible is true are her allies, not her antagonists. It is largely because of their fanatical commitment to the Bible that the South is different. Through biblical stories the South has been conditioned to see reality the Hebrew way and not the Greek way. "Our response to life is different if we have been taught only a definition of faith than it is if we have trembled with Abraham as he held the knife over Isaac," O'Connor explains (*CW*, 859). Thus the anti-modern conditioning that is already a part of the life of the South can help the Catholic novelist to be both a better novelist and a better Catholic, because "in the last four or five centuries we in the Church have over-emphasized the abstract and consequently impoverished our imagination and our capacity for prophetic insight. The circumstance of being a Southerner, of living in a non-Catholic but religiously inclined society, furnishes the Catholic novelist with some very fine antidotes to his own worst tendencies" (*CW*, 859).

The "mythic dimensions" of shared story must not be confused with "myth." Whether the stories told are factually true or false, "myth" gives meaning and provides explanations, but the story itself often falls away in favor of the ideas presented. As other scholars have noted, O'Connor's method is more parabolic than mythic, but her particular use of the parabolic method must be defined carefully.[37] O'Connor's conception of the parable is rooted in Hebrew logic that does not leave the sign itself behind as a "shadow." Her view is that of Claude Tresmontant: "The *mashal* [parable] is either a sensible material fact or a historical event which signifies some invisible reality. The meaning is contained *in* the signifying fact, *in* the concrete reality. We do not have to flee the sensible in order to reach the intelligible. The teller of parables invites us to discern a meaning not affixed to the fact from without, but actually immanent in it, a constituent part of the fact."[38] The fact itself is not just a vehicle of an idea's transmission: the Word became flesh and is known only through the flesh, never purely as word. Some critics have dangerously reversed this logic, suggesting that O'Connor's aim is to draw the reader's attention to the "centrality of [the fiction's] interpretative language."[39] O'Connor believes that God is knowable and that her stories have meaning, but not as reduced to intelligible word. She does not offer a hermeneutics of certainty in either her fiction or in reading Scripture. She does not offer a hermeneutics at all.

IT MUST BE ANCIENT

Of course, the story one tells is just as important as the fact of story. And O'Connor's stories, as many have noted, have a favorite plot. Against an American literary tradition that congratulates its heroes for striving for autonomy and freedom, O'Connor spurns her protagonists for their arrogance.[40] When her protagonists try to

---

[37] See Sallie McFague, "The Parabolic in Faulkner, O'Connor, and Percy," *Notre Dame English Journal* 40 (1983).

[38] Tresmontant, *Study of Hebrew Thought*, 59.

[39] In his study of O'Connor's fiction, John May writes that "the crucial question related to the meaning of O'Connor's fiction deals with the centrality of its interpretive language. The parabolic form dictates the religious limits of that language; the hermeneutic core of her narratives guides the interpreter to their meaning and specifies the awareness they call the reader to as word" (May, *The Pruning Word: The Parables of Flannery O'Connor* [Notre Dame IN: University of Notre Dame Press, 1976] 18).

[40] O'Connor deliberately told stories that defy the mainline American literary

assert themselves in the standard American fashion, they fail miserably and learn the limits to their sovereign selves. In other words, O'Connor's stories tell tales of people who make anti-modern discoveries in anti-modern ways. Carol Shloss explains that O'Connor wrote with a sensibility "radically removed from either Joyce's or Woolf's," in that "she seemed to feel more of an affinity with the ancient concept of epiphany, and hence she tended to emphasize a divine movement-human response pattern, whereby people are no longer agents of epiphany through the movements of their minds but the recipients of some great and even unsought knowledge."[41]

Since O'Connor's stories emphasize divine movement, Shloss rightly concludes that they lead many readers to see their violence as victimization, not as the grace O'Connor claims for it. O'Connor knew her readers would react this way. We have been trained by our culture to see individual autonomy as the highest good and to see pain and disability as obstacles to be overcome. Any outside agent that comes deliberately to do violence to our plans must be against us, not for us.

That interpretation of God will particularly be the case for a culture that has reinvented God—even the God of the church—according to our needs. As we have seen, the modern self as conceived by the *cogito* must birth itself in detachment from the world, the world medievals had considered to be both mysterious and feminine. The goal of medieval philosophy had been union with God through

---

tradition. From Huckleberry Finn to Jay Gatsby, the American hero is congratulated for at least trying to break free from restraints into a new world, since such freedom is what most interests his creator. O'Connor believed that to be the artist's romantic fantasy. M. A. Klug explains the connection between the Romantic theory of the imagination and the types of heroes it produces: "the prototype of the spiritual hero becomes a kind of artist whatever the hero's occupation might be. The hero is a romantic artist of the self, furiously laboring to give birth to his or her own perfected being through the achievement of a personal destiny" (Klug, "Flannery O'Connor and the Manichean Spirit of Modernism," *Southern Humanities Review* 17/4 [1983]: 304). For a complete study of this issue see Brian Abel Ragen, *A Wreck on the Road to Damascus* (Chicago: Loyola University Press, 1989).

[41] Carol Shloss, "Epiphany," in *Modern Critical Views: Flannery O'Connor*, ed. Harold Bloom (New York: Chelsea House Publishers, 1986) 69.

union with that world, so modern philosophy, seeing the autonomous self as its ultimate goal, had to remake God. In their hands God became a distant father figure, in part to "alleviate the epistemological anxiety" that resulted from the separation.[42] God became authoritarian, judgmental, and distant. Ultimately he became, as Brian Ingraffia has argued, a God that "has been understood through Greek conceptuality," that is, God as immaterial essence, intelligence, pure understanding, spirit.[43] He is God as idea—he is not a God who would stoop to become a real man in order to redeem creation.

The modern concept of God has had rather insidious effects on O'Connor scholarship. Reading O'Connor through this philosophical grid, critics look for a distant and paternal God and for an authoritarian narrator to speak his judgments for him. When those critics are feminists, they tend to see in O'Connor's characters "women [who] are chastised by satanic male agents of the Heavenly Father, who demands allegiance and submission."[44] If they cannot find an authoritarian narrator, as Carol Shloss cannot, O'Connor as an artist becomes a contradictory figure whose "excessive indirection" seems to them to controvert her Catholic aims.[45]

But modernism's God is not O'Connor's God. In her stories, God is not a distant authoritarian figure who passes judgment on sinners, but a being whose primary aim is revelation (and not necessarily explanation). When O'Connor's God permits violence, it is always to

---

[42] Susan Bordo argues that the idea of the self birthing itself is largely a male Cartesian fantasy, in part derived from fear of the female body and its mystery (Bordo, *Flight to Objectivity,* 58). Bordo explains that "in the absence of a sense of connectedness with the natural world—and that includes, for Descartes, a sense of connectedness with one's own body—only a guarantee 'from above' can alleviate the epistemological anxiety. The change may also be described in terms of separation from the *maternal*—the immanent realms of earth, nature, the authority of the body—and a compensatory turning toward the *paternal* for legitimization through external regulation, transcendent values, and the authority of law" (ibid.).

[43] Brian D. Ingraffia, *Postmodern Theory and Biblical Theology: Vanquishing God's Shadow* (Cambridge & New York: Cambridge University Press, 1995) 5.

[44] Louise Hutchings Westling, "Fathers and Daughters in Welty and O'Connor," in *The Female Tradition in Southern Literature,* ed. Carol S. Manning (Urbana & Chicago: University of Illinois Press, 1993) 117–18.

[45] Shloss, "Epiphany," 66.

prove to her protagonists that they are created beings who are not as independent as they would believe. Her characters discover that they need God and they need each other. In these stories, the triumphant birth of the self is replaced by a much lowlier birth at the hands of others, a birth usually triggered by a humiliating encounter with the physical world. O'Connor's characters become aware of their dependency and therefore learn to judge themselves more accurately and to judge others less harshly. They also discover (or are poised to discover) new freedom and self-worth in the notion that Christ is an engaged physical presence, living in the bodies of believers here in temples of the Holy Ghost.

One way to recognize the pre-modern notion of revelation at work in O'Connor's fiction is to note that the wills of the characters have been virtually removed from the project, but their intellects, bodies, and emotions participate fully.[46] Cartesian minds rely on the will of the self to alleviate error. In contrast, O'Connor's fiction is a poetics of radical intervention that takes on characters in body and mind—as souls. A flying book and flying bullets, a goring bull, and a mind-arresting hermaphrodite: lowly objects and even lowlier people are agents of change. Characters do not read concepts in Scripture to come to knowledge of God; they get thrown off of a tractor or gored by a bull. They have been deeply poisoned, so their antidote must be radical. Their shock as characters and our shock as readers are meant to operate in the same way: as a wakeup call. "I'm always highly irritated by people who imply that writing fiction is an escape from reality," O'Connor wrote. "It is a plunge into reality and it's very shocking to the system" (*MM*, 77–78).

IT MUST DISPLACE

When you talk about fiction that shocks the system, you are talking about the grotesque. The grotesque is O'Connor's ultimate way of

---

[46] This is why I find puzzling Marshall Bruce Gentry's insistence in *Flannery O'Connor's Religion of the Grotesque* that O'Connor's characters "lay the tracks for their transport toward a redemptive experience they perceive as an annihilation" (Jackson: University Press of Mississippi, 1986, 4).

employing the method of the Incarnation to defy modern dualism. It is the antidote to the poison of the modern world in three essential ways, each of which will be illuminated in this book.

First, O'Connor's grotesques draw attention to the body. Physical abnormalities—especially disabilities—serve as constant reminders of our embodiment, even to a culture that would rather ignore those bodies. In his foreword to Mitchell and Snyder's *The Body and Physical Difference: Discourses of Disability,* James I. Porter explains why this reminder makes us uncomfortable: "Viewed in itself...a disabled body seems somehow *too much* a body, *too real,* too corporeal: it is a body that, so to speak, stands in its own way. From another angle, which is no less reductive, a disabled body appears to lack something essential, something that would make it identifiable and something to identify with; it seems too little a body: a body that is deficiently itself...."[47] Whatever else the grotesques may represent in O'Connor's fiction, they never cease to be physical bodies and to make us vividly aware of that fact. They are never merely symbols. When O'Connor's characters, poisoned by the modern world, try to act as if what they do in the body (or to other bodies) does not matter, the grotesque body violently insists that it does. Grotesque bodies get into characters' and readers' faces alike in *Wise Blood,* "Good Country People," and "Parker's Back."

Second, the grotesques defy the modern effort to attain conceptual purity, to live in a tidy world wherein all mysteries are explained. More often than not, O'Connor's grotesques shout out—through their marginality, their inutility, their being "extra"—that there will always be something in excess of our philosophical systems, something we cannot accommodate or explain. The essence of being is that it cannot be reduced to its essence.[48] This is the meaning of the word "mystery" for O'Connor,

---

[47] James I. Porter, foreword to *The Body and Physical Difference: Discourses of Disability,* ed. David T. Mitchell and Sharon L. Snyder (Ann Arbor: University of Michigan Press: 1997) xiii.

[48] Etienne Gilson warned that modernism is in error when it tries to reduce being by encompassing it into thought. Gilson asks, "are we to encompass being with thought, or thought with being? In other words, are we to include the whole in

and the mystery of being is the story of *The Violent Bear It Away*, "The Displaced Person," "The Life You Save May Be Your Own," and others.

Finally, by representing the part of reality that cannot be tidied up and explained away, the grotesque in O'Connor's fiction functions to displace characters (and readers) from the illusion of the autonomous self. O'Connor turned to the grotesque again and again because its appearance creates an epistemological crisis. It cannot be explained; it can only be encountered. It forces movement and change. In his book *On the Grotesque*, Geoffrey Galt Harpham defines the grotesque by its inexplicability. He writes,

> as a practical matter we commonly adhere to several tacit assumptions about ideas: that they can be clearly expressed; that they have kernels or cores in which all is tidy, compact, and organized; and that the goal of analysis is to set limits to them, creating sharply defined, highly differentiated, and therefore useful concepts. We assume that, however complex an idea may be, it is essentially coherent and that it can most profitably be discussed in an orderly and progressive way. The grotesque places all these assumptions in doubt.[49]

The grotesque is that which will not fit the system. It works by antagonisms, by defying easy solutions; its logic most resembles that of paradox, which in Harpham's description turns language against itself by insisting that both sides of a contradiction be kept. It

---

one of its parts, or one of the parts in its whole? If intellectual evidence is not enough to dictate our choice, history is there to remind us that no one ever regains the whole of reality after locking himself up in one of its parts" (*Unity of Philosophical Experience,* 323). He argues that "everything is what it is, and nothing else, existence belongs to each and every thing in a truly unique manner, as its own existence, which can be shared in and by nothing else. Such is the first principle, both universally applicable, and never applicable twice in the same way. When philosophers fail to perceive either its presence or its true nature, their initial error will pervade the whole science of being, and bring about the ruin of philosophy" (ibid., 321–22).

[49] Geoffrey Galt Harpham, *On the Grotesque: Strategies of Contradiction in Art and Literature* (Princeton: Princeton University Press, 1982) xvi.

therefore forces us to make new discoveries in the realm of experience, not of conceptual truths.[50]

O'Connor relied on the grotesque to bring characters and readers to a desperately needed "paradigm crisis."[51] Specifically it challenges the conventional wisdom of the age, which O'Connor described as tending "more and more to the view that the ills and mysteries of life will eventually fall before the scientific advances of man" (*CW*, 815). The grotesque challenges this naïve realism by operating in the margins, in skips and gaps, in the unconventional and inexplicable.[52] This is why in the best of O'Connor's stories, the grotesque represents both the Incarnation *and* the incarnational work of art. When God became man, he displaced our categories by appearing in a completely incongruous and unexpected form. The Incarnation is, in short, grotesque. So the incarnational artist follows this lead, disrupting our easy explanations and forcing growth. The artist follows God's logic not by usurping his role as creator, but by emulating the surprise of his appearance as man. O'Connor would agree with Erasmo Leiva-Merikakis that God is "more artist than philosopher" because he speaks to us "not in propositions and syllogisms, but in stern commands, in images, signs, gestures,

---

[50] Ibid., 19–20.

[51] Harpham writes that "in a larger sense confusion lies at the heart of all scientific discoveries of a revolutionary character. This is the position of T. S. Kuhn, who has opened up an extremely fertile area of inquiry by exploring the time of transition when scientists shift from one explanation of a given set of phenomena to another. This pregnant moment is a 'paradigm crisis,' when anomalies have emerged to discredit an old explanatory paradigm or model, and to make it impossible to continue adhering to it, but before the general acceptance of a new paradigm. The paradigm crisis is the interval of the grotesque writ large" (Harpham, *On the Grotesque*, 17).

[52] O'Connor writes that "in these grotesque works, we find that the writer has made alive some experience which we are not accustomed to observe everyday, or which the ordinary man may never experience in his ordinary life. We find that connections which we would expect in the customary kind of realism have been ignored, that there are many strange skips and gaps which anyone trying to describe manners and customs would certainly not have left. Yet the characters in these novels are alive in spite of these things. They have an inner coherence, if not always a coherence to their social framework. Their fictional qualities lean away from typical social patterns, toward mystery and the unexpected" (*CW*, 815).

whisperings of love, by both his manifest presence and his tangible absence, by both his words and his dramatic silences, *always* upsetting, overturning, the ordinary meanings of words and things. God's logic may thus be compared to the *logic of fire*, which enkindles everything it touches, not obeying any preexistent rule."[53]

O'Connor knew that when your goal is to displace rather than to confirm or defend, you create chaos. Fiction's purpose is not to "give order."[54] She knew that all kinds of people would read her fiction and that some of these readers would accept the grotesques she designed to be rejected, while others would reject the ones she designed to be accepted. Perhaps most prescient of all, she knew that the particular idea she wanted her grotesques to displace—the idea of the autonomous self—would lead to the greatest misunderstanding.

Take Harold Bloom for example. In his introduction to the collection of essays on O'Connor that he edited, Bloom quotes the following well-known passage from "Some Aspects of the Grotesque in Southern Fiction": "I think it is safe to say that while the South is hardly Christ-centered, it is most certainly Christ-haunted. The Southerner, who isn't convinced of it, is very much afraid that he may have been formed in the image and likeness of God. Ghosts can be very fierce and instructive. They cast strange shadows, particularly on our literature. In any case, it is when the freak can be sensed as a figure for our essential displacement that he attains some depth in literature."[55] Bloom quotes this passage in order to argue that O'Connor's fiction actually works against her ideas. He writes that "the freakish displacement here is from 'wholeness,' which is then described as the state of having been made in the image or likeness of God. But that mode, displacement, is not what is operative in O'Connor's fiction."[56] Instead, Bloom argues, "it is the interplay

---

[53] Erasmo Leiva-Merikakis, *Fire of Mercy, Heart of the Word: Meditations on the Gospel According to St. Matthew*, vol. 1 (San Francisco: Ignatius Press, 1996) 44.

[54] While it may and certainly does point to a created order, it does not impart or recreate that order.

[55] Harold Bloom, introduction to *Flannery O'Connor: Modern Critical Views* (New York: Chelsea House Publishers, 1986) 8.

[56] Ibid.

between Tarwater fighting to be humanly free, and Tarwater besieged by his great-uncle's training, by the internalized Devil, and most of all by O'Connor's own ferocious religious zeal, that constitutes O'Connor's extraordinary artistry."[57] Bloom cannot tolerate that old man Tarwater is O'Connor's hero. Who would possibly celebrate a cantankerous old man who wants to indoctrinate a poor young boy to such a limited view of Christian calling? Instead, for Bloom the power of fiction resides in its celebration of characters who strive to transcend all limits to the self and to ascend on the strength of their imaginative vision. And so he concludes that O'Connor's novels had this power in spite of her views, and that she "would have bequeathed us even stronger novels and stories, of the eminence of Faulkner's, if she had been able to restrain her spiritual tendentiousness."[58]

I doubt O'Connor would have been surprised that her fiction could not displace as grand a proponent of the Gnostic imagination as Harold Bloom. But I believe she did hope some readers would find themselves as uncomfortably displaced from their worldviews as she displaced her characters from theirs. Displacement *is* the operative mode in O'Connor's fiction. It is the story she tells more than any other.

"The Displaced Person" tells this story by way of two characters who claim to have a god's-eye view of the world—Mrs. Shortley and Mrs. McIntyre. Although they occupy different positions in the farm's hierarchy, each wants desperately to protect her place. But when a priest arrives with a new worker—the Polish displaced person, Mr. Guizac—they both encounter a disrupting other who does not play by their rules. Mr. Guizac's physical presence on the farm becomes an unavoidable, grotesque challenge to their autonomous selves. They each try to displace him before they get displaced themselves.

The opening paragraph presents one of O'Connor's clearest pictures of the monstrosity that is the sovereign American self:

---

[57] Ibid.
[58] Ibid.

The peacock was following Mrs. Shortley up the road to the hill where she meant to stand. Moving one behind the other, they looked like a complete procession. Her arms were folded and as she mounted the prominence, she might have been the giant wife of the countryside, come out at some sign of danger to see what the trouble was. She stood on two tremendous legs, with the grand self-confidence of a mountain, and rose, up narrowing bulges of granite, to two icy blue points of light that pierced forward, surveying everything. She ignored the white afternoon sun which was creeping behind a ragged wall of cloud as if it pretended to be an intruder and cast her gaze down the red clay road that turned off from the highway. (*CW*, 285)

Mrs. Shortley has proclaimed herself monarch-of-all-I-survey. Her prominence depends upon her ability to become as large and unmovable as a mountain while her icy gaze penetrates, measures, and dominates everything but herself. In the wider view the narrator affords the reader, we see that Mrs. Shortley ignores the white afternoon sun that could illuminate *her*. She wants to be all gaze, and when she trains that gaze on the intruding Guizac family, "her look first grazed the top of the displaced people's heads and then revolved downwards slowly, the way a buzzard glides and drops in the air until it alights on the carcass. She stood far enough away so that the man would not be able to kiss her hand" (*CW*, 288). Other people are only carrion she uses to feed her monstrous self. She determines her bodily distance from people, and when she wants to make her presence felt by Mrs. McIntyre, she trains her gaze on her back until she turns around (*CW*, 287). Although Mrs. Shortley has a massive body, her goal is always to look without being looked at, so that when she enters the barn she approaches from "an oblique angle that allowed her a look in the door before she could be seen herself" (*CW*, 291).

This sovereign self constructs and maintains that self by demonizing others. Mrs. Shortley therefore immediately links the Guizac family with newsreel images from the Holocaust—some distant evil event that she feels they will bring with them like a disease: "watching from her vantage point, Mrs. Shortley had the sudden intuition that the Gobblehooks, like rats with typhoid fleas, could have carried all those murderous ways over the water with them directly to this place. If they had come from where that kind of thing was done to them, who was to say they were not the kind that would also do it to others?" (*CW*, 287). Mrs. Shortley's imagination reduces the family to an undifferentiated, mangled, and dirty mass of bodies that would be better kept "over there." When the Guizacs are finally standing in front of her, she is surprised to discover that they look like people. "Every time she had seen them in her imagination, the image she had got was of the three bears, walking single file, with wooden shoes on like Dutchmen and sailor hats and bright coats with lots of buttons" (*CW*, 286).

Mrs. Shortley will grudgingly acknowledge them as people and not bears, but giving them too much shared ground will threaten the inviolable self she has constructed. She wants above all to avoid the kind of self-recognition that comes to the grandmother in "A Good Man Is Hard to Find" when she looks at the Misfit and says "why, you're one of my babies. You're one of my own children!" (*CW*, 152). So she constructs violent binaries of self versus other, us versus them, clean versus dirty. Since the displaced people surprise her by not looking like animals, physical difference will no longer be enough to differentiate, as it is with the black workers on the farm. So the purity must be maintained in language, as Mr. Shortley would explain later: "you go to these other places and the only way you can tell is if they say something. And then you can't always tell because about half of them know the English language. That's where we make our mistake...letting all them people onto English" (*CW*, 324). Mrs. Shortley thus begins to think of a race war as a word war, and the result is one of the most interesting passages in O'Connor's fiction:

> With two of them here, there would be almost nothing spoken but Polish! The Negroes would be gone and there would be the two families against Mr. Shortley and herself! She began to imagine a war of words, to see the Polish words and the English words coming at each other, stalking forward, not sentences, just words, gabble gabble gabble, flung out high and shrill and stalking forward and then grappling with each other. She saw the Polish words, dirty and all-knowing and unreformed, flinging mud on the clean English words until everything was equally dirty. She saw them all piled up in a room, all the dead dirty words,

theirs and hers too, piled up like the naked bodies in the newsreel. God save me! she cried silently, from the stinking power of Satan! (*CW*, 300)

A good fundamentalist, Mrs. Shortley demonizes what she cannot understand. She fears a loss of control over what she has clearly defined as good and evil. To think of their invasion as a language invasion shows how deeply threatened Mrs. Shortley feels, for her distinct categories of self and other can only remain intact when words are abstract and controlled as *sentences*, not when they become mangled and mangling *bodies* (uncontrolled words), distorted and disordering, out of her control. Since the dirty Polish words threaten to disrupt everything by flinging mud on the clean English words until all is equally dirty and unrecognizable, the challenge is to keep the words she knows pure and separate, ordered into logical propositions. So she does what a good fundamentalist will do: she turns to Scripture with new zeal. Scripture is not for her the book that Leiva-Merikakis had described, with power to displace her. It becomes instead a text she thinks is stable, pure, and on her side. From that day forward, records the narrator, Mrs. Shortley starts to read her Bible more closely, particularly the Apocalypse and the Prophets. Soon she believes she knows the whole plan of the mystery of the universe, and "she was not surprised to suspect that she had a special part in the plan because she was strong...right now she felt that her business was to watch the priest" (*CW*, 300).

Since the priest brought the displaced person to begin with, he cannot be trusted. As a symbol of authority, tradition, and mediation, he is a real threat to Mrs. Shortley's special place as defender of the absolute propositional truths she has discovered. He is a demonic other, his religion being no different from that of the "unreformed" Europeans. "They're full of crooked ways. They never have advanced or reformed. They got the same religion as a thousand years ago. It could only be the devil responsible for that" (*CW*, 297). Mrs. Shortley is a sort of ultimate liberal Protestant: God is at her service. She does not want a mediator because she believes she knows God's plan and her place in it. In a scene that seems to be derived from Bloom's description of Baptist Gnosticism in the hymn "I walk in the garden alone" ("He walks with me and He talks with me and He tells me I am His own"),[59] Mrs. Shortley ascends a hill to have her first vision:

> Suddenly while she watched, the sky folded back in two pieces like the curtain to a stage and a gigantic figure stood facing her. It was the color of the sun in the early afternoon, white-gold. It was of no definite shape but there were fiery wheels with fierce dark eyes in them, spinning rapidly all around it. She was not able to tell if the figure was going forward or backward because its magnificence was so great. She shut her eyes in order to look at it and it turned blood-red and the wheels turned white. A voice, very resonant, said the one word, "Prophesy!"

> She stood there, tottering slightly but still upright, her eyes shut tight and her fists clenched and her straw sun hat low on her forehead. "The children of wicked nations will be butchered," she said in a loud voice. "Legs where arms should be, foot to face, ear in the palm of hand. Who will remain whole? Who will remain whole? Who?" (*CW*, 301)

Visions are a significant part of O'Connor's characters' discoveries, but it is important to distinguish between those internally willed and interpreted and those externally given. Mrs. Turpin, for instance, has no desire to find herself at the end of a long line ascending into heaven as she sees in "Revelation." But in this scene from "The Displaced Person," Mrs. Shortley has a vision while "pleased with herself" on top of a hill; it is a vision she stole from Ezekiel, and most significant of all, it is a vision she "shut her eyes in order to look at." The resultant individual "prophecy" is nothing but a declaration of the unified self against that which threatens to displace its carefully-formed whole. In the cosmic irony of O'Connor's story the vision does, of course, eventually come to describe her. But for now Mrs. Shortley controls the vision and she means to stand against the evil displaced people. When she comes off the hill, she sees the priest's car: "'Here again,' she muttered. 'Come to destroy'" (*CW*, 302).

---

[59] See Harold Bloom, *The American Religion* (New York: Simon & Schuster, 1992) 200–233, for a discussion of the Gnostic elements of Southern Baptist and other fundamentalist beliefs.

In this story the peacock symbolizes everything grotesque "other" or unnecessary "extra" that does not fit into Mrs. Shortley's system. The priest compares the birds to Christ and to the displaced person and finds them all beautiful. But for Mrs. Shortley, peacocks are fine if they follow in her wake as the bird in the opening paragraph did, but far be it from her actually to look at them. That's a problem, because they have a point of view she does not know she desperately needs; that first peacock had his attention "fixed in the distance on something no one else could see" (*CW*, 285). After a conversation with one of the farm workers, Mrs. Shortley "stood a while longer, reflecting, her unseeing eyes directly in front of the peacock's tail. He had jumped into the tree and his tail hung in front of her, full of fierce planets with eyes that were each ringed in green and set against a sun that was gold in one second's light and salmon-colored in the next. She might have been looking at a map of the universe but she didn't notice it any more than she did the spots of sky that cracked the dull green of the tree. She was having an inner vision instead" (*CW*, 290–91). If she would only look she would see in the peacock's tail a fierce vision—indeed, she would see a map of the universe through many more eyes and with shifting colors—but she chooses instead to close her eyes and leave her myopic vision unchallenged.

Mrs. Shortley is not the only one who cannot see the true beauty of the "extra" peacocks. While Mrs. Shortley is the story's fundamentalist, Mrs. McIntyre, the farm owner, is the rational objectivist. She snaps, "I'm not theological. I'm practical!" (*CW*, 316). But she has exactly the same vision problem as Mrs. Shortley. She cannot see the beauty of the peacock and its "map of the universe" either. A good utilitarian, she lets the peacocks in which her husband delighted die off one by one because they are "extra." The priest's declaration that "Christ will come like that"—beautiful and extra, useless in the world's categories—is lost on her. When the priest admires the peacocks, she "wondered where she had ever seen such an idiotic old man" (*CW*, 317). Likewise, at first she welcomes Mr. Guizac because he is such a productive a worker, but as soon as he arranges a marriage between his white cousin and one of the "shiftless niggers" who work on the farm, he becomes an unacceptable monster. When Mrs. McIntyre looks at him with this new information, she looks at him "as if she were seeing him for the first time.... His whole face looked as if it might have been patched together out of several others" (*CW*, 313). The similarity to Frankenstein's monster is evident; and like Dr. Frankenstein, Mrs. McIntyre feels suddenly that she has brought something into being that she can no longer control. She climbs up a hill just like Mrs. Shortley, narrowing her gaze on Mr. Guizac "until it closed entirely around the diminishing figure on the tractor as if she were watching him through a gunsight. All her life she had been fighting the world's overflow and now she had it in the form of a Pole" (*CW*, 315). Anyone who is a threat to her way of life is "overflow" and "extra." Her place is being threatened; she has a dream that she becomes trash like the Shortleys. So she fights back, puts on a violent warring attitude no different from Hitler's:

> "He's extra and he's upset the balance around here," she said, "and I'm a logical practical woman and there are no ovens here and no camps and no Christ Our Lord and when he leaves, he'll make more money. He'll work at the mill and buy a car and don't talk to me—all they want is a car."
>
> "The ovens and the boxcars and the sick children," droned the priest, "and our dear Lord."
>
> "Just one too many," she said. (*CW*, 322)

The pronoun "one" in Mrs. McIntyre's declaration "just one too many" has an ambiguous antecedent. The context for the passage suggests that Mrs. McIntyre is still talking about Mr. Guizac and is ignoring the priest's remarks, letting him blather on. The priest equates the peacock with Mr. Guizac, Christ, Holocaust victims, and unwanted children. For Mrs. McIntyre, they are each "one too many"—others who must be eliminated at the first hint of threat to her ordered world. In O'Connor's view there is no difference between a fascist who kills Jews, people who kill Christ, and a white Southern woman who kills a Polish man: they each operate in fear, believing they've got to displace the pests or be displaced themselves.

Thus Mrs. McIntyre does not shout a hint of a warning at Mr. Guizac when a tractor rolls toward him and then over him, snapping his spine. She finds an easy and clean solution to a messy problem. But it does not stay clean and easy for long. Soon the physical violence and her complicity with it do their own work and displace Mrs. McIntyre in spite of herself. When she sees a pile of mangled bodies—and walking among them, the priest covered with Guizac's blood—"she felt she was in some foreign country where the people bent over the body were natives, and she watched like a stranger while the dead man was carried away in the ambulance" (CW, 326). Only Guizac's real blood, and Mrs. McIntyre's complicity in his actual death, can displace her from the world she has set up. The violence jars Mrs. McIntyre out of the frame of her own life for a moment and allows her, in effect, to become a grotesque stranger to herself. She loses her place but takes a step toward redemption.

Mrs. Shortley also loses her place and takes a step toward redemption. Earlier in the story she persuades her family to leave in order to avoid the embarrassment of being fired. When her husband asks her "where are we going," she is suddenly made aware that she is now a displaced person according to her own definition. She has a second vision, but this time it is not one she wants. The eyes that had only penetrated others from afar now look deep within herself: "all the vision in them might have been turned around, looking inside her. She suddenly grabbed Mr. Shortley's elbow and Sarah Mae's foot at the same time and began to tug and pull on them as if she were trying to fit the two extra limbs onto herself" (CW, 304). Mrs. Shortley sees herself now as one of the mangled and dirty bodies heaped in a pile. The fact that she grabs onto "extra limbs" and also Mr. Shortley's head, the cat, and other things makes no sense in this story without a clear understanding of the way bodies, particularly grotesque ones, function epistemologically in O'Connor's writing. As Mrs. Shortley's solid self disintegrates, her mind cannot preserve the hierarchy it had imagined; it cannot preserve the rigid distinction between self and other it had inhabited. As a result she finds herself reaching for the bodies of others to fit them onto herself, as if she now knows that those bodies—so grotesquely other, mangled, and everything she had been afraid of—are exactly what she needs. Mrs. Shortley has to be torn apart, seen as the grotesque she really is, before she can be put back together. "Wholeness" is achieved only by way of acknowledged brokenness. It is the paradox that resides at the heart of Christianity: no one who strives to "remain whole" can be redeemed. In the violence of her stroke and her displacement, Mrs. Shortley "seemed to contemplate for the first time the tremendous frontiers of her true country" (*CW*, 305).

But what about this "true country"? For many contemporary critics, as soon as O'Connor insists on a displacing God and a "true country," she performs the "god trick" herself. After all, her narrative voice is authoritarian and cannot escape the judgments she hands down to the characters. What gives O'Connor the right to displace? To insist upon a "true country"?

This view depends upon the largely tacit assumptions we have when we approach the modern novel—particularly the modern American novel. We assume that the writer construes a modern version of the self and will either show that self as beaten down to an isolated death or as fighting to be freed from constraints. We assume growth will come by way of his or her own heroic epiphany. Since this story is largely what American fiction gives, we can hardly be blamed for expecting it.

But scholars have found an alternative in the work of M. M. Bakhtin. Bakhtin offers critics a theory of the novel and of language that originates in an orthodox Christian tradition and rejects Enlightenment premises about the relation of subject and object, writer and world. Bakhtin insists that a novelist does not rule a story simply by telling it. Unlike the monologic world of Aristotle's *Poetics*, the novel, claims Bakhtin, "orchestrates all its themes, the totality of the world of objects and ideas depicted and expressed in it, by means of the social diversity of speech types and by the differing individual voices that flourish under such conditions."[60] According to Bakhtin,

---

[60] M. M. Bakhtin, *The Dialogic Imagination: Four Essays*, ed. Michael Holquist, trans. Caryl Emerson and Michael Holquist (Austin: University of Texas Press, 1981) 263.

the novelist permits a multiplicity of voices—*heteroglossia*—that allows for new links and different connections. In a way, the novelist sets a dispute in motion, embodies different views in his characters, and lets them duke it out on the page.

These theories have contributed immeasurably to the sophistication of O'Connor scholarship. [61] Critics now pay more attention to the subtleties of her characterization and narrative point of view, especially as they differ from authorial voice. Robert Brinkmeyer turns to Bakhtin's theories of dialogism in *The Art and Vision of Flannery O'Connor* to enrich our understanding of the complexity of novelistic interaction between O'Connor's "Catholic voice" and her "fundamentalist voice." But at times Brinkmeyer's study has an apologetic feel, as if he is trying to make concessions for the same "spiritual tendentiousness" that bothers Bloom.[62] We can deal with O'Connor's convictions about God much more easily when we think that the author and her narrator hold just one point of view among many and that their views are constantly under the pressure of other views. If the narrator's point of view has the same characteristics as the proud character and is dismantled along with his, as Brinkmeyer claims, we can walk away with the confidence that the narrator did not really know more than the character, that we have not really made any harsh judgments alongside him. Since fiction lets the conflict live for us—indeed, elevates that conflict as inherently

---

[61] Through Bakhtin's theories, Marshall Bruce Gentry emphasizes the way in which the characters' views rival those of the narrator and suggests that Bakhtin's theories help expand our understanding of O'Connor's grotesques beyond the usual negative categories. Gentry argues that "O'Connor took it as her artistic enterprise, I would suggest, to transform the images of negative modern grotesquerie into part of a redemptive process" (*Religion of the Grotesque,* 13). And Anthony Di Renzo's treatment of the medieval grotesque draws upon Bakhtin's discussion of Rabelais and the communal and redemptive nature of carnivalesque humor. Di Renzo writes that "God for her is not found in vapor but in sweat, not in the sublimity of the mind but the comedy of the body" (Di Renzo, *American Gargoyles* [Carbondale: Southern Illinois University Press, 1993] 81). Readers interested in a discussion of O'Connor's humor should look there.

[62] For a compelling analysis of the shortcomings of Brinkmeyer's argument, see Sarah Gordon, *Flannery O'Connor: The Obedient Imagination* (Athens: University of Georgia Press, 2000) 39–47.

irreducible—no one will tell us how to see. This, after all, is what we want from our fiction.

That safety is not what O'Connor wanted. She insisted on the irreducibility of fiction, but she also insisted that writers not separate judgment from vision. She believed that art, though it does not teach morals, demands a kind of moral answerability to the situations it depicts. Is the narrator's judgment necessarily equivalent to the poor and selfish judgments of many of the characters? Is the author as harsh as we think she is? Do we have to chastise O'Connor for judging her characters without love?

Bakhtin's early works can help us with these questions. In *Toward a Philosophy of the Act* and *Art and Answerability*, he advances a unique apologetic for aesthetic activity from a perspective that defies modernism without taking the postmodern turn toward viewing the text as always displacing its own meaning. The important difference in Bakhtin's approach is that it focuses on human embodiment, which "Bakhtin regards as more fundamental than either spirit or text."[63] In these essays, Bakhtin describes a relationship between the artist and the hero in which the hero, although free of and completely "other" to the artist, cannot author himself according to his desire. Instead, he must rely on the artist's "grace gift" of his "excess of seeing." Bakhtin defines "aesthetic activity" and "aesthetic seeing" rather broadly, as any embodied stance outside of an "other" that is able to see more than the other—he called it "excess of vision"—because of that outside stance. Bakhtin's theory differs radically from the romantic, in which the author is some transcendental genius with God-like power to de-create and re-create the world in his imagination. For Bakhtin, aesthetic activity instead reminds us, as nothing else can, that *because* we are embodied we need others to see us. Art teaches us that while no one can achieve the "immaculate perception" of a god's-eye view, we can and *must* help others see what they cannot see.

---

[63] David Dawson, *Literary Theory, Guides to Theological Inquiry Series* (Minneapolis: Fortress Press, 1995) 85.

One of the first moves Bakhtin makes is to distinguish aesthetic activity from theoretical cognition. Art, precisely because it never claims (or should never claim) to see all from nowhere, *can* claim to see something from somewhere. The author does not judge his own characters in the way a court of law might, by applying a universal standard from an outside point of view. Instead the author, through the narrator, enters into the consciousness of the characters before she steps outside of them. And she must step outside of them or it is not art at all. Bakhtin defines the term "aesthetic" by this otherness, by the fact that the author is able to do what the hero cannot: to see the hero's life as a whole. Bakhtin writes that "an aesthetic event can take place only when there are two participants present; it presupposes two noncoinciding consciousnesses."[64] There are thus two steps in artistic creation. The first is to empathize with the hero, to "penetrate him and almost merge or become one with him from within."[65] But "aesthetic activity" has not even begun until a second step is taken, for "aesthetic activity proper actually begins at the point when we *return* into ourselves, when we *return* to our own place outside the suffering person, and start to form and consummate the material we derived from projecting ourselves into the other and experiencing him from within himself."[66]

This return to the self enables the artist to supply a lack in the character's vision. The power and import of storytelling comes from this double vision, from what is learned in the overlap. Thus the artist sees the world as the character does but then "renders his horizon complete" by supplying the lack. In this assessment "framing" is not negative—it is an essential good. Bakhtin explains that "I must enframe him, create a consummating environment for him out of this excess of my own seeing, knowing, desiring, and feeling."[67] To enframe a character is not an act of hatred, especially if the end result

---

[64] M. M. Bakhtin, *Art and Answerability: Early Philosophical Essays*, ed. Michael Holquist and Vadim Liapunov, trans. Vadim Liapunov (Austin: University of Texas Press, 1990) 22.

[65] Ibid., 26.

[66] Ibid.

[67] Ibid., 25.

is that the character sees more, or even becomes more, than he or she did or was to begin with. Flannery O'Connor is not writing *Tess of the D'Urbervilles* that her narrative framework should push down on the characters, determine their fates, and ultimately crush them.[68] She had a strong sense of the impossibility of fiction in a determined world. Even if the novelist "writes about characters who are mostly unfree, it is the sudden free action, the open possibility, which he knows is the only thing capable of illuminating the picture and giving it life" (*MM*, 115). Instead, it is for O'Connor an act of love that she brings characters into being; she *consummates*, not determines, them.

This unique term is Bakhtin's. Consummation is a gift from the author to the character, a gift predicated on the author's bodily position outside the hero. The gift is a "whole that descends upon" the character, and it does not come from the transcendental genius but from an other's "active consciousness."[69] Bakhtin calls the excess of vision a "gift" to emphasize that to consummate is not to dominate. It is instead to provide a needed view of the self from the outside. Because of her position outside the hero, the author can render a whole event in a character's life so that we see it front and back—a view that we, like the characters, can never have of ourselves. Because it is something we cannot do for ourselves, it is an act of love that we receive in a dependent position. And because the artist's attention does not reduce a character to an abstract type but lets him be a whole person, the artist loves the object of her attention, whether good or bad. Seen through the realm of art, love,

---

[68] It is instructive also to think of Henry James's *The Portrait of a Lady*, which raises these issues by contrasting the deterministic framing of Osgood with the desire of Ralph Touchett, the narrator, and James.

[69] "The author's consciousness is the consciousness of a consciousness, that is, a consciousness that *encompasses* the consciousness and the world of a hero—a consciousness that encompasses and *consummates* the consciousness of a hero by supplying those moments which are in principle transgredient to the hero's consciousness and which, if rendered immanent, would falsify this consciousness. The author not only sees and knows everything seen and known by each hero individually and by all the heroes collectively, but he also sees and knows *more* than they do; moreover, he sees and knows something that is in principle inaccessible to them" (Bakhtin, *Art and Answerability,* 12).

in other words, goes well beyond the categories of good and evil, beautiful and ugly, but without erasing them. It argues that the human subject is worthy of the attention paid to it (a high compliment indeed), and for O'Connor it illustrates God's view of us. Bakhtin explains that even the fully "bad" character is the central object of aesthetic seeing, for "it is upon him that my *interested* attention is riveted in aesthetic seeing, and everything that constitutes the best with respect to content is disposed around *him*—the bad one—as around the one who, in spite of everything, is the sole center of values. In aesthetic seeing you love a human being not because he is good, but, rather, a human being is good because you love him."[70] The difference is crucial. In the creation of the work of fiction, both morally good and morally reprehensible characters are worthy of attention, worthy of the story told about them.

O'Connor never read Bakhtin, but she encountered something similar to his argument in Lynch's *The Image Industries*. Lynch argues that entertainment differs from art in that entertainment invites our identification with anyone to "avoid ultimate identification with our own selves, or own reality" whereas art elicits our collaboration with the dramatic expositor—the artist—who shows us ourselves by showing us others. The paradox of art lies in maintaining our distinctness from each other while learning of our dependence upon one another to see who we really are. For this reason Lynch calls our experiences liturgical—we are united in an act of sensibility.[71] Mr. Head and his grandson share such a redemptive moment in front of the plaster figure in "The Artificial Nigger." Because of her insistence on the value of the body, O'Connor, like Lynch, promotes a Bakhtinian sense of a productive relationship with the other, expressed aesthetically, that differs fundamentally from both modern definitions and their postmodern inheritors.[72]

---

[70] M. M. Bakhtin, *Toward a Philosophy of the Act* (Austin: University of Texas Press, 1993) 62.

[71] William F. Lynch, S. J., *The Image Industries* (New York: Sheed and Ward, 1959) 65.

[72] David Dawson agues that though they come to different conclusions about art, both Harold Bloom and Paul de Man insist on disembodied selves: "although

Incarnational art insists that being does have real presence, that the world is not illusory, and that God—the ultimate other—is not silent. But the incarnational artist does not claim that she has explained or played God. Through Bakhtin's early essays and O'Connor's work we will see that she did not claim that the artist imitates God's creative power. The most the artist can do is point to the creation's God-given significance as seen in the particular and compel the reader to look hard. Art is revelation, and revelation is often unexpectedly grotesque. While other artists strive to give meaning to a meaningless world by creating whole new worlds, usurping the prerogative of God in a triumph of the human imagination, O'Connor focuses upon the strange and displacing forms that will be revealed if she dares to see by a light that is not entirely her own.

Bloom's hyperspiritualized (and therefore disembodied) self wills to overcome a precursor, and de Man's hypertextualized (and therefore disembodied) 'renouncer of seductions' knows in the Socratic sense of being self-aware of his or her lack of knowledge, both conceptions focus on the singular self locked in a polar either-or, a situation in which what proves other to the self can only be threatening or seductive" (Dawson, *Literary Theory*, 107).

CHAPTER 2

WISE BLOOD AND THE POISON
OF THE MODERN WORLD

The novelist will have to do the best he can in travail with the world he has. He may find that in the end that instead of reflecting the image at the heart of things, he has only reflected our broken condition and, through it, the face of the devil we are possessed by. This is a modest achievement, but perhaps a necessary one.

—MM, 168

Whenever I'm asked why Southern writers particularly have a penchant for writing about freaks, I say it is because we are still able to recognize one. To be able to recognize a freak, you have to have some conception of the whole man, and in the South the general conception of man is still, in the main, theological.

—CW, 817

In 1949 Flannery O'Connor worked on *Wise Blood* in a room over Robert and Sally Fitzgerald's garage in their Connecticut home. She spent her mornings painstakingly revising her tale of Hazel Motes, her first incarnation of a character who, though determined to deny Christ and live life as he chooses, finds Christ inescapable in the end. She spent her evenings socializing with the Fitzgerald family, part of the time discussing Robert Fitzgerald's current work—the translation of Sophocles' Oedipus plays. When O'Connor read them in 1950, they apparently provided her with the novel's tragic resolution.[1] Recognizing that he is not clean as he had at first declared, Hazel Motes would blind himself, wander in a strange land away from home, and die alone.

At first glance this ending appears to be all that *Wise Blood* shares with Greek tragedy. Impossible to classify in any simple way, *Wise Blood* is one of the strangest novels ever written—even for O'Connor. It claims a kind of realism but takes place in a town that feels more animal than human. It has, as a prominent character, a prurient adolescent male who carries around a shrunken corpse that he worships as "the new jesus," and who finds solace in an ape suit. It ends with a man who blinds himself and wanders around with rocks in his shoes until he dies—but not before a woman tries to seduce him in a plot twist that could have come from a soap opera.

But O'Connor borrowed from the Oedipus plays something far more essential than their dramatic structure. In his book *Violence and the Sacred*, René Girard argues that modern scholars often miss the primitive aspects of Greek drama, the ways in which these plays adapt mythological themes.[2] Girard reads many of the Greek tragedies as reenactments of a primitive "sacrificial crisis" of which the Oedipus plays are exemplary. The city of Thebes suffers from plagues that come because Oedipus is a morally polluted being, having broken the cultural taboos of incest and parricide. In the primitive world, the breaking of taboos constitutes the community's loss of the distinction between the morally pure and impure, a loss that precipitates a crisis and makes corrective violence necessary. It is called a "sacrificial crisis" because Oedipus must claim responsibility for the city's woes and be banished and sacrificed before the community can be restored to order.

I believe *Wise Blood* feels so strange to us because it is the most unexpected of hybrids: it is a realistic novel with beliefs that are

---

[1] See Sally Fitzgerald's chronology in *CW*, 1244.
[2] René Girard, *Violence and the Sacred*, trans. Patrick Gregory (Baltimore: Johns Hopkins University Press, 1977).

defiantly more mythic than modern.[3] More than that, it insists that mythic thinking comes closer to reality and that the primitive world still enters this one with violence, in spite of our beliefs that we have "advanced" beyond it.[4] It depicts with monstrous detail a landscape—clearly meant to be modern America—that has been morally polluted and is in need of sacrificial redemption. To be specific, Taulkinham is a world grown monstrous because it has lost its primitive religious understanding of the essential unity of mind and body. It has become Gnostic. When the community believes that what its members do in the body has no impact on the soul, all distinctions between pure and impure are lost—especially in sexual life—and the community is in crisis. The crisis of Taulkinham is the crisis of the modern world.[5]

O'Connor believed that only an encounter with the primitive world and its instinctual insistence on the sanctity of the body can lead us to the point where we can even recognize that there is a crisis.

---

[3] The novel has mythic beliefs because the solutions offered to the sacrificial crisis are spiritual, as we shall see. But when it comes to the problems it illustrates, the landscape of *Wise Blood* is as modern as T. S. Eliot's "The Waste Land," as Sarah Gordon reminds us (Sarah Gordon, *Flannery O'Connor: The Obedient Imagination* [Athens: University of Georgia Press, 2000] 85).

[4] For a revealing analysis of the similarities between Girard's views and those of writers and residents of the South, see Laura Barge, "René Girard's Categories of Scapegoats and Literature of the South," *Christianity and Literature* 50/2 (2001): 248. Barge writes that "Girard's perspective on Christian narrative is more in line with Southern views: he does not consider the Passion of Jesus as only a religious concept but instead as an historical event. Even as early as *Violence and the Sacred* Girard puts forth his claims that religious myth not only can but must refer to something outside of itself and thus relate in a realistic sense to history."

[5] O'Connor's plan for *Wise Blood* indicates that she wanted to write about the breakdown of a community and the loss of home. "The principle [*sic*] character, an illiterate Tennessean, has lost his home through the breakdown of a country community. Home, in this instance, stands not only for the place and family, but also for some absolute belief which would give him sanctuary in the modern world. All he retained of the evangelical religion of his mother is a sense of sin and a need for religion.... This sense of sin is the only key he has to finding a sanctuary and he begins unconsciously to search for God through sin" (Gordon, *The Obedient Imagination*, 98–99).

So she brought the conflict between mythic and modern to bear in a body—that of the novel's protagonist, Hazel Motes, whom she describes as a "primitive" who is "full of the poison of the modern world" (*HB*, 403). While Haze is not solely responsible for the decay of Taulkinham as Oedipus is of Thebes, he participates bodily in it. Finally the corruption overwhelms him and he repents, becoming a kind of redemptive sacrifice. Although he himself dies, it is clear that in Haze's *body* the primitive story—the story of the wisdom of blood and of the veracity of an ancient sacrifice—wins.

When the primitive makes its appearance in the modern world, it will necessarily look grotesque. The bizarre world of *Wise Blood* is thus best explained by Geoffrey Galt Harpham's observation that the grotesque embodies the tension between the archaic and the advanced. The grotesque, he argues, "consists of the manifest, visible, or unmediated presence of mythic or primitive elements in a nonmythic or modern context."[6] It appeals to a primitive way of knowing in which the self was not separated from bodily life and defined by abstract thought. Myth addresses the "*illud tempus*, or the sacred time of the Beginnings, before history and profane time," Harpham writes "it offers even to many people today a release from the tensions and alienations of abstraction, healing the self divorced from the raw material of life and providing a tonic affirmation of the wholeness of existence...it is one of the large paradoxes of wholeness that it cannot be imagined or figured except as a violation of natural laws, in monstrous or distorted form."[7] The grotesques in *Wise Blood* evoke the primitive in exactly this way. They operate viscerally, sometimes unconsciously, in both characters and readers. The way they do so is to insist, in a primitive way that is also Christian, on the unity of mind and body, on the incarnational reality of a spiritual realm. As they operate in a primitive pre-modern way on Haze's wise blood, they become themselves symbols of the way incarnational fiction

---

[6] Geoffrey Galt Harpham, *On the Grotesque: Strategies of Contradiction in Art and Literature* (Princeton: Princeton University Press, 1982) 51.

[7] Ibid., 54–55.

operates on the readers, violently purifying us of the poisons of the modern world.

THE SACRIFICIAL CRISIS

When we are first introduced to Haze, we see the anger of an insecure man struggling against himself. The first sentence describes him "looking one minute at the window as if he might want to jump out of it, and the next down the aisle at the other end of the car" (*CW*, 3). He verbally assaults everyone, claiming intellectual superiority to people who do not even challenge him. He insults the porter unprovoked. He is a man on a mission—to go to Taulkinham in order to deny Jesus and live in sin. No one talks to him, but he responds with the anger of one accused: "Do you think I believe in Jesus? …Well I wouldn't even if He existed. Even if He was on this train" (*CW*, 7). In *Oedipus Rex*, Oedipus had first entered Thebes in order to save it; he was unaware of himself as the incestuous murderer of his father and the cause of the city's ills. But like a normally mild-mannered businessman might go to Mardi Gras in New Orleans today, Haze goes to Taulkinham deliberately to pursue immorality, to "do some things [he has] never done before." He goes in order to shake his Eastrod fundamentalist roots and his training to be a preacher. And he succeeds—at first. In a few short days he becomes grotesquely promiscuous, seduces a child, preaches nihilism, and murders a man. He is a notch worse than Jonah: he not only refuses to preach God's salvation to Nineveh; he becomes a Ninevite himself.

René Girard explains that the ancient narratives of Jonah and Oedipus tell the same story of a "sacrificial crisis." When Jonah is on the way to Tarshish to escape his calling to Nineveh, God sends a raging storm to the ship. Each man on board prays to his own god: the community is in religious disorder. Jonah knows his disobedience is the cause and tells the crewmen to cast him into the sea. They do so, appealing to Jonah's God, and the tempest stops. Thebes is in a similar crisis because of Oedipus's actions, and he must be exiled before Thebes can be redeemed. In both cases the community must be cleansed of its polluted being; in both cases, an act of violence is necessary for the cleansing.

The city of Taulkinham in *Wise Blood* is in this kind of religious disorder, but Haze participates in it willingly. As a result, Taulkinham becomes increasingly monstrous because, as Girard explains, in mythology there is no difference between the morally monstrous and the physically monstrous.[8] As many have noticed, Taulkinham is a place of easy metaphoric metamorphosis between the animal and the human.[9] People look and act like animals. Cars are "rat-colored," and even a block of white houses each sit "with an ugly dog face on a square of grass" (*CW*, 41). As a woman climbs out of the pool, she seems not even to be in control of her own body, which is practically becoming that of a dog's: "first her face appeared, long and cadaverous, with a bandage-like bathing cap coming down almost to her eyes, and sharp teeth protruding from her mouth. Then she rose on her hands until a large foot and leg came up from behind her and another on the other side and she was out, squatting there, panting" (*CW*, 47).

This animal world is the modern world gone sexually berserk. When Enoch Emery watches the bathing woman, "He moved from the clearing up a slope to some abelia bushes. There was a nice tunnel under them and he crawled into it until he came to a slightly wider place where he was accustomed to sit. He settled himself and adjusted the abelia so that he could see through it properly. His face was always very red in the bushes. Anyone who parted the abelia sprigs at just that place, would think he saw a devil and would fall down the slope and into the pool" (*CW*, 45). This deliberately Freudian scene emphasizes that the modern world is a world Freud has helped to

---

[8] Girard, *Violence and the Sacred*, 252.

[9] Frederick Asals notices that "animals and objects take on the qualities of each other and of the human" (*Flannery O'Connor: The Imagination of Extremity* [Athens: University of Georgia Press, 1982] 49). Asals argues that the density of such images makes *Wise Blood* read like a "naturalistic novel gone berserk," with O'Connor's adopting a "stock naturalistic device of applying animal and mechanical metaphors to her characters" to push the novel to "an extremity of comic horror" (ibid., 50).

make. Having lost all distinctions between pure and impure sexual behavior, people have become mere animals. After he crawls through the vaginal tunnel to voyeuristic titillation, Enoch's next words tell it all: "Well, I'll be dog" (*CW*, 46).

Thus the primal, mythic, and earthy grotesquerie of *Wise Blood* metaphorically depicts the moral degradation of man who denies God, is blind to his own depravity, and is given over to lust. The novel follows the trajectory given by the apostle Paul in Romans, where he describes how a godless world given over to its own depravity is foolish: "Because that, when they knew God, they have not glorified him as God or given thanks: but became vain in their thoughts. And their foolish heart was darkened. For, professing themselves to be wise, they became fools." Fools follow a path of increasing corruption, as Paul continues: "And they changed the glory of the incorruptible God into the likeness of the image of a corruptible man and of birds, and of four-footed beasts and of creeping things. Wherefore, God gave them up to the desires of their heart, unto uncleanness: to dishonour their own bodies among themselves."[10] As Haze descends into his rebellion, suppressing his belief in God, the world of *Wise Blood* becomes increasingly characterized by corrupted men, four-footed beasts, and creeping things. A zoo is at the center of the town; pigs roam the landscape; men ape the apes. Order has dissolved, violence escalates, promiscuity reigns—the world is plagued. But where did this poison come from? What has precipitated the crisis in which Haze participates?

In the world of Taulkinham, the answer is clear. Modern man's denial of the fundamental connection between body and soul has enabled him to dismiss the idea of sin, which is dependent upon maintaining categories of purity and impurity. Without sin there is no need for God, and so acts against purity are committed without shame, repentance, or redemption. But primitive religion shares with Christianity a belief in the wholeness of man and of the purity or impurity of acts done in the body. In a passage O'Connor underlined in *Patterns in Comparative Religion*, Mircea Eliade notes that what

---

[10] Romans 1:18–24.

separates "the people of the early cultures from people today is precisely the utter incapacity of the latter to live their organic life (particularly as regards sex and nutrition) as a sacrament...for the modern they are simply physiological acts, whereas for primitive man they were sacraments, ceremonies by means of which he communicated with the force which stood for Life itself."[11]

So much of *Wise Blood* centers on sex and sexual sin that many critics have argued that the novel reveals O'Connor's Jansenist horror of sex itself.[12] But just because O'Connor chose not to depict sex in its lawful context does not mean she *could* not. O'Connor more often chose to illustrate rottenness than wholeness, and sex is simply an easy avenue through which to illustrate the degradation of the modern world. Sexual sins are sins obviously committed against the wholeness of mind and body, and committed by modern men out of utter disregard for the sacred power or ultimate value of sex. The glutton eats to excess because he too little values food, not because he overvalues it. Modern man has become a sexual glutton, and the value of sex has decreased with its abuse. G. K. Chesterton explains that "to complain that I could only be married once was like complaining that I had only been born once. It was incommensurate with the terrible excitement of which one was talking. It showed, not an exaggerated sensibility to sex, but a curious insensibility to it."[13] If man believed in the sacramental force of sex, he would be a good deal less cavalier about it.

Haze tries his hardest to be cavalier about sex. But he has an innate conviction—which he represses—that sex is connected to life, that it reveals the unity of body and soul, and that sexual sins are sins

---

[11] Mircea Eliade, *Patterns in Comparative Religion*, trans. Rosemary Sheed (New York: Sheed and Ward, 1958) 31.

[12] Shortly after O'Connor's death, Warren Coffey wrote, "as an American Catholic, Flannery O'Connor was, of course, a Jansenist.... I think that Jansenism, more than anything else, explains both her very considerable power at the short story and her limitations. The pride of intellect, the corruption of the heart, the horror of sex—all these appear again and again in her books, and against them, the desperate assertion of faith" (Warren Coffey, "Flannery O'Connor," *Commentary* 40/5 [1965]: 96).

[13] Gilbert K. Chesterton, *Orthodoxy* (New York: Doubleday, 1990) 58.

against his own person. Most important, his wise blood teaches him that removed from its sacramental context, sex will lead to death. This innate understanding is why Haze remembers his childhood immediately after one of his nights with the prostitute, Leora Watts. He remembers the "SINsational" circus show, where as a young boy he paid fifteen cents to view a spectacle along with other men from the community:

> They were looking down into a lowered place where something white was lying, squirming a little, in a box lined with black cloth. For a second he thought it was a skinned animal and then he saw it was a woman. She was fat and she had a face like an ordinary woman except there was a mole on the corner of her lip, that moved when she grinned, and one on her side.

> "Had one of themther built into ever' casket," his father, up toward the front, said, "be a heap ready to go sooner." (*CW*, 35)

Though only a young boy, Haze knew something was not right about this. By rendering a woman's body into a grotesque spectacle, the men illustrated the link between illicit sex and death—her body looked like a skinned animal in a coffin—that would stay with Haze forever. When Haze heard his father's voice implicated in this scene of illicit desire, he scrambled out of the tent with a load of guilt. When he returned home, his mother knew he had seen something and hit him across the legs with a switch, saying "Jesus died to redeem you." When she approached him, his mind substituted his mother's tall thin body for the body of the fat woman he had just seen in the casket. Filled with a "nameless unplaced guilt," he filled his shoes with rocks and walked a mile in a primitive penance.

The clear link Haze makes between death, sex, and his mother make this passage a favorite among psychoanalytic critics.[14] Much of

---

[14] James M. Mellard writes that "Hazel Motes is still beset by the desire of the (m)other, that he still must find some way to escape her devouring gaze, and that he must find an Oedipal Other, an Other of the Law, an Other who will properly impose the law of lack (that is, castration), in order to cure those horror-ridden dreams" ("Framed in the Gaze: Haze, Wise Blood, and Lacanian Reading," in *New Essays on "Wise Blood,"* ed. Michael Kreyling [Cambridge: Cambridge University Press, 1995] 59).

their analysis rests on an assessment of Haze as a pathological character and of this early experience as trauma, concluding that O'Connor was afraid of sex. If this early experience is pathological, Haze's move at the end of the novel to put stones in his shoes again can only be seen as regression. But O'Connor clearly sees the return to this kind of thinking as Haze's redemption, because it illustrates his conviction that the body does matter and that he is not free to escape it. Haze has always had "a deep black wordless conviction in him that the way to avoid Jesus was to avoid sin" (*CW*, 11)—in other words, he knows that to acknowledge sin is to acknowledge need for redemption, just as he did in that early scene. O'Connor celebrates Haze's knowledge of Christ, the moral law, and the unity of body and soul that is purely practical, preconscious, and noncognitive. As a force in life decisions it is anything but abstract.[15] In *Approaches to God*, Jacques Maritain insists that such "primordial" or "prephilosophic" knowledge of God is valid—though intellectually unsophisticated—because it is based on the "solidity of existence."[16]

For O'Connor the modern world, not Haze, is pathological. Driven by desire and numb to any spiritual consideration of their bodies, Haze's friends encourage him to ignore his "wise blood" and go with them to a brothel. At first Haze's homespun training kicks in and he puts on his mother's glasses and refuses to join them. But his convictions fail him when the modern world begins its poisoning. When he tells his friends he would rather refrain and keep his soul, they laugh at him. "They told him he didn't have any soul and left for their brothel" (*CW*, 12). Shunned by his fellows, Haze begins to blind himself to his instincts so that he can be "free" to follow their

---

[15]Marshall Bruce Gentry argues that Haze's grandfather taught him to put a heavy emphasis on the physical such that "abstractions became a torment to him" and sin remained incomprehensible without a physical association (*Flannery O'Connor's Religion of the Grotesque* [Jackson: University Press of Mississippi, 1986] 126). When Haze connects sin to sex, argues Gentry, he pursues a strange logic of committing more sin in order to prove to himself his need for Jesus, and thus prepares the way for his own redemption.

[16]Jacques Maritain, *Approaches to God, World Perspectives*, vol. 1 (New York: Harper, 1954) 15. In *The Range of Reason* Maritain writes that such knowledge will remain unfruitful if it remains ignorant (New York: Scribner, 1952).

way of life.[17] "He took a long time to believe them because he wanted to believe them. All he wanted was to believe them and get rid of it once and for all, and he saw the opportunity here to get rid of it without corruption, to be converted to nothing instead of to evil" (*CW*, 12). With distance between him and his hometown ("he was gone four years; he didn't get back, even for a visit"), Haze can assert his will to believe according to these new desires. He wants to believe in "nothing" because it is a good deal easier to bear than a load of sin and guilt—and the memory of his mother's switch. He wants to live in a place in which free sex carries no guilt. So from this point forward, Haze tries to abandon his soul and his memories in favor of what he wills to "know." "He had all the time he could want to study his soul in and assure himself that it was not there. When he was thoroughly convinced, he saw that this was something that he had always known" (*CW*, 12–13).

The word "soul" has philosophical as well as theological significance in O'Connor's work. Etienne Gilson argues that the primary problem of the modern world is that we have effectively lost our souls by an illegitimate act of mental fiat. To save himself from what he cannot know, Gilson argues, Descartes substituted the word "mind" for "soul" because "soul" assumes an inexorable link to the body.[18] Man is a thinker; his body is a mere machine; therefore, what he does with his body is not important. By insisting that he could study anything away or will a truth to live by, Haze becomes the quintessential inheritor of the *cogito ergo sum*—I think; therefore, I am. The further he moves from the life of the body in Eastrod to the life of the mind in "Talking"ham, the more firmly he believes in modern philosophy's next step: "I think; therefore, the world can be as I think."

---

[17] Brian Abel Ragen argues that Haze's journey thus resembles that of the mythic American Adam with his insistence on individual male autonomy. *Wise Blood*, he argues, subverts that myth (Ragen, *A Wreck on the Road to Damascus: Innocence, Guilt, & Conversion in Flannery O'Connor* [Chicago: Loyola University Press, 1989]).

[18] Etienne Gilson, *History of Christian Philosophy in the Middle Ages* (New York: Random House, 1955) 163.

Haze puts his new beliefs to the test right away. On his first night in Taulkinham, Haze enters the world of modern sexuality through its most representative portal: a phone number written on the door of the men's toilet. The scenes depicting Haze's encounters with Leora Watts are among the most grotesque and comic in the novella. When he arrives at the house she was "sitting alone in a white iron bed, cutting her toenail with a large pair of scissors. She was a big woman with very yellow hair and white skin that glistened with a greasy preparation. She had on a pink nightgown that would better have fit a smaller figure. ...His senses were stirred to the limit" (*CW*, 17). Which of his senses are actually stirred is left to us to decide. But for his part, Haze is bound and determined to fornicate; he is not even deterred later when Leora grins to reveal teeth that were "small and pointed and speckled with green and there was a wide space between each one" (*CW*, 18).

In O'Connor's fiction, grotesque bodies do not always represent sin and impurity—in "A Temple of the Holy Ghost" the hermaphrodite's body represents the Eucharist. But in the monstrously mythical world of *Wise Blood*, the grotesque body of the prostitute clearly matches the moral monstrosity of prostitution. Haze's turn to Leora Watts's grotesque body also illustrates his self-degradation, for the apostle Paul's reasoning against prostitution is based on the body's being the residence of Christ. "Know you not that your bodies are the members of Christ? Shall I then take the members of Christ, and make them the members of a harlot? God forbid. Or know you not, that he who is joined to a harlot, is made one body?"[19] Paul means to make believers shudder at the incongruity of what is holy being united with a prostitute. O'Connor makes Leora's body grotesque to emphasize Haze's deliberate refusal to acknowledge that sex has any impact on his soul. It is not weakness in his flesh but deliberate defiance in his *will* that drives him to her. In her article "Carnal Abominations: The Female Body as Grotesque," Margaret Miles points to evidence that medieval Christian soldiers were instructed to think of the female body as grotesque in order to resist

---

[19] 1 Corinthians 6:15–16.

lust. Erasmus had instructed men to think of a prostitute's body as a "stinking hog wallow of lust."[20] That Leora's body is in fact hog-like and still does not repel Haze is thus ironic and emphasizes the extent of his willful self-degradation.[21] He is trying to drive Christ out of the temple of his body, and it is meant to appear to us as a rude and ridiculous trade. "What do I need with Jesus?" Haze says later, "I got Leora Watts" (*CW*, 31).

As Haze descends deeper into the moral morass of Taulkinham, he continues to try to prove to himself that the spiritual realities he has been taught have no real claim on him. He believes he can reduce Jesus to words and then declare his own redemption. It is not simply for humorous effect that Christ's name appears in *Wise Blood* only in imprecations. Haze curses "Jesus. My Jesus" whenever someone confronts him. While Haze means the words to be empty sounds, O'Connor makes us laugh at how they hit on the reality that Haze wants to deny: Jesus *is* Haze's Jesus, in spite of what he says. Christ teaches "let your yes be yes, and your no be no, or you will be condemned," in part to warn the faithful that to treat the Almighty lightly by bringing him into human oaths made with words is to deny the power of the larger reality that lies behind them.

Haze does not want reality; he wants words he can manipulate. When Onnie Jay Holy (Hoover Shoats) says he wants to see Haze's new jesus, because he had also "seen how a new one would be more up-to-date," Haze's response shows the heart of his problem: "listen here…there's no such thing as any new jesus. That ain't anything but a way to say something…no such thing exists!" (*CW*, 90). Haze is a man poisoned by the modern world. His ideas come first and he seeks a metaphor to explain them. Words are severed from

---

[20] Margaret Miles, "Carnal Abominations: The Female Body as Grotesque," in *The Grotesque in Art and Literature: Theological Reflections*, ed. James Luther Adams and Wilson Yates (Grand Rapids: W. B. Eerdmans, 1997) 106.

[21] Many critics with feminist concerns are understandably troubled by these degraded depictions of female sexuality. But O'Connor's goal was to depict the general degradation of sexuality in the modern world. Enoch Emery, for example, is equally sexually perverse and just as ugly. Haze cannot be considered a comparison because he is struggling against the degradation.

substances—they are tools for manipulation. In the new way of thinking that Haze is desperate to maintain, Jesus can be reduced to a story, a myth, an illustration to explain some abstract idea that one can think about with one's mind instead of know with one's soul.[22] Onnie Jay's remark makes O'Connor's point with the humor it deserves. When Haze cannot produce the new jesus, Onnie Jay quips, "That's the trouble with you innerleckchuls...you don't never have nothing to show for what you're saying" (*CW*, 90).

The boy who works in the car lot makes the same joke for O'Connor. When Haze asks how much the car costs, the boy curses: "Jesus on the cross...Christ nailed" (*CW*, 38). The curse touches reality in this case, too, for when Haze creates his "church of the truth without Christ," he particularly wants to emphasize that redemption through this new church will not *cost* anything. Haze wants to live in a world that has no need for Jesus to die for sin because sin is not real. Reduce sin to words, and God does not need to become an actual man and shed actual blood. In the Hebrew Scriptures, God's declaration "I AM" speaks to his self-sustaining, self-determining, sovereign reality—that God *is* the ultimate Being.[23] Haze mocks God and only looks ridiculous when he tries to play Jesus to himself and effect his own redemption by a constitutive speech act, emphasized with the same capital letters: "I AM clean" (*CW*, 52). In a conversation with Asa Hawks, he says, "'Listen...I'm as clean as you are.' 'Fornication and blasphemy and what else?' the blind man said. 'They ain't nothing but words,' Haze said" (*CW*, 29).

Haze's declaration that he is clean represents the nadir of the sacrificial crisis his descent into Taulkinham effects. With acts done in the flesh completely sundered from his soul, he no longer needs to

---

[22] Allen Tate describes this "angelic imagination" as that which "tries to disintegrate or to circumvent the image in the illusory pursuit of essence. When human beings undertake this ambitious program, divine love becomes so rarefied that it loses its human paradigm, and is dissolved in the worship of intellectual power, the surrogate of divinity that worships itself" (Tate, *The Forlorn Demon: Didactic and Critical Essays* [Chicago: Regnery, 1953] 37).

[23] Jesus declares his own divinity by using this phrase in reference to himself in the Gospel of John.

abide by any distinction between pure and impure. In fact, it is the effacement of these distinctions that most characterizes the doctrine of his new church. Sabbath Hawks, the hypocrite preacher's daughter, wants to join Haze's church so she can feel better about living any way she chooses. To test his church, she mentions to Haze that she was born out of wedlock. "Can a bastard be in it?" she asks. Haze replies that "there's no such thing as a bastard in the Church Without Christ.... Everything is all one. A bastard wouldn't be any different from anybody else" (*CW*, 69). That "everything is all one" is precisely the problem with the doctrine, and Haze knows it. He recognizes his own contradiction—"the thing in his mind said that the truth didn't contradict itself"—but he tries to convince himself of it anyway. "There wouldn't be any sense to the word, bastard, in the Church Without Christ" (*CW*, 69).

A world without bastards is a world without moral distinctions. It is, therefore, a world in crisis. Girard explains that primitive religion and classical tragedy share the implicit principle that "order, peace, and fecundity depend on cultural distinctions; it is not these distinctions but the loss of them that gives birth to fierce rivalries and sets members of the same family or social group at one another's throats."[24] Shakespeare illustrates this principle by opening *King Lear* with a reference to Edmund's bastard status. Edmund's insistence that the differences do not matter creates the sacrificial crisis that makes Gloucester's public blinding and death a purgative act of violence necessary to the restoration of order. The world of *Wise Blood* has descended much further into disorder. And the fact that Asa Hawks, Sabbath's father, only fakes his blindness shows that there is still a need for a valid act of redemptive violence.

But Haze will not yet own up to any of Taulkinham's sins. His denial of sin and his assertion of himself as clean make him the quintessential modern man in another exemplary way. He can laugh at the past out of which he has "advanced," for it has no hold on him. When he preaches his new church, he preaches modernity's church:

---

[24] Girard, *Violence and the Sacred*, 49.

we are all free from our primitive pasts. We are left in the placeless place of self:

> "I preach there are all kinds of truth, your truth and somebody else's, but behind all of them, there's only one truth and that is that there's no truth," he called. "No truth behind all truths is what I and this church preach! Where you come from is gone, where you thought you were going to never was there, and where you are is no good unless you can get away from it. Where is there a place for you to be? No place.

> "Nothing outside you can give you any place," he said. "You needn't to look at the sky because it's not going to open up and show no place behind it. You needn't to search for any hole in the ground to look through into somewhere else. You can't go neither forwards nor backwards into your daddy's time nor your children's if you have them. In yourself right now is all the place you've got." (*CW*, 93)

This is a Cartesian speech. Modern man, in order to live in the certainty of his own mind, must exile himself to placeless isolation. And he does so with pride, claiming himself to be the "demystifier" of primitive thought. Science has liberated us from the past, as Girard explains: "In severing the cord that attached us to the matrix of all mythic thought, this liberator of humanity will have delivered us from dark ancestral falsehood and led us into the luminous world of truth."[25] Haze's liberation speech also reminds us of Emerson's insistence that "good and bad are but names very readily transferable to that or this; the only right is what is after my constitution; the only wrong what is against it."[26] In the world of *Wise Blood*, this is no triumph. When good and bad are merely names, people inhabit an illusory mental space instead of their actual bodies, and the crisis descends.

But Haze, remember, is a primitive. The appearance of the grotesque is meant to ignite his primitive instincts. The grotesque assumes that the dark ancestral world still has power to challenge our neat categories, that acts done in and to the body can still penetrate

---

[25] Ibid., 233.

[26] Ralph Waldo Emerson, *Selected Essays*, ed. Larzer Ziff (New York: Penguin, 1982) 179.

and challenge our mental fictions. So O'Connor hits Haze—and the reader—with grotesque bodies of incredible mythic power. One such body is the new jesus.

ENOCH EMERY'S GROTESQUE GIFT

O'Connor probably learned from Edgar Allan Poe that the grotesque body could do this kind of primitive and challenging work. She wrote that as a child she went through an "Edgar Allan Poe period which lasted for years and consisted chiefly in a volume called The Humerous Tales of EAPoe," and added, "this is an influence I would rather not think about." After citing a formidable list of writers she read at Iowa and later, she concludes the paragraph "but always the largest thing that looms up is The Humerous Tales of Edgar Allan Poe. I am sure he wrote them all while drunk too" (*CW*, 951).

Poe's story "The Spectacles" predicts *Wise Blood*. In it, a young, myopic protagonist named Simpson vainly refuses to wear glasses. When he goes to the theater and falls in love with one of the actresses, he builds a rich imaginative life and makes himself the center of an elaborate plot to seduce and marry her. She eventually agrees, but on the condition that he wear his glasses on their wedding day. He does, and discovers not only that he had nearly married a wrinkled octogenarian grotesquely caked with makeup, but that he had also nearly married his great-great grandmother. She had decided to play along to teach Simpson a lesson.

In Poe's story, as in O'Connor's, the characters are so self-deluded that they must be shocked not by an event, a symbol, an idea, or a text, but by a physical body rendered grotesque. The reason is simple: the defining characteristic of Simpson's ideality is its separation of his mind from the world "out there." He can maintain his fantasy only by never looking at the woman's actual body. To actually see it is to be unable to appropriate it into his fantasies about himself. It would be to identify it as wholly and unpredictably other.

So Poe must make of the body a spectacle. He must render it grotesque for it to be seen at all. He must bring Simpson to the point of physical contact with the actual body of the other for him to discover the extent of his ideality. Simpson's fantasies are also uniquely modern in that their fulfillment would constitute a defiance of taboos regarding sexual life. Here it is both the incest prohibition and the conventional role of marriage in producing offspring; to marry his great-great grandmother would be to lose the distinction between pure and impure sexual relations. Poe clearly relies on his readers to still share those distinctions, and then to react to the older woman's body, *in this context*, as grotesque.

In *Wise Blood*, Haze gets his dose of the grotesque body through Enoch Emery. Critics have had a hard time with the ambiguity of this character—he is so animal-like and crude that many want to dismiss him as a comic or diabolic foil and reduce him to the merely animal, as if he exists only to reveal Haze's spirituality by contrast.[27] But this stance ignores the essential and active role Enoch plays in Haze's rediscovery of the necessary connection between the spiritual and the physical. It ignores what Haze must relearn from him. After all, Enoch's "wise blood" is similar to Haze's; he simply lacks the ability to temper it. Enoch Emery is the ultimate example of the foolish shaming the wise with a primitive, poetic, unironic wisdom that lies somewhere beyond the realm of the intellect. Enoch "knows" that

---

[27] O'Connor criticism has largely followed the lead of Carter W. Martin, who calls Enoch the "fully realized existentialist," a being so fully immersed in the world of the body that he shows Haze's spirituality by contrast (Martin, *The True Country: Themes in the Fiction of Flannery O'Connor* [Nashville: Vanderbilt University Press, 1968] 67). Kathleen Feeley says of Enoch that "his descent into animality shows—in caricature—the alternative Hazel could have taken" (Feeley, *Flannery O'Connor: Voice of the Peacock* [New Brunswick NJ: Rutgers University Press, 1972] 65). But in his reading of *Wise Blood* as a tale that chronicles Haze's search for redemption, Marshall Bruce Gentry has reassessed Enoch as a kind of secondary protagonist who is "at once an apostate and a disciple. "Even when critics condemn Enoch, Gentry argues, they prove his essential role in the story. Gentry points out that early manuscripts of *Wise Blood* indicate that O'Connor had designed an even more central role for Enoch, so that at first glance he appears to be the story's protagonist. Gentry argues that Enoch "degrades his oppressive religion to a physical level" but that ultimately he, like Haze, is equipped to "use the grotesque positively," and his story, although subordinated to Haze's, complements it (Gentry, *Religion of the Grotesque*, 136–40).

the mummified man—the grotesque "new jesus"—is important to Haze, that it is something he has to see, touch, be confronted with. His gospel, though perverse, has primitive wholeness and palpability. In its palpability lies its revelatory and redemptive power.

In terms of O'Connor's incarnational aesthetic, to call Enoch an idiot is to enhance his credibility as one innocent enough to be used of God, as O'Connor says, to "set the havoc in motion" (*CW*, 1147). In a letter to the Corinthians, the apostle Paul emphasizes the vast difference between the wisdom of God and the wisdom of man,[28] adding that the lowliest men by earthly standards have been chosen *specifically* to shame the wise of this world. "For see your vocation, brethren, that there are not many wise according to the flesh, not many mighty, not many noble. But the foolish things of the world hath God chosen, that he may confound the wise: and the weak things of the world hath God chosen, that he may confound the strong. And the base things of the world and the things that are contemptible, hath God chosen: and things that are not, that he might bring to nought things that are: That no flesh should glory in his sight."[29]

While Hazel Motes denies his instincts, Enoch Emery lives entirely by his. When Enoch begins his preparations for the new jesus, his wise blood takes over, and the narrator remarks, "If he had been much given to thought, he might have thought that now was the time for him to justify his daddy's blood, but he didn't think in broad sweeps like that, he thought what he would do next. Sometimes he didn't think, he only wondered; then before long he would find himself doing this or that, like a bird finds itself building a nest when it hasn't actually been planning to" (*CW*, 73).

While Enoch's extremes are ridiculous here, O'Connor does not completely disapprove of his instinctual (and active) response to the world. In fact, his instincts may even constitute the beginnings of a

---

[28] "...Jews require signs: and the Greeks seek after wisdom. But we preach Christ crucified: unto the Jews indeed a stumbling block, and unto the Gentiles foolishness: But unto them that are called, both Jews and Greeks, Christ, the power of God and the wisdom of God. For the foolishness of God is wiser than men: and the weakness of God is stronger than men" (1 Corinthians 1:22–25).

[29] 1 Corinthians 1:26–29.

kind of poetic wisdom. When O'Connor described how she wrote *Wise Blood*, she used the same phraseology she used to describe Enoch's actions. When she glossed Haze as a character that she meant to be full of the "poison of the modern world," she added "of course, that isn't all there is in it and when I wrote it my mind was not primarily on these abstract things but only on what would Haze and Enoch do next, they being themselves..." (*HB*, 403). And in another letter she made an explicit comparison: "as you must know I wrote the book just like Enoch would have, not knowing too well why I did what but knowing it was right. I think everything in the book is right and I am astounded by it" (*CW*, 919).

It would be easy to pass off O'Connor's sympathy with Enoch as a mere joke, but *Wise Blood* does not allow it. The novella suggests that the knowledge Enoch Emery has is the same *kind* of knowledge as poetic knowledge, although in Enoch it is misdirected, perverted, and incomplete. Consider O'Connor's use of Enoch to help her aestheticize the new jesus in this story. The new jesus is a shriveled man displayed in one of three glass cases; it stands in the middle of the floor in a room at the center of the museum. The museum is in the center of the park, and the park is in the heart of the city. Isolated in a museum, the new jesus is already a kind of *objet d'art*, removed from its context and waiting to be seen for its significance. Enoch, like a prophet or an artist, has a special (if limited) vision of the shriveled man, and his discovery compels him to reveal to others what he has seen: "There was something, in the center of the park, that he had discovered. It was a mystery, although it was right there in a glass case for everybody to see and there was a typewritten card over it telling all about it. But there was something the card couldn't say and what it couldn't say was inside him, a terrible knowledge without any words to it, a terrible knowledge like a big nerve growing inside him. He could not show the mystery to just anybody; but he had to show it to somebody" (*CW*, 45).

The wordless knowledge Enoch has of the mystery in the museum contrasts sharply with Hazel's wordy assertions of truth. Enoch has a mystical knowledge that this shriveled being can mean something to the right viewer and that this meaning cannot be

contained in words written on a card. According to the neo-Thomist
scholarship O'Connor admired, mystical knowledge like Enoch's is of
the same order as poetic knowledge; it is just mute (and in Enoch's
case revealingly misapplied). Maritain argues that mystical knowledge
and poetic knowledge both grasp their object through what Aquinas
called "connaturality." In other words, knowledge of the significance
of something in concrete existence comes not by "means of concepts
and conceptual knowledge, but by means of an obscure knowledge
which [is] knowledge through affective union."[30]

Enoch's "affective union" with the new jesus is absurd because
the new jesus in itself is unworthy of the attention, and Enoch's
eventual worship of this dead man constitutes one of the most
perverse scenes in the story. But at the same time, Enoch's instincts
are at least *whole*. He looks for mystery in the world around him. He
wants to do something, to act on what he sees. There is no ideality in
Enoch as there is in Haze, who only moves around a lot, getting
nowhere and doing nothing. Enoch may be an idiot, but his primary
action in the text, his instinct to show the new jesus and not to talk
about it, leads to the central confrontation that will begin Haze's
redemption. While one critic has argued that Enoch has "a diabolical
attraction to mystery," it might be more correct to say that he has an
"attraction to diabolical mystery"—his attraction to the significance
of what is out there is correct, but what he is interested in has
perverse spiritual content.[31]

Enoch's perverse attachment to a dead body makes him a
participant in the escalation of the sacrificial crisis in Haze's life and
in the community of Taulkinham. Girard points out that in primitive
cultures that dismiss the gods or render them insignificant, the dead
ancestors of the community start to show up to disrupt things.[32] He
explains that "when incest, adultery, and other social ills begin to

---

[30]Jacques Maritain, *Creative Intuition in Art and Poetry* (New York: Pantheon
Books, 1953) 115.

[31] See Feeley, *Voice of the Peacock*, 65.

[32] Girard writes that "...mythic ancestors, or the dead, take the place of the
missing divinities and are seen as the founders, guardians and, if need be, disrupters
of the cultural order" (Girard, *Violence and the Sacred,* 254).

proliferate, when family relationships begin to crumble, the dead are displeased and visit their displeasure on the living. They bring nightmares, madness, contagious diseases; they provoke discord among relatives and neighbors and instigate all sorts of perversions."[33]

O'Connor has Enoch bring a dead body to Haze because it will activate Haze's wise blood. Although Haze wants to believe the modern view he teaches in his church that "the dead are dead and stay that way," he can find no power in the doctrine to ameliorate his fear of death. Modernity's scientific view can only work to put off death or separate us from it as long as possible—it cannot prepare us for it. Haze, we find out, had never really dealt with his mother's death; he seems to expect to find her and other members of his family when he returns to Eastrod from the military. When he tries to sleep on the train, thoughts of death overwhelm him. The closeness of the sleeper's berth feels like a coffin to him, and as he drifts in and out of sleep, he thinks of his grandfather's, brother's, and mother's funerals in turn. In each case he had denied the reality of death by fantasizing that the people would spring out and escape their coffins (*CW*, 9–10). When Haze's thoughts turn to the memory of his mother in her coffin, Haze puts himself into her body, sees from her point of view, and feels the lid closing on him. He springs up and yells at the porter, "I'm sick! ...I can't be closed up in this thing. Get me out!" (*CW*, 14).

Through Enoch's primitive beliefs and violent interjections into Haze's life, O'Connor grotesquely foregrounds death and forbids Haze his modern escape from it. He *will* look at it, and it will appear to him as a mythic harbinger of the death his immorality has invited. When Enoch brings Haze to look at the shriveled man, we see Haze focus through Enoch's eyes: "All he could tell was that Hazel Motes's eyes were on the shrunken man. He was bent forward so that his face was reflected on the glass top of the case. The reflection was pale and the eyes were like two clean bullet holes. Enoch waited, rigid" (*CW*, 56). In a novel so much about seeing, this is an extraordinary moment, and Enoch contrives it all. He provides the opportunity for Haze, and he

---

[33] Girard, *Violence and the Sacred*, 254.

nervously prays that he will have time enough to react. When Enoch
hears footsteps, the narrator records, "Oh Jesus, Jesus, he prayed, let
him hurry up and do whatever he's going to do! The woman with the
two little boys came in the door. She had one by each hand, and she
was grinning. Hazel Motes had not raised his eyes once from the
shrunken man. The woman came toward them. She stopped on the
other side of the case and looked down into it and the reflection of
her face appeared grinning on the glass, over Hazel Motes's" (*CW*,
56).

The grotesque, as Harpham argues, highlights the act of
perception. It represents the "scene of transformation to and from
the realm of the meaningful" so that "looking at ourselves looking at
the grotesque, we can observe our own projections, catching ourselves,
as it were, in the act of perception."[34] Hazel's discovery here
operates the way that O'Connor considered her own art to operate on
the reader. When Haze looks into the case and sees his reflection and
the mother's transposed onto the dead man's, the vision jars him. He
cannot prevent his own death any more than he could his mother's or
anybody else's in the decaying town of Eastrod. From the standpoint
of the goals of incarnational art, one thing is clear. In *Wise Blood*,
Enoch performs and re-performs a literal *habeas corpus*—he
produces the body. Haze must experience, with his senses, an actual
dead body to remember that, for an atheist, real death is the necessary
and indisputable end of men. Haze must feel the power of literal death
in his gut before a literally resurrected Christ can mean anything.
O'Connor explained it simply: "The book is about somebody whose
insistence on what he would like to think is the truth leads him to
what he most does not want. As I see Haze, he most does not want to
have been redeemed. He most wants man to be shut of God. Enoch,
with his wise blood, unerringly lights on what man looks like without
God and obligingly brings it for Haze to have a look at" (*CW*, 920).
Haze does not have an aesthetic vision *per se*. But the readers do, and
that could not happen unless the event has some kind of compelling
reality for Haze. In other words, the reader has an experience because

---

[34] Harpham, *On the Grotesque,* 40, 43.

Haze does; as Bakhtin puts it, "an aesthetic reaction is a reaction to another reaction, and a reaction not to objects and to meaning in themselves, but to objects and to meaning as they are for a given human being, i.e., as correlated with the values of a given human being."[35] O'Connor cannot hope to strike a chord for all readers in the new jesus as a universal *symbol*, but she can let us experience Haze's reaction to its literal meaning for him. We experience aesthetically what he experiences concretely. The meaning cannot be divorced from the particular context of Haze's experience.

O'Connor shared with Gabriel Marcel the belief that the physical world could yield such experiences. In *The Mystery of Being,* Marcel argues that modern man lacks any sense of the transcendent and that the way to recover it is not to transcend experience, but to go through it. Artists already have this instinct, which is more primitive: "It is not a reference arrived [at] by way of abstract thought, but rather one that is grasped through intimate lived experience—experience, in the sort of case I am talking about, intimately lived in the inner awareness of the poet or the artist."[36] Marcel argues that because our experience of the transcendent (God) is an experience of a *being* as other, it stands against the philosophy of the last century that was "in a very large measure dominated by a prejudice...[that] consisted in admitting that all experience in the end comes down to a self's experience of its own internal states."[37] Like O'Connor's readers, Haze has been knocked over the head with something "other" to him, an exaggeration of reality—in this case, death writ large—to help him to see the rot in the self and the rot in

---

[35] M. M. Bakhtin, *Art and Answerability: Early Philosophical Essays,* ed. Michael Holquist and Vadim Liapunov, trans. Vadim Liapunov (Austin: University of Texas Press, 1990) 222.

[36] Gabriel Marcel, *The Mystery of Being*, vol. 1 (London: Harvill Press, 1950) 45.

[37] Ibid., 49. Stephen L. Tanner writes that both O'Connor and Marcel were "what might be called reflective empiricists who believed that concrete human experience is the only avenue to the mystery of being" (Tanner, "Flannery O'Connor and Gabriel Marcel," *Literature and Belief* 17/1–2 [1997]: 151).

the world. Hazel responds as one would expect: he runs away, knocking the pursuing Enoch Emery in the head with a rock.

Recall Girard's argument that in the absence of gods, primitive cultures substitute the worship of the dead. The rites reflect the primitive understanding of death as the ultimate violence against life. They also suggest the need for legitimate sacrificial violence that would be capable of restoring order. "The worship of the dead, like the worship of the gods, represents an interpretation of the role of violence in the destiny of a community. In fact, it is the most transparent of all such interpretations, the closest to what actually occurred the first time—except, of course, that it has misconstrued, as always, the mechanism of recovered unanimity. This interpretation states explicitly that the origin of any cultural order involves a human death and that the decisive death is that of a member of the community."[38] When Enoch brings the new jesus to a shrine in his house to worship him, the scene emphasizes how degraded Taulkinham has become, how much in need of a pure sacrificial victim, a real Jesus. Once again, the grotesque becomes revelatory of the true content of the perversions. The grotesque is brought from the margin to the center—the body is again made spectacle in order to teach.

Enoch prepares his room as a kind of second museum for the new jesus; he had never thought of cleaning it before, but now he does. The shrine he has reserved for the shriveled man is a washstand with grotesque decorations: "directly over this place for the treasure, there was a gray marble slab and coming up from behind it was a wooden trellis-work of hearts, scrolls and flowers, extending into a hunched eagle wing on either side, and containing in the middle, just at the level of Enoch's face when he stood in front of it, a small oval mirror. The wooden frame continued again over the mirror and ended in a crowned, horned headpiece, showing that the artist had not lost faith in his work" (*CW*, 74). O'Connor mocks this perverted version of the Hebrew ark of the covenant, the place where God literally resided between two "hunched" cherubim. While in the Hebrew

---

[38] Girard, *Violence and the Sacred*, 256.

tabernacle the craftsman's handiwork highlighted the transcendent, in Enoch's room the art absurdly highlights death, not life. By aestheticizing these perversions via grotesque defamiliarization, O'Connor renders the perverse tabernacle *revelatory*.[39]

Enoch, whose intellect is so underdeveloped that he thinks a dead man should be worshiped, must be sent off to his bestial ending. But as a Christian, O'Connor believed his primitive convictions to be more real than Haze's modern denials. O'Connor's convictions about the nearness of primitive religions to Christianity came largely from Mircea Eliade's *Patterns in Comparative Religion*. O'Connor reviewed the book in 1958 when she wrote that it "describes various religious hierophanies—rite, myth, cosmogony, god—in relation to and as a manifestation of the mental world of those who believed in them."[40] O'Connor advised readers of the book that although the hierophanies are "in general alien to the Judeo-Christian religious life," the book should be studied as a way to "understand the meaning of the sacred in primitive cultures."[41] She marked in her copy and quoted in her review the following passage: "That the dialectic of hierophanies of the manifestation of the sacred in material things

---

[39] The washstand's mirror, which sits "just at the level of Enoch's face," indicates that there is something to be learned about one's self by looking into an artistic rendition of what one worships when one believes in nothing. Enoch takes seriously both the washstand and the three pictures that are hanging in his room, and the humor in the narrator's description works as it does when Huckleberry Finn admires the "art" in the Grangerford home. One picture, given to Enoch by his nearly blind landlady, is of a moose with a smug face that Enoch feels watches him all the time. Instead of removing the picture, he "realized with a sudden intuition that taking the frame off him would be equal to taking the clothes off him (although he didn't have on any) and he was right because when he had done it, the animal looked so reduced that Enoch could only snicker and look at him out the corner of his eye" (*CW*, 75). Just as Enoch had given a dead body spiritual value, he has attributed more power to this meaningless picture than it actually has. But his belief that the heavy brown frame "added to [the moose's] weight and his self-satisfied look" at least illustrates his poetic instinct that framing—setting aside, recontextualizing, and centering—matters.

[40] Leo J. Zuber, comp., *The Presence of Grace and Other Book Reviews by Flannery O'Connor*, ed. Carter W. Martin (Athens: University of Georgia Press, 1983) 58.

[41] Ibid.

should be an object for even such complex theology as that of the Middle Ages serves to prove that it remains the cardinal problem of any religion. One might even say that all hierophanies are simply prefigurations of the miracles of the Incarnation, that every hierophany is an abortive attempt to reveal the mystery of the coming together of God and man."[42]

Although O'Connor had not yet read Eliade when she worked on *Wise Blood*, his book sheds considerable light on the complex function of Enoch's worship of the new jesus. Eliade's book (not unlike Jung's *Modern Man in Search of a Soul,* which O'Connor also read and partly admired) shows a respect for the primitive cultures as they chose various extraordinary objects to be considered as belonging to a "different order of being," contact with which will put the contemplator into "upheaval at the ontological level."[43] The object is chosen not out of concern for whether it is corporeal or not, personal or impersonal, but with whether it has *mana*—the "sacred force of being." These hierophanies, in other words, prefigure the Incarnation because they suggest that an object in the world can have otherworldly presence and significance. Bodies are not just rattling machines. Eliade does not define idolatry as the worship of these hierophanies *per se*, but as the practice of a culture that *remains* primitive and reverts to all previous manifestations without responding to new revelation. The conviction that the world out there contains something mysteriously other is not the problem.

By these descriptions, Enoch's worship of the new jesus is something far worse than idolatry, although it is that. Of all objects that Enoch as a primitive being could choose to worship, a dead man is least likely to contain *mana*. His choice of the new jesus as an object of worship is a perverted hierophany. As an object that is "all man, with no blood to waste," it has no presence, no *mana* at all. His primitive, poetic instinct to treat something in the world as having mysterious significance outside of what his own mind can conjure up is, nonetheless, precisely the instinct that Haze denies in himself and

---

[42] Ibid.

[43] Eliade, *Patterns in Comparative Religion*, 17.

that Enoch will help to recover. What Haze does not want to acknowledge is that by asking for a human new jesus, he is literally asking for the worship of death instead of life. When we laugh at what Enoch has chosen to worship, we actually laugh at Haze because Enoch, as one critic argues, lives out what Haze preaches.[44]

Enoch's worship of the new jesus is a powerfully grotesque entrance of the primitive into a modern context. But Enoch's next move—to bring the new jesus to Haze like a new baby to the family—is even more so. Haze and Sabbath Hawks had moved in together. Haze had seduced her for the same reason he had visited Leora Watts—in order to prove that no acts performed in the body are spiritually significant. But because Haze has erased the distinctions between pure and impure, his relationship with Sabbath becomes a part of the sacrificial crisis and all moral hell breaks loose. Sabbath becomes ultimately perverse in that she loses the ability to distinguish between the dead and the living. Girard writes that "this troubling confusion between living and dead is sometimes regarded as the consequence of the crisis and sometimes as its cause. The punishments that the dead inflict on the living are indistinguishable from the consequences of wrongdoing."[45] Sabbath is obsessed with the idea of the dead visiting judgment on the living. When Haze first encounters her preaching on the street with her father, she begins an odd sermonette:

> Listen…this here man and woman killed this little baby. It was her own child but it was ugly and she never give it any love. This child had Jesus and this woman didn't have nothing but good looks and a man she was living in sin with. She sent the child away and it come back and she sent it away and it come back again and ever' time she sent it away, it come back to where her and this man was living in sin. They strangled it with a silk stocking and hung it up in the chimney. It didn't give her any peace after that, though. Everything she looked at was that child. Jesus made it beautiful to haunt her. She couldn't lie with that man

---

[44] Frederick Asals writes "what Haze preaches, Enoch lives" (Asals, *Imagination of Extremity*, 47).

[45] Girard, *Violence and the Sacred*, 254–55.

without she saw it, staring through the chimney at her, shining through the brick in the middle of the night. (*CW*, 28)

The story is a mythic picture of the guilt associated with breaking cultural taboos and the violence that is its necessary corollary. In this case it predicts Sabbath and Haze's own relationship and the violent visitation from the dead that leads Haze finally to end it. At the end of chapter 10, Sabbath throws herself at Haze, promising to teach him how to get rid of the last vestiges of a sacramental view of sex: his guilt. She says, "From the minute I set eyes on you I said to myself, that's what I got to have, just give me some of him! …That innocent look don't hide a thing, he just pure filthy right down to the guts, like me. The only difference is I like being that way and he don't. Yes sir! …I like being that way, and I can teach you how to like it. Don't you want to learn how to like it?" (*CW*, 95). Haze says he wants to and gets into the bed. He can learn this; after all, he taught himself that he did not have a soul, either. "Take off your hat, king of the beasts," she says, and the chapter ends with them in bed in the dark.

Because their illicit liaison is a violation of the sanctity of sex, it can only bring death. And sure enough, in the next scene we find Enoch with the new jesus bundled up so that he was "carrying something about the size of a baby, wrapped up in newspapers…" (*CW*, 97). The swaddling clothes of Jesus Christ have become dirty newsprint, the "infant" is a feckless dead man, and the Mary to whom Enoch delivers the baby is hardly immaculate. In fact, when Sabbath Hawks receives the new jesus he is even more shriveled, with his eyelid split open and a pale dust seeping out of it. She stares for awhile and the narrator writes "she might have sat there for ten minutes, without a thought, held by whatever it was that was familiar about him. She had never known anyone who looked like him before, but there was something in him of everyone she had ever known, as if they had all been rolled into one person and killed and shrunk and dried" (*CW*, 104). Sabbath takes the new jesus into the crook of her arm, begins to rock him, and immediately considers Haze to be his daddy.

If O'Connor counts on our ability to laugh at the idea of the new jesus as Enoch's God, she counts no less on our visceral horror at the idea of the new jesus as Haze and Sabbath's baby.[46] The effect is like Poe's character who nearly marries his grandmother—it goes against what still remains of our sense of the life-giving purpose of the family. When Sabbath rocks the new jesus in her arms, she gives familial attention to a dead thing that will never reproduce. By the scene O'Connor suggests that casual, descramentalized sex produces literal death, not only death associated with judgment, but more fundamentally and instinctually the death humanity would die should sexuality ever be completely severed from procreation. The new jesus does have symbolic value for American culture: he is a perverted baby Jesus who obviously cannot save anything or anyone. But the scene affects us more powerfully in a visceral way because of our own wise blood: like Haze, we know *this is not right*.

Thus Enoch's act of *habeas corpus* cannot be understood unless it is first understood *literally*. As Tresmontant points out, Descartes and his Greek progenitor Plato believe a man's body is of a different substance than his soul, and that it is a "tomb" or a "prison" or a "stranger" he must escape.[47] But in Hebrew language, says Tresmontant, there is no word for "body" as defined this way. The word for a living person's form was the word "flesh" (with metaphysical weight in the Hebrew), and the only other word used for the physical body was "corpse," because "when the 'soul' is gone, what remains is not a 'body' but a corpse, the dust of disjoined elements which only provisionally, as though by reprieve, retain the deceptive appearance of a living body. A corpse is not even a thing in the philosophical sense: it is a *heap*."[48] Enoch's dusty heap is a literal picture of the Cartesian empirical "machine of bone and flesh," and when Enoch puts it in Sabbath's arms where a baby should be, we, like

---

[46] One of the benefits of John Huston's movie translation is that this scene has the visual horror it deserves.

[47] To use a term with some contemporary purchase, it is a "container" from which the soul needs to be set free.

[48] Claude Tresmontant, *A Study of Hebrew Thought*, trans. Michael Francis Gibson (New York: Desclee Company, 1960) 89.

Haze, *experience* the incredible difference.[49] A corpse is a corpse is a corpse. As Tresmontant continues, "in a living organism there *is* a *potential* multiplicity within a real unity, but it is only potential and abstractly conceived. This potential multiplicity is the 'matter,' the 'body' of the concrete living being. Death makes real this potential multiplicity *seen in* a living organism. While it might perhaps be conceded that the corpse is a thing, we can never say that the body is a thing. It is a metaphysical, not an empirical, *view* of a multiplicity which is potential...."[50]

The disintegration of the corpse also reflects the disintegration of the social order Sabbath and Haze have willfully perpetuated. Girard explains that in primitive cultures the final decomposition of a corpse was related to the ultimate loss of cultural distinctions—societal death. "Like the violent disintegration of a society, the physiological decomposition of the corpse leads gradually from a very complex system of differentials to undifferentiated dust. The forms of the living revert to formlessness."[51] O'Connor assumes that her readers will react not like Sabbath, who literally embraces death. She hopes we will react like Haze, who retains enough of what his mother gave him to recognize this perversion for what it is, especially now that he has an undeniable incarnation of it right in front of his eyes. When Sabbath takes her new baby to Haze and says, "Well, let's go give him a jolt" (*CW*, 105), we know that this will be Haze's moment of reckoning—his moment of grace. Just before Sabbath arrived with the

---

[49] Tresmontant quotes Descartes (*Study of Hebrew Thought*, 90).

[50] Tresmontant, *Study of Hebrew Thought*, 89. The shriveled man does not have a name; he is not (or not any longer) a person created for his own sake, with the "unique and irreplaceable" essence Tresmontant emphasized in his discussion of Hebrew metaphysics and its relation to Christian personalism. Tresmontant distinguishes between creation and fabrication; creation "unfolds from a unity which grows with the assimilation of outer elements" and is explosive. But fabrication, such as the fabrication of an idol, starts from the "preexisting multiplicity of matter" and is organized externally. His point is to argue that "many" in creation is found only at the end, in dust and death (ibid., 39). Although Tresmontant's book was published after O'Connor's novel, her description of the new jesus shows an affinity with this idea.

[51] Girard, *Violence and the Sacred*, 256.

"baby" Haze was packing up to continue his meaningless wanderings. He picks up his duffel bag and rummages around in it, careful as he always was to not touch the Bible "that sat like a rock in the bottom of the bag for the last few years." But he does grab the case with his mother's glasses in it. He puts them on, and he sees "his mother's face in his, looking at the face in the mirror. He moved back quickly and raised his hand to take off the glasses but the door opened and two more faces floated into his line of vision; one of them said, 'Call me Momma now'" (*CW*, 106).

Haze has forgotten that he has the glasses, that he has a history and a means of seeing things clearly. But when he dons them the first thing he can see is himself, and he notices his similarity to his mother. The scene clearly repeats the one in the museum; he sees his mother's face in his, boring into him, revealing his soul. This makes him nervous enough, and just as he is about to deny the vision and remove the glasses, Sabbath comes in with the shriveled corpse to which she says "call me Momma now," a phrase that literally names Haze as the father of death.

The grotesque does its most shocking work in that moment. Haze's primitive, sacramental instincts, like ours, have been fully activated by the sick substitution of a corpse for a baby. Having once again been given a picture of death without any promise of life behind it, Haze responds with physical violence and throws the new jesus against the wall. O'Connor could not understand why readers tended to take the scene as anticlimactic; she believed the rejection to be pivotal. "That Haze rejects that mummy suggests everything. What he has been looking for with body and soul throughout the book is suddenly presented to him and he sees it has to be rejected, he sees it ain't really what he's looking for. I don't regard it in any abstracted sense at all..." (*HB*, 404).[52] Like a doubting Thomas, Haze has

---

[52] For O'Connor to say she does not regard the new jesus as an abstraction is not to say the figure has no symbolic value. Instead it indicates she clearly saw that the shriveled figure's main importance lies in its physical, decaying, dusty, *real* existence. It is literally a dead man that, when aesthetically taken out of its usual context (the grave), becomes loaded with meaning for Haze, who, afraid himself of death, denies Jesus Christ as the giver of life. As a mere symbol, existing only in

opportunity to see, touch, and handle the inevitable, actual result of his rejection of eternal life in Christ: death.

Baron von Hügel's essays address this issue in terms similar to O'Connor's dramatization of the new jesus. In his first series of essays von Hügel pinpoints the dangers of what he called Feuerbach's radical Hegelianism: that man essentially consists of mind alone, that there is no supreme reality external to him. Von Hügel argues that philosophy must start with the elementary facts of the world (such as historical evidence), "to which it must ever be willing to grant appeal, that man is not simply mind, but also sense, imagination, feeling, will," and that man achieves real knowledge of himself only by his contact with things other to him that act upon him.[53] In other words, it is less human *action* (the mind's originating its own reality) than human *reaction* (the whole self's responding to revelation of any sort) that matters. When O'Connor gives Haze the new jesus via her perverse prophet, she gives him literal death with the power the primitive world attributed to it. The more real it is to him the more real will be his response. Haze's rational activity has met an end. As von Hügel writes, "it is the action of all that objective world upon this human subject, and the manifold reaction of this human subject to that world's action, which is primary; whereas the abstracting activity is secondary and instrumental, and necessarily never fully catches up or exhausts those primary informations. The more real is the subject

---

literary or mythological space, it could not reach Haze (or the reader) where he most needs to be reached. The abstract idea that Haze's atheism leads to death is no more meaningful than the abstract idea that God became man to redeem creation. As an idea, it means nothing. As a physical reality with analogical significance, it means everything. This focus on the new jesus' physical reality evokes 1 John, a letter written by John to contradict the Gnostic teachings that had infected the early church. The letter begins, "that which was from the beginning, which we have heard, which we have seen with our eyes, which we have looked upon and our hands have handled, of the word of life. For the life was manifested: and we have seen and do bear witness and declare unto you the life eternal, which was with the Father and hath appeared to us. That which we have seen and have heard, we declare unto you: that you also may have fellowship with us and our fellowship may be with the Father and with his Son Jesus Christ" (1 John 1:1–3).

[53] Baron Friedrick von Hügel, *Essays and Addresses on the Philosophy of Religion: First Series* (New York: E. P. Dutton, 1928) 32.

thus stimulated and thus reacting, and the more real is the object thus stimulating and thus acting, the more 'inside' does the subject and the object possess, and the more rich will be such stimulation and such response."[54] Haze's stimulation and response are rich indeed: he slams the new jesus against the wall and begins his redemption by its rejection.

THE SACRIFICIAL CRISIS RESOLVED

All of O'Connor's grotesques displace characters and readers by insisting upon a reaction. In *Wise Blood*, O'Connor committed herself to the "negative grotesque"—to making rejection the necessary reaction.[55] She eventually found this definition of the grotesque limiting and would retell *Wise Blood* in order to transform the grotesque into a body that must be accepted. That retelling is *The Violent Bear It Away*. Perhaps O'Connor made this change because she came to understand that she chose a difficult route when she wrote a novel in which the character "negates his way back to the cross." She had to be able to show that rejection of rot can be a way to acceptance of the truly good. And many do not believe she succeeded, arguing that the ending promotes a kind of Manichaeism. If incarnational art assumes the body is good, as I have argued, it seems to make no sense for a character to receive his redemption by mortifying the flesh and literally blinding himself as Haze does. But within the context of this story, which focuses on Haze's efforts to blind himself to his own instincts, his body, and his past, it makes perfect sense. He placed rocks in his shoes as a young man because he understood that what he does in the body matters. When he returns to that activity in the end, however misdirected and extreme, he does so to acquiesce again to that truth. And his self-blinding has mythic and literal importance. With this act, Haze becomes an Oedipus who acknowledges how he had blinded himself to his own participation in

---

[54] Ibid., 33.

[55] "Haze is repulsed by the shriveled man he sees merely because it is hideous. He has a picture of his new jesus—shriveled as it is. Therefore it certainly does have meaning for Haze. Why would he throw it away if it didn't? Its meaning is in its rejection" (*HB*, 403).

Taulkinham's moral degradation.[56] In an effort to purify himself he becomes a kind of sacrifice for the community as well. The story practically requires that the blinding be literal, because the act has to be genuine enough to restore integrity to a landscape that has almost completely disintegrated. Asa Hawks's fake blinding proves that he does not believe in the literal existence of the Christ he peaches; Haze's appropriation of that act in a literal way thus returns him to his integrity and sets himself up as an exemplary sacrifice for the entire community of Taulkinham.

Finally, while self-blinding and self-mortification may seem to be a turn away from the physical world, it can actually be a turn toward it. Critics note that when Haze blinds himself, he does so as a medieval ascetic might: he repudiates the physical world in favor of the spiritual. But ascetics are not necessarily Gnostics. Medieval asceticism in particular acknowledges the body's essential and inescapable role in our spiritual lives at the same time it acknowledges that the body tries always to claim undue absolute sovereignty. In short, ascetics know better than anyone how important the body is.[57]

---

[56] Haze acknowledges the limits of his own vision and his need for new light. As Erasmo Leiva-Merikakis writes, "faith rejoices in a natural blindness that is the precondition for the vision of God. Even the Greeks had an intuition of this: in the figure of Sophocles' Oedipus we see the necessity of first becoming blind in order to be able really to see. Our own native lights must be extinguished if Jesus is to light his lamp in our souls" (Leiva-Merikakis, *Fire of Mercy, Heart of the Word: Meditations on the Gospel According to St. Matthew*, vol. 1 [San Francisco: Ignatius Press, 1996] 493–94).

[57] Umberto Eco defends medieval asceticism against those who would say that ascetics thereby reject the sensuous world. "Ascetics, in all ages," he writes, "are not unaware of the seductiveness of worldly pleasures; if anything, they feel it more keenly than most" (Eco, *Art and Beauty in the Middle Ages*, trans. Hugh Bredin [New Haven: Yale University Press, 1986] 6). Robert Brinkmeyer also defends the sacramentalism of Haze's actions by drawing upon Elaine Scarry's and Geoffrey Harpham's work on the meaning of the body to asceticism. Brinkmeyer concludes that Haze's abuse of his body "represents not a rejection of the body but a plunge into it, so that on a broad level his and Enoch's final acts are similar in their celebration of the physical. What is different is what they hope to achieve in terms of their spiritual lives by plunging into the physical" (Robert H. Brinkmeyer Jr., "'Jesus, Stab Me in the Heart!': *Wise Blood*, Wounding, and Sacramental Aesthetics," in *New Essays on "Wise Blood,"* ed. Michael Kreyling [New York: Cambridge

Likewise it is the literally blind who, ironically, live in a world in which the problems of perception are foregrounded. Only people who never think to question the limits of what they can see with their eyes may be tempted to a self-selected vision.[58] Haze has learned that he will actually see the world more clearly when he follows the figure of the ragged Jesus around in the dark, where he could not possibly be sure of his footing.

University Press, 1995] 83). One must wholly reconnect one's body to one's soul before one can recognize sin as a corruption to be fought against, not a meaningless activity to be freely indulged in. By blinding himself, Haze finally acknowledges that he never stopped believing sin matters. It matters because the body is a part of the soul. As such, writes Brinkmeyer, "Haze's violent self-mutilations collapse the external world into himself, paving the way for an unmediated relationship between the body and the divine" (ibid., 83).

[58] In Cormac McCarthy's *The Crossing*, a blind character reflects that the truly blind are those who choose what to see and what not to see. But the literally blind have no choice; the blind character in this novel, reports the narrator, "said that men with eyes may select what they wish to see but for the blind the world appears of its own will. He said that for the blind everything was abruptly at hand, that nothing ever announced its approach. Origins and destinations became but rumors. To move is to abut against the world" (McCarthy, *The Crossing* [New York: Alfred A. Knopf, 1994] 291).

CHAPTER 3

BODY MATTERS:
BOYS WITHOUT MOTHERS

> *Metaphysics snatches at the spiritual in an idea, by the most abstract intellection; poetry reaches at it in the flesh, by the very point of the sense sharpened through intelligence.*

—Jacques Maritain, *Creative Intuition in Art and Poetry*

Flannery O'Connor used the grotesque to make the body visible. But readers continue to ignore the bodies in her fiction by emphasizing what we think they symbolize. In doing so we turn again and again to O'Connor's insistence that "when you can assume that your audience holds the same beliefs you do, you can relax a little and use more normal ways of talking to it; when you have to assume that it does not, then you have to make your vision apparent by shock—to the hard of hearing you shout, and for the almost blind you draw large and startling figures" (*CW*, 805–806). Yes, O'Connor felt her readers were blind to her beliefs. But she did not inscribe those beliefs onto grotesque bodies, as if the bodies were meant to be read only as symbols. Instead the grotesque insists that the modern world has become blind to something that was for O'Connor the only way to reach the spiritual: the body itself. We tend to think O'Connor's stories shout out her beliefs; what they actually shout out is the body.

Blindness to the body is an epistemological problem. As we have seen, modern philosophy is predicated on the definition of self as a mind separated from the individual body and from the body of the world. The body, then, has nothing to do with the achievement of knowledge and can only be seen as an impediment to the self. Since Descartes believed the body to be the primary source of prejudice and error, he also believed that children—absorbed in the body and dependent upon outside information for discovery—represent human nature in its highest susceptibility to error. For Descartes, the medieval era was philosophy's childhood; it naively looked for participation in and connection to a universe it perceived as feminine. The Cartesian ideal, therefore, is an adult male consciousness that sees clearly when it frees itself from both a childish dependence on its own body and a childish goal to connect with a feminine universe.

When philosophy "grew up," the body and the universe became an object for detached, scientific study. The adult male mind takes a "god's-eye" view of that body, penetrating it from afar, studying it, dominating it. And as some feminist scholars have recently pointed out, such a detached view has the paradoxical effect of rendering the body invisible. Rosi Braidotti explains that "western sciences put forward the assumption that a body is precisely that which can be seen and looked at, no more than the sum of its parts. Modern scientific rationality slipped from the emphasis on visibility to the mirage of absolute transparence of the living organism...."[1] Because science thinks it can be placeless, that it can see all from a position that is nowhere, the body itself disappears from view.

O'Connor brings the body back. What is more, she does it by way of children. Children, immersed in the body, nearly always see better than adults. They seek connection, not separation. Although they often start out lost, characters such as Francis Tarwater, Norton Sheppard, Nelson Head, and the "child" in "Temple of the Holy Ghost" always instinctively look for the right things in the right

---

[1] Rosi Braidotti, "Mothers, Monsters, and Machines," in *Writing on the Body: Female Embodiment and Feminist Theory*, ed. Katie Conboy, Nadia Medina, and Sarah Stanbury (New York: Columbia University Press, 1997) 73.

places. In fact, their spiritual growth hinges upon experiences in their bodies and on their search for connection with the feminine universe—that which is concrete, particular, embodied, grotesque, and often mysterious. In contrast, spiritual blindness and death comes from a turn to abstract intellectual thought that claims to be independent from the body. Grown men who define themselves against their mothers receive O'Connor's scorn: Julian, Asbury, Mr. Shiftlet, and Thomas, among others. Women who behave this way, like Joy/Hulga, receive equal scorn. To deny one's connection to one's own body and to the world's body is to destroy the self in an act of solipsism. To long for it is to long for connection to the world of spirit and ultimately to God.

Because we need the humility our bodies teach us—and because we need connection, not separation—we need first to acknowledge that we are the children of our mothers. To be motherless or to behave as a motherless child is thus a spiritual danger of particular interest to O'Connor. "The Life You Save May Be Your Own," "The Artificial Nigger," "The River," and "The Lame Shall Enter First" depict the cold and isolated worlds men create in the absence and/or denial of embodied love from mothers. In each case, a grotesque body serves to insist that connection must be accepted and isolation shunned for spiritual growth to take place. Some of the characters learn, and some do not. Some learn too late.

The motherless Tom T. Shiftlet of "The Life You Save May Be Your Own" might be the most offensive major character in any of O'Connor's stories. He mercilessly dupes an old woman into giving him her retarded daughter as a wife, and then he steals the family car in order to continue his shiftless life. In this story O'Connor employed the full range of the grotesque—as an image of spiritual deformity (Shiftlet's own body) and as the face of the divine as seen in an otherwise useless body (Lucynell Crater). This story practically requires that body to be female, for if ever there was a character in O'Connor's fiction with the desire to flee the feminine body and all that it stands for, it is Tom T. Shiftlet. His chance for redemption— the development of a genuine moral intelligence—comes through the body of Lucynell Crater, who becomes a reminder of his mother and consequently an avenue for potential spiritual growth.

Mr. Shiftlet lives a life defined by separation and isolation. As John Desmond has aptly summarized, the story describes a Gnostic attempt to "transcend history by flight, the reverse of the incarnational movement downward into the concrete to discover its transfiguring possibilities."[2] Mr. Shiftlet spends most of his time on the move, trying to escape himself, responsibility, and, it would appear, all women. When he does slow down long enough to approach the Crater farm, he sees rottenness everywhere he looks, a rottenness he intends to fix with his toolbox. "'There ain't a broken thing on this plantation that I couldn't fix for you, one-arm jackleg or not. I'm a man,' he said with a sullen dignity, 'even if I ain't a whole one. I got,' he said, tapping his knuckles on the floor to emphasize the immensity of what he was going to say, 'a moral intelligence!'" (*CW*, 176).

Mr. Shiftlet's "moral intelligence" is neither moral nor intelligent, and it shifts to suit his purposes. His primary purpose is to become an ultimately free spirit that is not bound by his body or by any body. Mrs. Lucynell Crater, desperate to marry off her daughter (also named Lucynell Crater), tells him that if he would accept her as his wife and stay with them he could get a "permanent house and a deep well and the most innocent girl in the world." Mrs. Crater wants so much to believe Mr. Shiftlet will be a good match for her daughter that she fails to hear the warning bells in his response: "Lady, a man is divided into two parts, body and spirit…the body, lady, is like a house: it don't go anywhere; but the spirit, lady, is like a automobile: always on the move…" (*CW*, 179). Mr. Shiftlet's language strongly differentiates her as a "lady" from him as a man. A "man" knows that the feminine and domestic—the body/house—is a prison, it "don't go anywhere." The women can only be to him a crater, an abyss that will drop him into the earth to stay, or a crate designed to cage him. Even as Shiftlet agrees to Mrs. Crater's proposal, then, he reveals his true

---

[2] John F. Desmond, *Risen Sons: Flannery O'Connor's Vision of History* (Athens: University of Georgia Press, 1987) 49.

intentions. He will follow his whims: "I'm only saying a man's spirit means more to him than anything else. I would have to take my wife off for the week end without no regards at all for cost. I got to follow where my spirit says to go" (*CW*, 179–80).[3]

When a man's spirit means more to him than anything else, the value of all bodies with which he comes into contact depends upon their exchange value. Shiftlet sees the two women only as a means to a car. The car is the key to masculine mobility; Mrs. Crater remarks that "the day my husband died, it quit running" (*CW*, 173). It is really no surprise that the day Shiftlet marries Lucynell he leaves her in a restaurant and drives off without remorse. She could only be dead weight to him. But the pity we may feel for her or the scorn we may feel for him is not the primary story O'Connor wants to tell. The real story is the strong, unconscious, and barely acknowledged effect the doubled mother/daughter female bodies have on Shiftlet, in spite of himself. For with Lucynell Crater, O'Connor begins to explore what will be the strongest characteristic of the grotesque in her fiction: the value of all created beings. It is a value we can only learn from our dependence upon and connection to others.

Shiftlet, defining himself against his own body and interested only in an illusion of perpetual freedom, does not believe people are valuable simply because they exist—least of all someone like Lucynell who cannot function normally in the world. Consequently Shiftlet tries to "fix" Lucynell by teaching her how to speak. For her to acquire language would mean separation, entrance into the symbolic order, a disruption of the mute community and practical identity of the two women.[4] But Lucynell can learn only one word—bird. It is an

---

[3] One of the many articulations of placelessness as a defining feature of American culture can be found in Philip Fisher, *Still the New World: American Literature in a Culture of Creative Destruction* (Cambridge: Harvard University Press, 1999). Fisher argues that American democracy creates a "Cartesian social space" to which "the right to enter or exit is equally fundamental" (ibid., 44).

[4] The mirrored names and the fact that neither woman does much suggests a kind of ultimately female place, a place of stasis ("home") that is not necessarily negative for O'Connor and is an important aspect of her critique in this story. For a thorough discussion of the implications of such a separation, see Julia Kristeva, *Desire in Language* (New York: Columbia University Press, 1980).

apt one, for she is described throughout as if she were a peacock. Lucynell watches Mr. Shiftlet with "her head thrust forward and her fat helpless hands hanging at the wrists. She had long pink-gold hair and eyes as blue as a peacock's neck" (*CW*, 173). She behaves remarkably like the peafowl on O'Connor's farm: "Terrible noises issued from the shed" where Lucynell was "sitting on a chicken crate, stamping her feet and screaming, 'Burrddtt! bddurrddtttt!'" (*CW*, 178). Lucynell will remain as useless as the peafowl at Andalusia who do nothing but holler, prance around, and eat the flowers. And that is exactly the point. In her essay "The King of the Birds," O'Connor presents the peafowl she collects on her farm as a subtle metaphor for the "useless" human grotesques she collects and presents in her fiction. She begins by relating her story of a bantam chicken she owned at age five that could walk forward or backwards. After that, "what had been only a mild interest became a passion, a quest. I had to have more and more chickens. I favored those with one green eye and one orange or with over-long necks and crooked combs. I wanted one with three legs or three wings but nothing in that line turned up" (*CW*, 832). The weirder the better, and the more the merrier. "When I first uncrated these birds, in my frenzy I said, 'I want so many of them that every time I go out the door, I'll run into one'" (*CW*, 834).

The birds' inutility makes them a good symbol of O'Connor's grotesques. But their surprising and sudden beauty—revealed only to those with eyes to see—make them an even better one. While at first the chickens look as if they "might have been put together out of a rag bag by an unimaginative hand," they prove to be immensely beautiful for those willing to wait. "Analyzing the appearance of the peacock as he stands with his tail folded, I find the parts incommensurate with the whole. The fact is that with his tail folded, nothing but his bearing saves this bird from being a laughingstock. With his tail spread, he inspires a range of emotions, but I have yet to hear laughter" (*CW*, 835).

Like the priest on Mrs. McIntyre's farm in "The Displaced Person," it is the artist who can see the body as beautiful and important in its own right. And like Mrs. McIntyre and Mrs. Shortley, those enmeshed in worlds of their own making will miss the show. In

"The King of the Birds" O'Connor relates that some visitors who came out to Andalusia could see the beauty, and some could not. One man, not unlike Mr. Shiftlet, nearly drove off in impatience until O'Connor screamed after his car, "he's doing it!!" (*CW*, 837). The man stopped in time to get the full display, but when O'Connor asked him what he thought, he said he "never saw such long ugly legs...I bet that rascal could outrun a bus" (*CW*, 837).

When visitors to her farm, like visitors to her fiction, miss the beauty of the grotesques, O'Connor treats their response as both a moral and an aesthetic problem. These visitors have turned off their imaginations to see only with their minds, their definition of beauty controlled by society's definition of perfection. "Many people, I have found, are congenitally unable to appreciate the sight of a peacock. Once or twice I have been asked what the peacock is 'good for'—a question which gets no answer from me because it deserves none" (*CW*, 836). To speak of nature, humanity, and the work of art in utilitarian terms is to miss its true beauty. So when Mr. Shiftlet and Lucynell's mother treat Lucynell as a bargaining chip, they share in the most deplorable of abusive acts—to trade others' lives for personal advantage. When it comes to the peafowl O'Connor raised, she was also tempted to let economics dictate: "I do not like to let my thoughts linger in morbid channels but there are times when such facts as the price of wire fencing and the price of Startena and the yearly gain in peafowl all run uncontrolled through my head" (*CW*, 842). She then describes that she had a dream that she herself was "five years old and a peacock. A photographer has been sent from New York and a long table is laid in celebration. The meal is to be an exceptional one: myself. I scream, 'Help! Help!' and awaken" (*CW*, 842).

O'Connor's fantastic substitution of her own body with that of a peacock about to be eaten is not a simple joke. With her lupus in full gear, she might herself be one of the useless grotesques, the imperfect and the expendable. She, like Lucynell, could be seen as one of what Patricia Yaeger calls the "throwaway bodies" that the fiction of

Southern women centralizes.[5] The protection of the throwaway peacocks is akin to the protection of all life. "I intend to stand firm and let the peacocks multiply, for I am sure that, in the end, the last word will be theirs" (*CW*, 842).[6] On the farm and in her fiction, it is truly the last who shall enter first.

Tom T. Shiftlet, on the contrary, inhabits a dualism that prevents him from seeing any value in maimed bodies, even and especially his own. Immediately after a waiter draws his attention to the beauty of the sleeping Lucynell who looks like "an angel of Gawd," Shiftlet abandons her in the restaurant and heads toward Mobile (*CW*, 181). He refuses to acknowledge that his body is also, in its own way, radically dependent and contingent; his movement away from her is as much self-hatred as it is disregard for her. He notices but does not accept the message on the roadside sign: "Drive carefully. The life you save may be your own."

That's the lesson Shiftlet *almost* learns. Through a deep and nearly unconscious connection of the doubled Lucynell Crater to his own mother, Shiftlet's real moral intelligence begins to emerge. His conscience working overtime, Shiftlet tells a completely uninterested hitchhiker that "it's nothing so sweet...as a boy's mother. She taught him his first prayers at her knee, she give him love when no other would, she told him what was right and what wasn't, and she seen that he done the right thing.... I never rued a day in my life like the one I

---

[5] Yaeger writes that through the grotesque, Southern women's writing "provokes the uncanny presence of disposable bodies," bodies that suggest, among other things, "the ways in which southern women's writing opens up a different way of thinking about the relation between American history and the body—particularly, what happens to the body within a culture of neglect" (Yaeger, *Dirt and Desire: Reconstructing Southern Women's Writing, 1930–1990* [Chicago: University of Chicago Press, 2000] 67).

[6] O'Connor's desire to let the birds reproduce unchecked (and actually seeking after the deformed ones) illustrates how different her view of life and creation was from that of the romantics. In her provocative essay "The Monster in the Rainbow: Keats and the Science of Life," Denise Gigante argues that the romantic definition of the monstrous includes the idea of reproduction out of control. She writes that "to imagine life as an autonomous power with the capacity to exceed its material dimensions...is to imagine something monstrous" (Gigante, "The Monster in the Rainbow: Keats and the Science of Life," *PMLA* 117/3 [2002]: 443).

rued when I left that old mother of mine" (*CW*, 182). Shiftlet knows that in rejecting his mother and her morals, he rejects the chance for redemption through genuine connection. In defining himself by autonomy and movement of his spirit, he rejects the necessary perspective that others have on him—on his *body*. In "Author and Hero in Aesthetic Activity," Bakhtin calls this other perspective "aesthetic seeing." Without it, we can never possess the true value of our own bodies, and by extension the bodies of others. Bakhtin writes that there is a "profound difference between my inner experience of my own body and the recognition of its outer value by *other* people—my right to the loving acceptance or recognition of my exterior by *others*: this recognition or acceptance descends upon me from others like a gift, like grace, which is incapable of being understood and founded from within myself. And it is only in this case that certainty in the outer value of my body is possible, whereas an immediately intuitable experience of that value is impossible—all I can do is have pretensions to it."[7]

The first "other" to value an individual's body is his mother. Bakhtin emphasized that a child receives all his early self-determination—particularly regarding his body—from his mother and those closest to him: "It is from their lips, in the emotional-volitional tones of their love, that the child hears and begins to acknowledge his own *proper name* and the names of all the features pertaining to his body and to his inner states and experiences."[8] O'Connor does not give enough information to let us determine whether Shiftlet's mother failed him or he simply abandoned her. But he certainly rejects whatever name he had been given and chooses to define himself as close to a nonentity as possible—as if he could be all free-floating energy and no matter. The three other names he had considered calling himself were "Sparks," "Speeds," and "Bright" (*CW*, 174). As soon as he was married he was trying to be released from the

[7] M. M. Bakhtin, *Art and Answerability: Early Philosophical Essays,* ed. Michael Holquist and Vadim Liapunov, trans. Vadim Liapunov (Austin: University of Texas Press, 1990) 49.
[8] Ibid.

bond, eschewing all connection and definition that may come from it: "that didn't satisfy me none...that was just something a woman in an office did, nothing but paper work and blood tests. What do they know about my blood? If they was to take my heart and cut it out...they wouldn't know a thing about me" (*CW*, 180).

One of the painful things about this story is how much Mrs. Lucynell Crater fails as a mother. She could have been a mother to Shiftlet, but instead she uses him. When trying to convince him to stay, she says "'Lemme tell you something: there ain't any place in the world for a poor disabled friendless drifting man.' The ugly words settled in Mr. Shiftlet's head like a group of buzzards in the top of a tree" (*CW*, 179). Mrs. Crater fails to recognize the problem in seeing her daughter as a "basket of jewels" and a "prize." Although she does ultimately recognize that her daughter means more to her than can be described in trading terms, this knowledge comes only after she uses her to scheme, giving Shiftlet no reason to break his cycle of abusing women. He continues to build a chain of escapes out from loving relationships and from being "placed," a chain that includes his escape from a relationship with the ultimate other—God. Breaking away from all connections with his own body, the body of his mother, and the body of the world, Mr. Shiftlet leaves God with the only role possible for a Cartesian thinker: the judging paternalistic figure whom he begs to "break forth and wash the slime from the earth." And the reader knows that Shiftlet himself, the rain chasing him as he flees to Mobile for a life of more movement, is still that slime.

Many consider "The Life You Save May Be Your Own" to be O'Connor's most despairing story and "The Artificial Nigger" her most optimistic. Although the stories have different outcomes, their protagonists share the same initial problem: they are men who wander around in a disembodied and motherless world, sorely in need of spiritual connection. "The Artificial Nigger" tells the story of Mr. Head and his grandson Nelson. Mr. Head takes Nelson—whom he considers to be uppity—to Atlanta to teach him a lesson. It is Mr. Head who gets the lesson when fear leads him to betray Nelson, and he finds that through humility he can and must enter into the suffering of others.

Like Norton of "The Lame Shall Enter First," Nelson suffers at the hands of a confused male who has to parent him without any female input. Mr. Head's world is characterized by disconnects—subject from object, self from other—because he has defined maturity as one's ability to assert independence and superiority. The greatest danger illustrated by this story is that Mr. Head will effectively pass his version of self-actualization, with its spiritual blindness and racist inevitabilities, onto the next generation. The real horror of "The Artificial Nigger" is the horror of bad parenting.

Mr. Head is head and center of a world of his own making. He believes he has reached the epitome of maturity in his sixty years, and in the story's first paragraph he awakens to find the moon "five feet away in his shaving mirror, paused as if it were waiting for his permission to enter" (*CW*, 210). This moon casts a "dignifying light on everything" and sets him up as a king. Even the chair stands "stiff and attentive as if it were awaiting an order" (*CW*, 210). The relationship Mr. Head imagines between himself and everyone around him is clear. He considers himself to be "one of the great guides of men," perhaps "Vergil summoned in the middle of the night to go to Dante, or better, Raphael, awakened by a blast of God's light to fly to the side of Tobias" (*CW*, 210).

But there is trouble in Mr. Head's paradise. We quickly discover that the relationship between him and his grandson is not characterized by leadership, but by games of one-upmanship. Each claims to know more about the big city of Atlanta than the other: Mr. Head brags that he has been there three times; the boy claims he has already been there twice, the first being his birth. Like so many of O'Connor's characters, Mr. Head intends to carry out a "moral mission" to prove to Nelson that he is not as smart as he thinks he is. "It was to be a lesson that the boy would never forget. He was to find out from it that he had no cause for pride merely because he had been born in a city. He was to find out that the city is not a great place" (*CW*, 211).

Mr. Head claims his superiority—and evinces his poor parenting skills—by bragging that he has knowledge of "niggers," whereas Nelson has never seen one: "'If you seen one you didn't know what he was,' Mr. Head said, completely exasperated. 'A six-month-old child don't know a nigger from anybody else'" (*CW*, 213). Mr. Head intends to teach Nelson how to define himself as a white man over against the black other that will serve to affirm his identity and worth. Mr. Head's childishness here perfectly illustrates that when the self is defined by autonomy instead of by connection, it necessarily "remains frozen in a defensive infantile need to dominate and/or repress others in order to retain individual identity."[9] Mr. Head finds opportunity to teach his "lesson" on the train when a black man walks by them and Nelson does not react. Mr. Head questions him, "What was that?" To each of Mr. Head's probing questions ("what kind of a man?"), Nelson innocently answers "a man...a fat man...an old man" (*CW*, 216). Race as physical difference clearly does not inherently compel Nelson to construct a new category for people. That behavior must be learned. "You never said they were tan. How do you expect me to know anything when you don't tell me right?" (*CW*, 216). Mr. Head's lesson is devastatingly effective. "Nelson turned backward again and looked where the Negro had disappeared. He felt that the Negro had deliberately walked down the aisle in order to make a fool of him and he hated him with a fierce raw fresh hate; and also, he understood now why his grandfather disliked them" (*CW*, 216). Nelson has been ushered into his grandfather's gnosis. When they later see the colored section of the dining car, Nelson easily accepts Mr. Head's explanation: "they rope them off" (*CW*, 217).

The story O'Connor tells in "The Artificial Nigger" is that Nelson still has characteristics unique to children that mitigate against the elder's lessons, though Nelson is losing those characteristics rapidly. Immersed in the body and not yet completely given over to his grandfather's abstract categories, Nelson has sympathetic instincts toward all other people. When the two get lost in the black section of the city, they are afraid. But Nelson is still child enough not to fear the black body, even after he has been taught to hate it. When he asks

    [9] Sandra Harding, "From Feminist Empiricism to Feminist Standpoint Epistemologies," in *From Modernism to Postmodernism: An Anthology*, ed. Lawrence E. Cahoone (Cambridge: Blackwell, 1996) 626.

a matronly black woman for directions, he looks at her and finds himself drawn in:

> His eyes traveled up from her great knees to her forehead and then made a triangular path from the glistening sweat on her neck down and across her tremendous bosom and over her bare arm back to where her fingers lay hidden in her hair. He suddenly wanted her to reach down and pick him up and draw him against her and then he wanted to feel her breath on his face. He wanted to look down and down into her eyes while she held him tighter and tighter. He had never had such a feeling before. He felt as if he were reeling down through a pitchblack tunnel. (*CW*, 223)

This curious passage has generated considerable critical discussion, the best of it interpreting the woman as suggestive of the boy's "generosity of spirit" common to humanity.[10] Nelson, like so many of O'Connor's characters, has wise blood. He needs a mother and turns to this woman instinctively, his need for connection far exceeding his need for separation based on race that he learned to effect that morning. Led aimlessly around the city by the lost Mr. Head—to whom he is afraid to cling and appear weak—Nelson is now desperate to be picked up, nurtured, and held securely. As in "The Life You Save May Be Your Own," a solid, feminine, and embodied place offers redemptive respite from constant one-upmanship and drift. O'Connor explained that "I meant for her in an almost physical way to suggest the mystery of existence to him—he not only has never seen a nigger but he didn't know any women and I felt that such a black mountain of maternity would give him the required shock to start those black forms moving up from his unconscious" (*CW*, 931).

What are the "black forms" O'Connor believes are found in the unconscious of a white child, activated by contact with a maternal body? They represent something mysterious and other about the very

---

[10] Robert Brinkmeyer argues that the woman is an embodiment of a hidden self that has at its center "a generosity of spirit toward others—a form of charity whereby one both gives oneself to others and also takes them into oneself—that ties people of all description in a common bond of humanity" (Brinkmeyer Jr., *The Art & Vision of Flannery O'Connor*, Southern Literary Studies [Baton Rouge: Louisiana State University Press, 1989] 79).

fact of human existence that Nelson senses he needs. The *physical* presence of motherhood, so lacking in Nelson's life, activates good instincts for him, the instincts that displace the artificial by means of the real. Only these instincts are strong enough to shock Nelson out of the categories of the self and other and mind and body that his grandfather tries so hard to construct for him. The "pitchblack tunnel" Nelson feels himself falling into here suggests the same kind of subconscious place Joe Christmas finds when he gets lost in the black part of town in Faulkner's *Light in August*. It is a place where racial distinctions—constructions of the abstract, rational mind—are subsumed by the physical sensations of the connectedness of all humanity that reign there.

But Mr. Head, sensing the woman's threat to the authority he asserts, wants to pull Nelson back to his world with its rigid categories: "Nelson would have collapsed at her feet if Mr. Head had not pulled him roughly away. 'You act like you don't have any sense!' the old man growled" (*CW*, 223). Mr. Head's "sense" belittles any other ways of knowing, and he criticizes the child for living purely in the physical realm like an animal: "...standing there grinning like a chim-pan-zee while a nigger woman gives you directions. Great Gawd!" (*CW*, 224). But O'Connor chastises Mr. Head's independent and disembodied ego by letting him experience the inevitable results of his philosophy. When separation and one-upmanship become the order of the day, the self can do nothing but swell up monstrously, sacrificing any connection with the other that might threaten its identity. This is precisely what happens to Mr. Head. When accused that his boy has contributed to a woman's breaking her ankle, he betrays and abandons Nelson: "this is not my boy...I never seen him before" (*CW*, 226).

Mr. Head's severance from Nelson is total—physical, emotional, and intellectual. Mr. Head "felt Nelson's fingers fall out of his flesh," and the horrified women cleared a circle of ignominy for him "as if they were so repulsed by a man who would deny his own image and likeness that they could not bear to lay hands on him" (*CW*, 226). A man who lives in a fearful solipsism and who fails to see the interconnectedness of all humanity is but a step away from denying even the strongest blood connections. The young boy follows Mr.

Head from a distance, unresponsive to any of his attempts to make up for his betrayal. Robert Brinkmeyer explains that "the two are thoroughly isolated, each driven into a separate realm of consciousness that dominates their thoughts and redefines their existence."[11] Nelson's eyes become cold, and he feels homeless: "home was nothing to him" (*CW*, 229). Mr. Head "felt he knew now what time would be like without seasons and what heat would be like without light and what man would be like without salvation" (*CW*, 229). He has fully entered the hell of his own making.

In "The Artificial Nigger" O'Connor does not leave the characters to perish in this hell of isolation. Instead they reconnect in the oddest of ways: by looking together at a plaster figure of a black man on a suburban lawn. The moment confuses many first-time readers of the story, and a common complaint of critics is that the experience does not seem weighty enough to effect the evident change in Mr. Head and in his relationship with Nelson. For as many times as critics mention the scene, it is also as many times strangely glossed over. And as an *aesthetic* experience of two "readers"—Mr. Head and Nelson—it is hardly treated at all. John Desmond comes closest to doing so when he argues that the statue "best realizes all the anagogical potentialities for the image" and that "the image's anagogical force is explicitly manifested through Mr. Head's radical change of vision."[12] While true, Desmond's remark does not explain *how* a racist statue would give them the sense of their link with fallen humanity.

O'Connor offers no explanation. Although she writes that what she "had in mind to suggest with the artificial nigger was the redemptive quality of the Negro's suffering for us all" (*CW*, 931), she does not explain how the plaster figure could be interpreted that way. But later in the same letter, O'Connor writes that she is "interested in making up a good case for distortion," since she has become

---

[11] Brinkmeyer, *Art and Vision*, 76.

[12] Desmond, *Risen Sons*, 49: Desmond also writes that the statue "embodies an immediate historical reality: the whole history of the sin of racial prejudice adumbrated in the attitudes of Nelson and Mr. Head."

convinced that it is "the only way to make people see" (*CW*, 932). Distortion turns out to be a good clue here. As a normal piece of yard art, this statue would have no power, but through distortion—the making of a grotesque—O'Connor gives it the power to displace. Although the original image of the Negro eating a watermelon and grinning was designed for white men to put in their yards to further the illusion of the black man's happiness, time and the elements changed the object so that Nelson and Mr. Head now see something entirely different. For them "it was not possible to tell if the artificial Negro were meant to be young or old; he looked too miserable to be either. He was meant to look happy because his mouth was stretched up at the corners but the chipped eye and the angle he was cocked at gave him a wild look of misery instead" (*CW*, 229). Consistent with the operation of the "new jesus" in *Wise Blood* and with many of O'Connor's early grotesques, this image represents the rotting of an illusion. Its distortion renders the invisible—in this case, the repressed history of racial inequity—visible.

Through the grotesquely defaced statue, Mr. Head and Nelson suddenly see a history of Negro suffering at the hands of white men: "they stood gazing at the artificial Negro as if they were faced with some great mystery, some monument to another's victory that brought them together in their common defeat. They could both feel it dissolving their differences like an action of mercy" (*CW*, 230). Perhaps O'Connor expects too much of her readers with these two sentences. But understanding O'Connor's effort to defy Cartesian categories of self and other can help us read the scene. Like Ozymandias in the sand, this "monument to another's victory," now completely effaced, shows how thin a victory it had really been. When Mr. Head sees it, it changes him—or, more accurately, helps him name the changes he has already experienced. Instead of seeing his identity as defined against the other, frozen in a cold rationality, he stands now with the suffering community in identification and sympathy. O'Connor's language emphasizes Mr. Head's and Nelson's similarities: "the two of them stood there with their necks forward at almost the same angle and their shoulders curved in almost exactly the same way and their hands trembling identically in their pockets.

Mr. Head looked like an ancient child and Nelson like a miniature old man" (*CW*, 230).

Mr. Head could not see himself in the grotesque statue unless he had some basic, instinctual ability to identify with others' defeat and misery. Mr. Head has that ability in part because of his own recent humiliation, and in part because of his participation in a Southern community that has experienced defeat and therefore has no pretense to idealism. The South, O'Connor writes, has been "traditionally opposed to the idea of Enlightenment perfectibility that still characterizes this age." Instead of inheriting Northern idealism, the South's beliefs and qualities have been absorbed part from the Scriptures and part "from her own history of defeat and violation." Those beliefs include a "distrust of the abstract, a sense of human dependence on the grace of God, and a knowledge that evil is not simply a problem to be solved, but a mystery to be endured" (*CW*, 862). Mr. Head, it seems, needed a reminder of his Southern heritage, and he got one. The experience drives him away from the city, back to Nelson, back to his community, and—through all three—back to God.

O'Connor's convictions about the qualities and beliefs of Southern communities explain how Mr. Head's return home is a return to Eden of sorts. The moon still floods the area with light as it did in the opening scene, when Mr. Head thought he could direct it, but now it is "restored to its full splendor," and "as they stepped off [the train], the sage grass was shivering gently in shades of silver and the clinkers under their feet glittered with a fresh black light. The treetops, fencing the junction like the protecting walls of a garden, were darker than the sky which was hung with gigantic white clouds illuminated like lanterns" (*CW*, 230). Mr. Head learned the one lesson he wanted Nelson to learn: to "stay home." But now home affords him a different meaning. Instead of all the bustling around of the Cartesian king who would dictate to nature, he becomes still and speechless. "Mr. Head stood very still and felt the action of mercy touch him again but this time he knew that there were no words in the world that could name it" (*CW*, 230).

Mr. Head now also understands that the unnamable action of mercy "grew out of agony, which is not denied to any man and which is given in strange ways to children" (*CW*, 230). It was from the suffering dependence of a child that Mr. Head had to learn of his own dependence. He gives up on his "adult" project of separation and individuation and, like a child, accepts his position of dependence upon the grace of others—in this case, the supreme other—that is the necessary component of true repentance.[13]

Failed male parental figures in O'Connor's fiction always live up to the irony of their names. Mr. Head heads up a family expedition that gets them lost, and Mr. Sheppard of "The Lame Shall Enter First" fails in his calling to care for and nurture his own flock. Sheppard is the father of another motherless boy, Norton. And like another failed parent—Rayber of *The Violent Bear It Away*—he has completely embraced the Enlightenment project of education. He sees the world as one big arena for his reformation projects. Sheppard so intellectually invests himself in the reform of Rufus Johnson, a troubled youth with a clubfoot, that he ignores the emotional needs of his own son. By the end of the story Norton has hanged himself in an effort to return to his mother, and Sheppard is left with the guilt.

As we have seen, Cartesian internalism insists that a childlike immersion in the body prevents the development of the autonomous self, which is the goal of modern philosophy. Susan Bordo argues that read psychoanalytically, this insistence that the self define itself as a mind constituted against the world's body can be linked to the child's need to overcome aggressively the pain of separation from his mother. Rather than feel the pain of dependency on the maternal, the

---

[13] This conclusion modifies that reached by Mary Neff Shaw, who argues that the final movement in the narrative is for the RT (the Represented Thought of Mr. Head) to break away from the NS (Narrator's Sentence-judgments about the character). She writes that by this move the "RT realizes his internal freedom" (Shaw, "'The Artificial Nigger': A Dialogical Narrative," in *Flannery O'Connor: New Perspectives* [Athens: University of Georgia Press, 1996] 148). But I believe the evidence better shows that Mr. Head accepts full responsibility for himself the moment he realizes he has taken internal freedom too far—which seems to be the narrator's position.

self prefers to effect its separation through aggressive self-assertion. The self plays out a fantasy of self-parenting, "of 'rebirthing' the self, playing the role of active parental figure rather than passive, helpless child."[14] The human being is the "engineer and architect" of the detachment, thinking himself born into complete independence.

Sheppard may believe that he has effectively parented himself, but his entrapment in this kind of thinking makes him a terrible—and terribly tragic—parent to his child. When the story opens, we find him looking with disdain upon ten-year-old Norton (as Norton spreads peanut butter and ketchup on a piece of chocolate cake) because Norton is so "selfish." So Sheppard makes plans. He thinks Norton will come around if he helps him reform the juvenile delinquent, Rufus Johnson. Sheppard tries to win his son's help through rational arguments. He tells him to think of what he has, how his material needs are met, and how he has been taught the truth. "And your mother is not in the state penitentiary," he concludes (*CW*, 597). The penitentiary remark reminds Norton of his mother and he begins to cry, moaning that if she was in the pen, at least he could see her. Sheppard, seeing Norton's "childish" behavior, "sat helpless and miserable, like a man lashed by some elemental force of nature. This was not a normal grief. It was all part of his selfishness. She had been dead for over a year and a child's grief should not last so long. 'You're going on eleven years old,' he said reproachfully" (*CW*, 597).

Sheppard's belief that his young son could get over the death of his mother in a year is perverse. It also indicates that Sheppard associates growth and maturity with the ability to separate oneself from a childish attachment to the maternal world and to develop a cold and clinical care for others. "'If you stop thinking about yourself and think what you can do for somebody else,' Sheppard said, 'then

---

[14] Susan Bordo, *The Flight to Objectivity: Essays on Cartesianism and Culture* (Albany: State University of New York Press, 1987) 107–108. Bordo argues that the "Cartesian project of starting anew through the revocation of one's actual childhood (during which one was 'immersed' in body and nature) and the (re)creation of a world in which absolute separateness (both epistemological and ontological) from body and nature are keys to control rather than sources of anxiety can now be seen as a 'father of oneself' fantasy on a highly symbolic, but profound, plane."

you'll stop missing your mother'" (*CW*, 597). As the story progresses we see that the "truth" Sheppard has taught Norton is that his mother, since she is dead, is gone forever. When Rufus Johnson, who turns out to be quite a Bible-thumper, refuses Sheppard's attempt to inspire him and insists that he is going to hell when he dies, Sheppard responds, "nobody has given reliable evidence there's a hell" (*CW*, 611). But Norton believes Rufus when he invokes the Bible's authority in the matter, and he wails in despair: "'Is she there?' he said in a loud voice. 'Is she on fire?'" Sheppard responds, "your mother isn't anywhere, she's not unhappy. She just isn't" (*CW*, 611). Sheppard gives Norton the rational atheist's concession to his spiritual needs by telling him that her spirit lives on in other people, "and it'll live on in you if you're good and generous like she was" (*CW*, 612).

Some critics argue that Sheppard, like Rayber, fails as a character because he is too much of a straw man. Indeed Sheppard is so coldly rational that he is almost inhuman. But that is the point: he simply lives out his enlightened humanistic convictions with integrity. Without God and the Christian tradition to teach that human life has eternal value for its own sake, man is necessarily left to create the meaning of his existence. Since that meaning is measured by a person's utility, the sooner children can grow up to make a contribution to the world, the better. So Sheppard focuses on Johnson's "potential" to be a "new self"—potential that he locates in Johnson's high IQ. He encourages mastery of the mind through exertion of the will: "I believe you can make anything of yourself that you set your mind to," he tells him. Sheppard's plan for Johnson's education is the perfect design of the enlightened male intellect who wants to see, separate himself from, and control the world as other. "Instinctively he concentrated on the stars. He wanted to give the boy something to reach for besides his neighbor's goods. He wanted to stretch his horizons. He wanted him to *see* the universe, to see that the darkest parts of it could be penetrated. He would have given anything to be able to put a telescope in Johnson's hands" (*CW*, 601). Sheppard sees himself as Mr. Head did, as "a guide to men." Under his tutelage, Johnson will birth a new self as he penetrates the darkest parts of the female universe, explaining every mystery with detached scientific vigor. His mind will dominate, and he will be free. Eventually Johnson's primitive beliefs in the devil, heaven, and hell will prove to be illusions.

Once again, only the body rendered grotesquely visible can effectively challenge the tidiness of Sheppard's worldview. In "The Lame Shall Enter First," the monstrous appears in Johnson's unsightly clubfoot. Sheppard cannot permit any infirmity or freakishness; such things must be fixed or hidden. "The unsheathed mass of foot in the dirty sock made Sheppard feel queasy" (*CW*, 620). To Sheppard, Johnson's clubfoot stands for everything deformed or childish about him, especially his conviction that Jesus is real and that hell is an actual place. When Sheppard buys Johnson a special shoe so that "he won't know he don't have a normal foot," he thinks of his act as if he has become a superior god, "as if he had given the boy a new spine" (*CW*, 621). When Johnson refuses to wear it, Sheppard's response to the clerk says it all: "I had thought he was less of a child" (*CW*, 621).

Here again children, immersed in the body and accepting its grotesqueries and imperfections, see better than adults. Johnson has biting insight into Sheppard's true character: "Yakkety, yak...and never says a thing...I don't care if he's good or not. He ain't *right*." And most revealingly: "He thinks he's Jesus Christ" (*CW*, 604, 609). Johnson bucks the "truth" Sheppard tries to teach him and insists instead on his brutal narrative of the truth of hell and of Christ. When Sheppard tries to tell Johnson he does not really believe all that because he's "too intelligent," Johnson responds, "even if I didn't believe it, it would still be true," and eats the pages of Scripture as if to affirm their physical reality as an echo of Christ's (*CW*, 627). The boy reveals the ugliness of Sheppard's soul; he gets through the thin layer of self-perfection Sheppard wears. When Sheppard looks at Johnson, his "eyes were like distorting mirrors in which he saw himself made hideous and grotesque" (*CW*, 624).

In spite of Sheppard's shepherding, Johnson's story of heaven and hell and eternal life compels Norton. Not ashamed of his needs, Norton asks the right questions, groping around for answers beyond what his father will teach him. He follows a valid spiritual instinct for connection when he looks for his mother's body in the sky. But with no one to shepherd him, Norton is left to interpret Johnson's teaching in his own way. While Norton is upstairs at the telescope, looking for his mother in the stars, Sheppard is downstairs quarreling with Johnson. The quarrel leads Sheppard to insist upon himself as a self-sacrificing martyr for Johnson, and when he does, it finally dawns on him that it is not good that he "had done more for Johnson than he had done for his own child" (*CW*, 631). In horror he recognizes that he had "stuffed his own emptiness with good works like a glutton. He had ignored his own child to feed his vision of himself" (*CW*, 632). The image he had constructed of himself "shriveled until everything was black before him" and by contrast, he has a vision of his son Norton at the telescope, suffused with light. "The little boy's face appeared to him transformed; the image of his salvation; all light. He groaned with joy. He would make everything up to him. He would never let him suffer again. He would be mother and father" (*CW*, 632). It is a colossal spiritual advance for Sheppard to want to be a *mother* to Nelson. He finally understands that he needs to give himself instead of abstract ideas. But it comes too late. When he runs upstairs to kiss Norton, he finds him hanging "just below the beam from which he had launched his flight into space" (*CW*, 632).

This shocking death may be too much for this story—and it is not the only child death in O'Connor's *oeuvre*. In "The River" the young Harry Ashfield, also blatantly neglected by his parents, gets baptized by a journeyman preacher who tells him that he now "counts." But unable to return to understanding parents at home (his mother is a passed out alcoholic and his father cares little), he later returns to the river and, wishing to be held inside that which gave him meaning, drowns himself.

I think it is unfortunate that O'Connor felt compelled to bring to tragic ends stories in which such an end is not truly required. The writers who trained her were steeped in the New Criticism, and certainly they led her to focus on endings that definitively closed the dramatic circle of the story. Caroline Gordon had at various times told her that her endings were too flat and that she must "gain some altitude and get a larger view" (*HB*, 78). As we have seen, O'Connor felt that her characters (and Americans in general) were hardheaded and needed to be violently displaced. But when death comes at the end of a story after difficult spiritual discoveries have already been made—as in "The Lame Shall Enter First," "The River," "Greenleaf," and perhaps even "A Good Man Is Hard to Find"—it often unnecessarily diverts attention from those earlier discoveries. Even Christian readers, convinced that death is not by far the worst thing that can happen to a person, stumble over the finality of it. Often O'Connor seems to use death not to bring a character to spiritual discovery, but to punish him or her for arriving at that discovery too late.

In "The Lame Shall Enter First" and "The River," the child deaths are even more problematic. They mitigate against O'Connor's desire to show how children often understand much more spiritual truth than do adults. They tax non-Christian readers too much because readers must be able to see that each death comes from ignorance that is an ever-so-slight misapplication of otherwise profound spiritual understanding. But through their dramatic finality the deaths illustrate that even in the ways the children are wrong, they are still more correct than their adult counterparts. Their "childish" literalness saves them from "adult" abstractions that would lead eventually to the end of Christianity. Without the literal death and resurrection of Christ, the apostle Paul taught, "then is our preaching vain, and your faith is also vain."[15] Harry Ashfield, wanting to be connected, wanting to be literally buried with Christ in his baptism, comes to understand the core of the gospel.

Norton's mother is dead, and Harry Ashfield's might as well be. For such a short story, O'Connor used a lot of space to develop the distance between this mother—often referred to simply as "she"—and her five-year-old child Harry. When the story opens the father is paying the baby-sitter, Mrs. Connin, while the mother shouts directions at him from another room. The narrator never gives a physical description of the mother beyond her dress. She had "long

---

[15] 1 Corinthians 15:14.

black satin britches and barefoot sandals and red toenails" (*CW*, 166). She rarely gets up from the sofa. She leaves the child to rummage among party leftovers for his meals, and her conversation with him serves only to determine her own reputation: "what did that dolt of a preacher say about me?" (*CW*, 168).

Although both parents neglect Harry, the mother's neglect is far more significant to him. When Harry first goes with Mrs. Connin to the baptisms, he takes for himself the preacher's name "Bevel," claiming that "my mother named me that" (*CW*, 165). O'Connor believed that the name given to a person—his *apax legomenon*—marks his distinctiveness as a valued human being.[16] It is the first act whereby the family—and particularly the mother—gives significance and value to a child. Since this child was a mistake, his parents just considered him another "Tom, Dick, or Harry" and named him accordingly. Thus Harry, in choosing the distinctive name "Bevel," expresses his need for what the preacher says to him at his baptism: "you count now...you didn't even count before" (*CW*, 165).

It is not surprising that he begins at this moment to transfer his need for connection to his mother onto an obsession with the river. Recall Bakhtin's explanation that the mother's love for her child is the earliest example of an aesthetic act through which one human being values the other simply because he is an other. Like other acts of aesthetic productivity and love, this act echoes God's love in its gratuity. Harry's parents could have taught him God's love through their love, but instead he has to leave the "ashfield" of his home to look for it. When he does, his instincts are unfailingly good, for they lead him to the living waters of the baptismal font. The sacrament of baptism defies the dualism that would deny Harry's best impulses here. First, it acknowledges (as do all sacraments) that man has a body and a soul and that the body is as deeply implicated in epistemological discovery and spiritual growth as is the mind.[17] More significant,

---

[16] See Arthur F. Kinney, *Flannery O'Connor's Library: Resources of Being* (Athens: University of Georgia Press, 1985) 22 for quotations O'Connor marked in Tresmontant's *Study of Hebrew Thought* regarding proper names.

[17] In *The Idea of Catholicism*, one of the writers explains that baptism "befits man, who has a body as well as a soul; it befits the Church, which is a supernatural

while dualistic thinkers insist upon the autonomous *will* as power to do and to know, baptism insists on an identification with Christ as the only way to true knowledge. It insists on childlike helplessness. The will is important, but identification is more so. Baptism "is not merely a question of moral attachment by the determination to obey His commandments and to walk in His footsteps. It means to identify oneself with Jesus Christ...."[18]

Baptism is so significant a topos in O'Connor's fiction because it enables her to play out the ways in which the spiritual is linked to the corporeal. Water is present at all births; water can be the cause of death. Baptism emphasizes both: "This sea [of baptism], as we have seen, is at the same time both deadly and regenerating. The baptismal fonts, that is to say, the waters of baptism, are at the same time a tomb and a maternal womb of inexhaustible fruitfulness."[19] Harry's return to the river illustrates his desire to be "buried with Christ in baptism" and into a new life.[20] But he is drawn there by his need for connection with his mother that he has been denied. His substitution of the river for his mother's body can be seen in O'Connor's control of the river metaphor below:

> She tiptoed lightly across the room and sat down on the edge of his bed. "What did that dolt of a preacher say about me?" she whispered. "What lies have you been telling today, honey?"
>
> He shut his eye and heard her voice from a long way away, as if he were under the river and she on top of it. She shook his shoulder.

---

society but also a human and visible one; and it befits Christ, the head of this Church, who is God made flesh and who died for us in the flesh," and that by the sacraments "we do not see Him, we touch Him" (Walter J. Burghardt, S. J., and William F. Lynch, S. J., *The Idea of Catholicism: An Introduction to the Thought and Worship of the Church* [Cleveland: Meridian Books, 1960] 190, 188).

[18] Burghardt and Lynch, *Idea of Catholicism,* 194.

[19] Ibid., 192.

[20] "For in him dwelleth all the fulness of the Godhead corporeally; and you are filled in him, who is the head of all principality and power: In whom also you are circumcised with circumcision not made by hand, in despoiling of the body of the flesh, but in the circumcision of Christ: Buried with him in baptism, in whom also you are risen again by the faith of the operation of God, who hath raised him up from the dead" (Colossians 2:9–12).

"Harry," she said, leaning down and putting her mouth to his ear, "tell me what he said." She pulled him into a sitting position and he felt as if he had been drawn up from under the river. "Tell me," she whispered and her bitter breath covered his face.

He saw the pale oval close to him in the dark. "He said I'm not the same now," he muttered. "I count."

After a second, she lowered him by his shirt front onto the pillow. She hung over him an instant and brushed her lips against his forehead. Then she got up and moved away, swaying her hips lightly through the shaft of light. (*CW*, 168)

Harry's mother is brutally distant. She sits on the edge of the bed, shakes him, lowers him by his shirt, and only brushes him with her lips. Harry, therefore, imagines himself embraced by the river with his mother a long way off. He has already chosen the river as a new womb, a place to be reborn. During his baptism Harry had been overcome by the "sudden feeling that this was not a joke. Where he lived, everything was a joke" (*CW*, 165). The mother's physical distance from the body of her child echoes the ironic distance she and her husband take from everything—they are literally "above it all." And this ironic distance parallels the other example in the story in which someone outside the river is laughing at someone inside of it: Mr. Paradise, hunched over like a gargoyle, who laughs at the idea of baptism.

But Harry is so eager to return to the river and bound in that he does not even see Mr. Paradise. Neither does he look for the preacher to help him. His need for wholeness and connection is so great that he cannot wait for a mediator, and there is no one around to give him the guidance he needs. He is calling himself Bevel now, for he "intended not to fool with preachers any more but to Baptize himself and to keep on going this time until he found the Kingdom of Christ in the river" (*CW*, 170). He plunges in only to discover that the river *physically* will not have him, and "he stopped and thought suddenly: it's another joke, it's just another joke" (*CW*, 171). Harry's confusion of literal death with spiritual death in the river, while tragic, reveals that he has a deeper understanding than the adults in his world. For him, spiritual need is real need, need for connection with the actual body of Christ, not for a story that can be deemed absurd, kept at arm's length, and simply laughed at. Justifiably afraid of the predatory "giant pig" Mr. Paradise he now sees coming after him, in faith Harry "plunged under once and this time, the waiting current caught him like a long gentle hand and pulled him swiftly forward and down. For an instant he was overcome with surprise; then since he was moving quickly and knew that he was getting somewhere, all his fury and his fear left him" (*CW*, 171). The "long gentle hand"—the touch of connection, meaning, and protection—was what he had wanted all along.

CHAPTER 4

BODY MATTERS:
"GOOD COUNTRY PEOPLE" AND
"A TEMPLE OF THE HOLY GHOST"

It is strange to think that all the great women of fiction were, until Jane Austen's day, not only seen by the other sex, but seen only in relation to the other sex. And how small a part of a woman's life is that....

—Virginia Woolf, *A Room of One's Own*

In the view of most feminist critics, Flannery O'Connor cannot win. She has been derided for abusing female characters, especially intellectual or powerful women, by having them raped by a masculine God.[1] She has been scorned for upholding a virulently patriarchal version of Catholicism. She has been taken to task for believing she can ignore or underplay sexual difference. Some scholars have argued that she thinks women are not fit to be artists.[2] Some have intimated that, there being no evidence of a love affair with a man, she must

---

[1] For the most characteristic of these arguments, see Louise Hutchings Westling, *Sacred Groves and Ravaged Gardens* (Athens: University of Georgia Press, 1985).

[2] Katherine Hemple Prown, *Revising Flannery O'Connor: Southern Literary Culture and the Problem of Female Authorship* (Charlottesville: University Press of Virginia, 2001) 3.

have repressed homoerotic desires.[3] For all of these arguments to be true, O'Connor would have to be someone deeply conflicted, her strong vocational sense of herself as a woman writer warring at all times against her support of patriarchy, and her love for women warring at all times against her need to illustrate that women in the church must not be strong and must be violently subdued. She must have been an unhappy woman indeed.

This story of churning inner conflict is fascinating, but is it accurate? Those interested in the question of O'Connor's personal life quickly discover that the resources available to help answer it have been carefully protected by the O'Connor estate.[4] In the meantime feminist critics have tended to take O'Connor's outspoken Catholicism like a battering ram to both her fiction and her life as a woman writer. What is assumed and rarely problematized in these treatments is what being a woman in the Catholic church meant to O'Connor. For nearly all these critics, to be a Catholic woman in the 1940s and '50s meant having only two choices: either acquiesce to or struggle subversively against a hierarchy that denigrates women and denies them any real agency. But O'Connor never seemed to see it that way. Part of the problem is that we have grown so accustomed to the story of O'Connor's writing life that we forget how radically

---

[3] Such rumors led Sally Fitzgerald to defend O'Connor's heterosexuality by describing "painful" episodes of unrequited love, for which she offers little evidence. I believe Fitzgerald's approach would have frustrated O'Connor because it acquiesces to the culture's assumption that there is no category for women beyond that which is constituted by sexual desire. Under this assumption, Mary Flannery O'Connor can be a woman if she loves men or if she loves women. To be defined by desire for neither would be—well—grotesque (see Fitzgerald, "Flannery O'Connor: Patterns of Friendship, Patterns of Love," *Georgia Review* 52 [1998]).

[4] In the absence of an official biography, we have the manuscripts and a robust collection of letters that have been mined by critics for fifty years. Taken as a whole, the letters reveal a remarkably self-assured and compassionate woman, bravely enduring considerable physical suffering, working as a writer in a rural community that largely did not understand her, and generously giving herself as a spiritual mentor to as many as wrote to her with sincerity. If she was an unhappy woman, having bitterly repressed sexual desire for women, or feeling uneasy as a woman writer in a male's world, it is not easy to find evidence of it—either in the lines or between them.

countercultural a woman she was. O'Connor managed to fashion herself a life that enabled her both to be in full communion with the Catholic church and to be the furthest thing from the 1950s woman Betty Friedan was soon to identify. She never married. She was bound to her home by lupus, not by her definition of femininity. She did not feel conflicted about being a professional woman (though certainly others felt conflicted about her), and neither did she deny her female identity. Regardless of how we view the teachings of the Catholic church on women (or how others viewed her life at the time), it is clear, if the letters are to be believed, that by and large she was satisfied with herself as a woman and as a Catholic—though little in her life can be construed as a conventional example of either.

And if we can accept her opinion that an independent Catholic woman writer is not an oxymoron, we might find something surprising. First we find that she is radically committed to her belief that in matters of the soul there is no difference between men and women. She was an egalitarian in her treatment of male and female characters: both are hardheaded, both tend to pride, both need redemption. O'Connor always thought of gender-neutral characteristics as the primary characteristics, and her fiction speaks to the truth of her epistolary quip that "on the subject of the feminist business, I just never think, that is never think of qualities which are specifically feminine or masculine. I suppose I divide people into two classes: the Irksome and the Non-Irksome without regard to sex" (*HB*, 176). Critics use this quotation to argue that O'Connor suppressed gender differences—a move that enables them to keep unchallenged their view that the Catholic church is misogynist. But to class people according to a different category from gender is not necessarily to ignore the category altogether. In fact, it is my conviction that a careful look at gender in O'Connor's work can give us a definition of woman many feminists long for: that a woman can be a woman without reference to her relationships with men or to the category of sexual desire. In other words, it is not a stretch to see O'Connor's insistence on a radically egalitarian spiritual measure of a person's value as a way to free us to find a productively different answer to the question Judith Butler poses at the beginning of *Gender Trouble*: "Is there a region of the 'specifically feminine,' one that is both differentiated from the masculine as such and recognizable in its difference by an unmarked and, hence, presumed universality of 'women'?"[5]

O'Connor is usually denied the chance even to pose that question.[6] In nearly every example of the critical claim that her stories endorse a "misogynist politics," we find arguments like Katherine Hemple Prown's: "The landscape that characterizes much of her published fiction is overwhelmingly masculinist. Although women appear in a number of her short stories, they most often serve as comical examples of peculiarly feminine and irrational forms of behavior that invariably leave them vulnerable to attack. Rare is the adult female character who enjoys narrative respect or who survives unharmed."[7] Yes, but rare is any character of O'Connor's who enjoys respect and survives unharmed—that is, if you accept Prown's definitions of respect and harm. And are we really so certain that female characters are attacked only when they act in "peculiarly feminine" ways?[8] Furthermore, if there are only three characters that O'Connor "truly admired" (as Prown goes on to argue) and they happen to be male, does that prove she was unable to admire strong women?[9]

Part of the problem is that we operate with strong cultural assumptions that O'Connor did not share. One of our most salient convictions—particularly as Americans—is that growth comes by way of transcendence of the autonomous individual. Although in

---

[5] Judith P. Butler, *Gender Trouble: Feminism and the Subversion of Identity, Thinking Gender* (New York: Routledge, 1990) 4.

[6] Cynthia Seel's *Ritual Performance* is a notable exception (Steel, *Ritual Performance in the Fiction of Flannery O'Connor* [Rochester NY: Camden House, 2001] 46–59).

[7] Prown, *Revising Flannery O'Connor*, 6.

[8] The argument is illustrative of how O'Connor cannot win on the feminist question because other scholars have argued that the women who are most likely to receive narrative attack are those that *break* the usual conventions.

[9] The primary problem we are always stumbling over is that O'Connor rarely gave "positive" portraits of humanity in general. That was simply not the story she felt it was necessary to tell.

O'Connor's fiction we do not find that kind of transcendence—by either male or female subject—we still criticize her for not allowing women to transcend. For example: "Because she associated the female with the particular, the mundane, and the trivial, she refused to allow women characters, particularly those who were ladies, to represent the universal, the transcendent, or the spiritually profound."[10] This conclusion reveals a tacit acquiescence to the assumptions that drive (to use one important example) Simone de Beauvoir's *The Second Sex*. De Beauvoir argues that men have claimed for themselves transcendence and have located immanence in the bodies of women, rendering them "other." Man demands that woman be his property and that she "represent the flesh purely for its own sake. Her body is not perceived as the radiation of a subjective personality, but as a thing sunk deeply in its own immanence; it is not for such a body to have reference to the rest of the world, it must not be the promise of things other than itself: it must end the desire it arouses."[11] De Beauvoir's decidedly modern and existential assumptions about the goal of human existence lead her to see in Christianity a separation of the spirit and the flesh, wherein the flesh is evil and the spirit good. Under these assumptions, Christianity is inevitably misogynistic: woman corresponds with flesh and death and is evil; man corresponds with spirit and life and is good. Indeed, de Beauvoir is happy to allow Tertullian to speak for the entire Christian church: "Woman! You are the gateway of the devil. You persuaded him whom the devil dared not attack directly. Because of you the Son of god had to die."[12] De Beauvoir then draws the astonishingly reductive conclusion that "all Christian literature strives to enhance the disgust that man can feel for woman."[13]

---

[10] Prown, *Revising Flannery O'Connor*, 7. Prown argues that O'Connor's rejection of ladyhood equates with a rejection of feminine embodiment (9), but these are rather significantly different things.

[11] Simone De Beauvoir, *The Second Sex*, rev. ed. (London: Everyman's Library, 1993) 166.

[12] Tertullian, quoted in ibid., 176.

[13] De Beauvoir, *The Second Sex*, 176.

Under these assumptions we will misread O'Connor's treatment of the flesh in general and of women in particular. De Beauvoir's Gnostic version of Christianity is not O'Connor's Christianity. That male and female characters seek to escape from the body and the limits of the physical and of death is always a spiritual problem and never a liberating triumph. So when Prown and others argue that O'Connor's female characters are associated with the "trivial and mundane," they fail to see how O'Connor championed the "trivial and mundane" as the only avenue for real growth, thereby putting women, particularly Southern women, a step closer to that growth than men.[14] The astonishing truth is that O'Connor's women fail when they *imitate men* who fail. And men fail most in their angelic attempts to transcend the realities of the body, of creaturely immanence.

Once we disengage ourselves from de Beauvoir's existential assumptions about the individual and about Christianity, we can see that O'Connor redefined the feminine within Catholic Christianity by wresting both the category of the feminine and the category of the Christian away from larger cultural limits. She did this through two apparently contradictory stories that directly address the subject of female desire: "Good Country People" and "A Temple of the Holy Ghost." Taken together, the stories suggest that a woman—no different from a man on this count—cannot and must not avoid her immanence. They also open up a way for woman to be defined as woman apart from her relationship to men. The stories clearly reveal—negatively, as they often do—that O'Connor pitied two types of women: those who deny their embodied selves to live in the mind, as if having a female body is of no import (Joy/Hulga), and those who define themselves only by sexual desire (the child's cousins in "Temple"), as if having a female body is of essentialist import. Both Joy/Hulga and the child make profound spiritual discoveries that

---

[14] Patricia Yaeger argues that Southern women writers have been unfairly accused of ignoring larger racial and political themes because of their tendency to focus on everyday things. "The epic status of the everyday is what southern women's writing is most about" (Yaeger, *Dirt and Desire: Reconstructing Southern Women's Writing, 1930–1990* [Chicago: University of Chicago Press, 2000] 112).

give them great future (though untold) potential. Joy/Hulga discovers that she is not a mind that can detach herself at will from her female body, and the child discovers the possibility of a female identity greater than what can be constituted by gender differences and the category of sexual desire.

"Good Country People" tells the story of Joy, a thirty-two-year-old with a Ph.D. in philosophy. Joy lives with her mother Mrs. Hopewell and their help Mrs. Freeman and her family. Joy, a characteristic O'Connor intellectual, thinks she is above it all and that she has nothing to do with everyone else's primitive existence. She renames herself Hulga and stamps around on a wooden leg (her leg having been shot off in a hunting accident) until a Bible salesman, who turns out not to be a Bible salesman at all, coaxes her leg from her and leaves her alone in a barn loft.

O'Connor said "Good Country People" was the easiest thing she wrote. "Technique works best when it is unconscious, and it was unconscious there," she explained in a letter (*CW*, 1000). Perhaps the story came from her pen so easily because of the scenario's obvious similarity to her own life: an intelligent young woman who has an outside education is forced, because of physical limitations, to live at home with her mother and the farm help. Joy/Hulga's mother does not understand her daughter's intellectual interests, and there are certainly humorous hints to the same effect in O'Connor's references to her own mother, whom O'Connor often gently mocked.

O'Connor herself admitted the similarities in a letter, but then reminded the recipient that she could not write Hulga if she were Hulga (*HB*, 106). Although O'Connor is not Hulga, the story has always felt to me like a kind of cautionary tale: Joy/Hulga is what O'Connor might have been if she were an atheist and put all her stock in her education instead of in her faith. O'Connor believed the church gave her a place to be a whole intellectual woman, a woman with a vocation, without denying her femininity. She found viable models in the atypical female saints. But the secular world, she believed, can only maim its intellectual daughters, because it defines the intellectual life by transcendence (which is a doomed formula anyway) and then proceeds to insist that women cannot achieve that transcendence.

"Good Country People" is thus a complex story with a double critique: it criticizes Mrs. Hopewell for adopting and propagating the culture's destructive gender binaries, and it criticizes Joy/Hulga for pursuing a faulty path to intellectual growth. Joy may have a wooden leg, but her real problem is that she is doubly maimed: first by her culture and then by her own choices.

"Good Country People" was written in the postwar era Betty Friedan would later criticize for reversing earlier advances in feminism by creating one acceptable role for women: that of wife and mother.[15] As an intellectual woman living against this milieu, Joy/Hulga was maimed at the outset by a culture that characterizes her as grotesquely unfeminine—a culture that lives in microcosm in her mother, Mrs. Hopewell.[16] Mrs. Hopewell can see her other daughters as "fine girls," but she thinks of Joy only as an unsexed "child." Glynese and Carramae—aptly renamed Glycerine and Caramel by Joy—fit the culture's definition of women as defined by male desire. Glynese is eighteen and has "many admirers," and Carramae is, at age fifteen, already married and pregnant.

A product of her time, Mrs. Hopewell simply does not know what to do with a thirty-two-year-old Ph.D. who does not seem to want any "*normal* good times" (*CW*, 266). Because Mrs. Hopewell defines femininity by that which is attractive to men, she cannot see anything beautiful or feminine in a daughter who will not play by the rules of that game. "Hulga always put her eggs on the stove to boil and then stood over them with her arms folded, and Mrs. Hopewell would look at her—a kind of indirect gaze divided between her and Mrs. Freeman—and would think that if she would only keep herself up a little, she wouldn't be so bad looking. There was nothing wrong with her face that a pleasant expression wouldn't help. Mrs. Hopewell said that people who looked on the bright side of things would be beautiful

---

[15] Betty Friedan, *The Feminine Mystique*, twentieth anniversary ed. (New York: Dell Publishing Company, 1984).

[16] Mrs. Hopewell is the perfect example of what Sarah Gordon has identified as the Southern mother's admonition that their daughters "do pretty" (Gordon, *Flannery O'Connor: The Obedient Imagination* [Athens: University of Georgia Press, 2000]).

even if they were not" (*CW*, 267). Mrs. Hopewell clearly believes her daughter is not actually beautiful, and she is now working on ways to manipulate appearances to the contrary. Frustrated in that attempt, she sets up for Joy a separate category—genderless—in which Joy is the only member: "It seemed to Mrs. Hopewell that every year she grew less like other people and more like herself—bloated, rude, and squint-eyed" (*CW*, 268).

Not finding any models or room for herself as feminine, Joy increasingly and deliberately defines herself in opposition to her mother's categories. To her mother's forced cheerfulness, Joy responds with constant outrage. She stamps noisily and heavily around the house on her wooden leg, wearing old and unattractive clothing, emphasizing how far she is from her mother's ideal of the feminine as coy and petite. Without an example of femininity that can accept the female body without accepting rigid gender roles—an example the church could provide—Joy selects a reasonable but fatal alternative. She adopts the modern intellectual's approach to identity by insisting that the mind is all, and the body is nothing. She works to convince herself and others that her body is unimportant and mechanical and that her leg might as well be a wooden one because it is just something to use. More important, Joy comes to believe that she has actually reduced everything to her mind. She acts as if nothing in the physical world can affect or move her—*particularly* as a woman. She refuses traditional pastimes, claiming that they have no appeal: "all day Joy sat on her neck in a deep chair, reading. Sometimes she went for walks but she didn't like dogs or cats or birds or flowers or nature or nice young men. She looked at nice young men as if she could smell their stupidity" (*CW*, 268).

Does this mean O'Connor necessarily dooms intellectual women? Not if we carefully examine the choices Joy has made for the use of her intellect. Joy, in the same manner as many of the male characters O'Connor most viciously mocks, has become a dualist. She believes her autonomous mind, having now disconnected itself from the prejudices and errors of the body, can "see through" to nothing. And now that the myths of her mother's naïve world have been proven to be illusory, the world has become completely transparent to

Science—ultimately penetrable, knowable, and dismissible. When her mother picks up one of Joy's books, she reads: "Science, on the other hand, has to assert its soberness and seriousness afresh and declare that it is concerned solely with what-is. Nothing—how can it be for science anything but a horror and a phantasm? If science is right, then one thing stands firm: science wishes to know nothing of nothing. Such is after all the strictly scientific approach to Nothing. We know it by wishing to know nothing of Nothing" (*CW*, 268–69).

O'Connor's humor works powerfully in this story, for here we laugh both at the seemingly nonsensical conclusion of Heidegger's argument and at Mrs. Hopewell's hopeless anti-intellectualism, as the words worked on her "like some evil incantation in gibberish" (*CW*, 269). But Joy has clearly taken this kind of thinking seriously. Free from any dependence upon the laws of the body, the autonomous self becomes everything and must give itself a new birth. This self insists upon "playing the role of active parental figure rather than passive, helpless child" in a "defiant gesture of independence from the female cosmos."[17] So Joy renames herself "Hulga" primarily in order to completely exit from the world of her mother and Mrs. Freeman. That world is mired in slavish and anti-intellectual dependence upon sensuality, generativity, the body and its relationships with other bodies. Hulga will instead give birth to herself, and fully own herself:

> She considered the name her personal affair. She had arrived at it first purely on the basis of its ugly sound and then the full genius of its fitness had struck her. She had a vision of the name working like the ugly sweating Vulcan who stayed in the furnace and to whom, presumably, the goddess had to come when called. She saw it as the name of her highest creative act. One of her major triumphs was that her mother had not been able to turn her dust into Joy, but the greater one was that she had been able to turn it herself into Hulga. (*CW*, 266–67)

As we have already seen, when a mother names a child, it is a communal act, wherein another confirms the child's value. Through Mrs. Hopewell's body and her early mothering, Joy's "dust" was

---

[17] Susan Bordo, *The Flight to Objectivity* (Albany: State University of New York Press, 1987) 107, 106.

literally turned into "Joy"—in spite of Joy's desire to the contrary. Joy wants her name, as her self, to be completely her own affair, a volcanic explosion of personal power. When Mrs. Freeman, seeing through Joy/Hulga's spite, begins to use the new name, Hulga "would scowl and redden as if her privacy had been intruded upon" (*CW*, 266). Joy/Hulga's refusal of her given name is a refusal to acknowledge that she is actually dependent upon the communal and corporeal world her mother's body represents. Ultimately, Joy/Hulga's "highest creative act" is to sever all ties to the body and live in a world her genius constructs.

I have argued that O'Connor's goal in her fiction was to provide her characters and readers with a shocking, bodily experience that would defy dualism and begin the process of spiritual growth. In *Wise Blood* Hazel Motes needs the corrupted body of the "new jesus" to see what his dualistic philosophy would actually produce. The problem with Joy/Hulga is not that she is an intellectual. It is that she has used her intellect to deny the physical reality of her body and to convince herself that nihilism is the world's whole truth. Joy/Hulga needs an encounter that will prove she is not above her body and that will give her a picture of the real results of her philosophical convictions.

Enter Manley Pointer. When he "inraduces" himself, he says he is "Manley Pointer from out in the country around Willohobie, not even from a place, just from near a place" (*CW*, 271). Rootless and drifting like Mr. Shiftlet, he also has used several aliases so that no one would learn his real name—the name his mother gave him that would have particularized him and linked him to a place. "I use a different name at every house I call at and don't stay nowhere long" (*CW*, 283). He has no respect for people, particularly women. When he absconds with Hulga's artificial leg, he tells her he has a history of collecting other "body" parts of women: "I've gotten a lot of interesting things.... I got a woman's glass eye this way" (*CW*, 283). Manley is Joy's male counterpart, an incarnation of what she thinks she believes. She had convinced herself that the soul/body connection does not matter, and suddenly she finds someone who really believes it, who has reduced people to instruments for his pleasure. Through his utter depravity, Joy/Hulga also comes to discover that she has some faith—wise blood—that is not in keeping with her own philosophical project.

Of her treatment of Joy/Hulga, O'Connor wrote that "it's not said that she never had any faith but it is implied that her fine education has got rid of it for her, that purity has been over-ridden by pride of intellect through her fine education" (*CW*, 1000). Strangled as Hulga is by this kind of pride, it is clear that more education or an intellectual argument would not work here to change her back into Joy. Only a displacing encounter could break down the separations she has made rigid, an encounter that rejoins body and mind and resuscitates her soul as a soul. O'Connor's answer is that of the incarnational artist: she drags Joy back through her own body.

Joy/Hulga arranges to meet Manley Pointer for a picnic in order to carry out a plan that she thinks will vindicate her beliefs. She imagines that she will disabuse him of his innocence by seducing and abandoning him, because "true genius can get an idea across even to an inferior mind. She imagined that she took his remorse in hand and changed it into a deeper understanding of life. She took all his shame away and turned it into something useful" (*CW*, 276). But when they get out into the countryside the next day, Joy/Hulga finds a much more aggressive Manley Pointer than she had anticipated. He pants after her and kisses her. She remains convinced that she is mentally in control of the entire situation:

> The kiss, which had more pressure than feeling behind it, produced that extra surge of adrenaline in the girl that enables one to carry a packed trunk out of a burning house, but in her, the power went at once to the brain. Even before he released her, her mind, clear and detached and ironic anyway, was regarding him from a great distance, with amusement but with pity. She had never been kissed before and she was pleased to discover that it was an unexceptional experience and all a matter of the mind's control. Some people might enjoy drain water if they were told it was vodka. (*CW*, 278)

Joy/Hulga believes she possesses the Cartesian mind—"clear and detached and ironic"—and that her will can overcome any experience in the body. Her error, however, can be seen in the last sentence. Although one might decide to *enjoy* drain water by calling it vodka, one cannot make drain water *function* like vodka by an act of the mind. Sex, like alcohol, has a force of its own. Here O'Connor agrees with René Girard that "sexuality is one of those primary forces whose sovereignty over man is assured by man's firm belief in his sovereignty over it."[18] O'Connor clarified in a letter that "it's not said that she's never loved anybody, only that she's never been kissed by anybody—a very different thing" (*CW*, 1000). It is different because love can be conceptually understood, even willed, but a kiss activates the body as well as the mind.

What happens to Joy/Hulga when the two go up into the hayloft moves quickly beyond her capacity to understand and control. Although the seduction scene between them is perverted and possibly burlesqued,[19] in it O'Connor again insists that sexual intercourse has spiritual significance whether the participants acknowledge it or not.[20] When Manley takes Joy/Hulga's glasses, she looks out the window and sees two green swelling lakes. She ignores them and returns to her insistence that "some of us have taken off our blindfolds and see that there's nothing to see" (*CW*, 280). But the sexual life, generativity, and the water of the womb are not "nothing," and Joy is drawn into their larger meaning in spite of herself. Soon Manley asks her to let him remove her artificial leg—an incredibly intimate request. The wooden leg came to signify her difference, her uniqueness. In a way it also represents her virginity, the loss of which would be a physical sign of an emotional surrender: "As a child she had sometimes been subject to feelings of shame but education had removed the last traces of that as a good surgeon scrapes for cancer; she would no more have felt it over what he was asking than she would have believed in his Bible. But she was as sensitive about the artificial leg as a peacock about his tail. No one

---

[18] René Girard, *Violence and the Sacred*, trans. Patrick Gregory (Baltimore: Johns Hopkins University Press, 1977) 34.

[19] Anthony Di Renzo, *American Gargoyles* (Carbondale: Southern Illinois University Press, 1993).

[20] The Christian church has always viewed marriage as the only legitimate place for sexual relations because through sex the "two become one flesh." Union with other bodies, therefore, degrades the marriage bond.

ever touched it but her. She took care of it as someone else would his soul, in private and almost with her own eyes turned away" (*CW*, 281). When Manley Pointer guesses this, it moves her to complete the surrender to him that her body had already begun. "This boy, with an instinct that came from beyond wisdom, had touched the truth about her" (*CW*, 281). She gives him the leg, and it "was like losing her own life and finding it again, miraculously, in his" (*CW*, 281).

This is the language of the Christian's surrender to Christ—Jesus taught that one must lose one's life to find it—and it is also the language used in Christian discussions of the sacrament of marriage. In Catholic theology, the Incarnation of Christ adds ultimate significance to the marriage relationship. In the words of one of the writers of Burghardt and Lynch's *The Idea of Catholicism*, "it is precisely because Christ inaugurated new relations between God and humanity that His coming has, without His having expressly said so, not changed but raised up tremendously the nature of marriage by making it a sign of a great mystery."[21] By the Incarnation, "the Son of God and the human race are no longer two, but one in the same flesh forever" so that marriage "is another example of the deep saying of the Gospel: he who seeks his life shall lose it; who loses his life shall find it. The bride and bridegroom must really give themselves to one another in a way that is unselfish."[22] In other words, for both partners marriage is the repudiation of independence, of the drive to define ourselves *against* others instead of *by* them. This process begins for Joy/Hulga when she thinks about someone else taking over the daily removal of her leg. She begins to think about her body's being for someone else. "She was thinking that she would run away with him and that every night he would take the leg off and every morning put it back on again" (*CW*, 281). This is not the satiric, ironic, and detached Hulga. Made keenly aware of her body, she is made aware of her dependence on others. "Without the leg she felt entirely dependent on him. Her brain seemed to have stopped

---

[21] Walter J. Burghardt, S. J., and William F. Lynch, S. J., *The Idea of Catholicism* (Cleveland: Meridian Books, 1960) 213.
[22] Ibid., 213, 216.

thinking altogether and to be about some other function that it was not very good at" (*CW*, 282).

This "other function" is what her mother and Mrs. Freeman are good at, and Joy/Hulga is shocked to discover that she is not so unlike them—she is a woman with a strong desire for relationship. But she also discovers that she shares the naiveté she often mocked. For when Manley Pointer reveals himself to be the scoundrel that he is, she protests, "aren't you just good country people?" (*CW*, 282). He responds, "You ain't so smart. I been believing in nothing ever since I was born" (*CW*, 283). Although he takes her leg and her pride, he leaves her with the much more precious gift of true self-knowledge. Like so many of O'Connor's characters, Joy has learned what she thought she could teach her own mother and the "innocent" Pointer: "we are not our own light."

But this is not the end of the story. To leave analysis here might tempt us to see O'Connor as some kind of propagator of the feminine mystique, as if Joy should abandon the life of the mind and become the frilly and unintellectual daughter her mother always wanted. The solution is not for Joy/Hulga now simply to enter the unironic world of the motherly Mrs. Hopewell. The story has also roundly dismissed that worldview as hopelessly naïve, as "simple" as Mrs. Hopewell thought the Bible salesman to be. After all, Mrs. Hopewell's binary categorization of everything, including a rigid essentialism in gender roles, largely led Joy/Hulga to her predicament in the first place. Her mother has something to teach Joy, but she also has something to learn from her, and the truth lies somewhere between them.

What that middle ground might look like is not the story O'Connor chooses to tell here. But by critiquing both Joy and her mother, O'Connor indicates the error of those who would make the embodied world the law of destiny and those who would make the embodied world irrelevant. The two errors, therefore, also symbolize similar pitfalls that face the artist. Deny the body and its laws and you will achieve only a false transcendence, but you will also fail if you do not see beyond the physical. O'Connor explained these two errors in a letter: "About the woman who is the Realist: this is a complicated subject but the only light I have to throw on it is that Poetry is always dependent on Realism, that you have to be a realist or you can't be a poet. Mrs. Hopewell is a realist but not a poet, whereas Hulga has tried to be a poet without being a realist" (*CW*, 975). *Both* pretensions must be pierced and their expositors displaced.

Some may think it a monstrous contradiction that O'Connor's most Catholic story—"A Temple of the Holy Ghost"—is also the one that most directly and controversially addresses the issue of gender. I believe it must be read as a complement to "Good Country People" because it presents a more complete picture of the choices we might imagine are now available to Joy/Hulga in her new self-awareness up in the loft. The protagonist is a twelve-year-old girl referred to only as "the child" who is clearly an intellectual, a sort of prepubescent Joy/Hulga. The story stymies critics who believe that O'Connor's fiction degrades women and women artists, for O'Connor reserves some of the greatest spiritual discoveries for an adolescent girl. Furthermore, it is through the child's artistic imagination—her metaphoric connection of the Holy Eucharist to the grotesque body of a carnival hermaphrodite—that the child enters true worship, an egalitarian space where *body* difference is fully accepted, but male/female *desire*—as constitutive of identity—is displaced.

The child, like Joy/Hulga, lives in a world primarily constituted by male/female desire, a world she mocks (though she does not understand it). The story opens with her second cousins, Joanne and Susan, coming from Mount St. Scholastica convent for a weekend visit. The girls could not wait to take off their androgynous brown uniforms, after which they "put on red skirts and loud blouses. They put on lipstick and their Sunday shoes and walked around in high heels all over the house, always passing the long mirror in the hall slowly to get a look at their legs" (*CW*, 197). The child, whose view the story primarily follows, seems to exult in her genderlessness in this environment so charged with female sexuality and desire. She "decided, after watching them for a few hours, that they were practically morons and she was glad to think that they were only second cousins and she couldn't have inherited any of their stupidity" (*CW*, 197). She herself has fat cheeks and braces and is proud of her intelligence and her thoughts toward a future career. She thinks them small for taking an interest only in boys: "Neither one of them could say an intelligent thing and all their sentences began, 'You know this boy I know well one time he...'" (*CW*, 197). The child even plays boyish pranks on her cousins, trying to find something "cold and clammy that she could hide in their bed," but doesn't have anything she can think of, "like a chicken carcass or a piece of beef liver" (*CW*, 205). O'Connor emphasizes the distance the child deliberately places between herself and the girls. She has not yet entered their world of lipstick and boys, so she will make them believe she does not care to. "If only one of them had come, that one would have played with her, but since there were two of them, she was out of it and watched them suspiciously from a distance" (*CW*, 197). She spies on them when they are on an outing with neighborhood boys, and she isolates herself in her room, from where she glares at them outside the window.

At one level, this story is about how intelligent girls are likely to be excluded from "typical activities of a girl her age," as one critic has argued.[23] But for O'Connor social failure in the world of shallow women is not much of a loss—as long as the child does not choose Joy/Hulga's path. For this story clearly celebrates the child's imagination as distinct from that of her cousins and as potentially productive of much greater joy than participation in that world alone would provide. Poised on the edge of adolescence, the child is dreaming up her identity, pondering her future. Although one of those daydreams involves seeing herself as the object of male desire (in her case, Wendell and Cory), the desire is less central to the dream than her own heroic activity. Indeed, her dream plays out a gender reversal; in it, a girl's act of heroism makes her attractive to the boys instead of the reverse: "I know them all right...we fought in the world war together. They were under me and I saved them five times from Japanese suicide divers and Wendell said I am going to marry that kid and the other said oh no you ain't I am and I said neither one of you

---

[23] Carla L. Verderame, "A Retreat Home: Flannery O'Connor's Disempowered Daughters," *The Flannery O'Connor Bulletin* 26–27 (1998–2000): 147.

is because I will court marshall you all before you can bat an eye" (*CW*, 200–201).

But a dream that involves male/female desire is the exception and not the rule for this child. The most significant thing about the child's imagination is that it consistently moves beyond the limits of the imaginations of those around her. Joanne and Susan dream only about boys; the child has a vision of herself as a professional woman and then as a saint, because "she felt she would have to be much more than just a doctor or an engineer. She would have to be a saint because that was the occupation that included everything you could know" (*CW*, 204). She feels immediately that she could never be a saint because she has problems with lying and sassing back, but she thinks she could be a martyr "if they killed her quick" (*CW*, 204).

It is precisely because the child can see beyond the gender roles played out by Joanne and Susan that she can begin to grasp profound spiritual concepts the girls only mock. Since the girls' reality centers on making themselves attractive to the opposite sex, they can only laugh when they report what they were taught about their bodies at the convent:

> Sister Perpetua, the oldest nun at the Sisters of Mercy in Mayville, had given them a lecture on what to do if a young man should—here they laughed so hard they were not able to go on without going back to the beginning—on what to do if a young man should—they put their heads in their laps—on what to do if—they finally managed to shout it out—if he should "behave in an ungentlemanly manner with them in the back of an automobile." Sister Perpetua said they were to say, "Stop sir! I am a Temple of the Holy Ghost!" and that would put an end to it. The child sat up off the floor with a blank face. She didn't see anything so funny in this. (*CW*, 199)

The child lacks a great deal of specific knowledge, but like many of O'Connor's child protagonists, she possesses an imagination that enables her to move beyond the limits that everyone else unblinkingly accepts. She sees her body in a completely new way. "I am a Temple of the Holy Ghost, she said to herself, and was pleased with the phrase. It made her feel as if somebody had given her a present" (*CW*, 199).

Her acceptance of this idea—that the female body, like the male body, was designed to be more than the locus of sexual attraction and reproduction—prepares her to be an interpreter of the grotesque body of the hermaphrodite. Hungry for information about the spectacle the girls had seen at the carnival, the child lies to them, telling them she would trade information about where babies come from (which she does not know) for a description of the event. They tell her the men were divided from the women in a circus tent, and the "you-know-what" moved from one side to the other, charging that "God made me thisaway and if you laugh he may strike you the same way" (*CW*, 206). The child does not understand how it can be a man and woman both—"you mean it had two heads?" So the child's imagination works instead on what she has just learned: that the human body is God's dwelling place of choice, his temple. As she lies in bed pondering the new information, she imagines the hermaphrodite in a church service, speaking to men and women together, telling them, "if anybody desecrates the temple of God, God will bring him to ruin and if you laugh, He may strike you thisaway. A temple of God is a holy thing. Amen. Amen" (*C W*, 207). The hermaphrodite becomes the priest—Christ's representative—and the congregation responds with "Amen": "so be it."

Joanne and Susan, content to live in a world of binaries defined by sexual desire, can be only repulsed and confused by the grotesque form. But the child lets it redirect her into making new connections, new discoveries. She lets it have the power that Geoffrey Harpham ascribes to the grotesque—the power of paradox. "If the grotesque can be compared to anything, it is paradox. Paradox has a way of turning language against itself by asserting both terms of a contradiction at once. Pursued for its own sake, paradox can seem vulgar or meaningless; it is extremely fatiguing to the mind. But pursued for the sake of wordless truth, it can rend veils and even, like the grotesque, approach the holy. Because it breaks rules, paradox can penetrate to new and unexpected realms of experience, discovering relationships syntax generally obscures."[24] The grotesque has

---

[24] Geoffrey Galt Harpham, *On the Grotesque: Strategies of Contradiction in*

displaced the child to a position of exceptional spiritual openness and potential fecundity. When she later goes to Mt. Saint Scholastica and enters the convent chapel, at the smell of incense, the sight of colors in springing arches, and the sound of singing, she "began to realize that she was in the presence of God" (*CW*, 208). She begins to pray in a new attitude. "Hep me not to be so mean…hep me not to talk like I do"—prayers for the very things she had felt were a block to her sainthood (*CW*, 208). And finally "her mind began to get quiet and then empty but when the priest raised the monstrance with the Host shining ivory-colored in the center of it, she was thinking of the tent at the fair that had the freak in it" (*CW*, 208).

The child's imagination is at once receptive and boldly creative. It powerfully connects like and unlike, equating the Eucharist—the body of Christ—with the body of the hermaphrodite, emphasizing the silencing mystery of both. The body of the hermaphrodite illustrates that something radical is going on here, something that breaks all the rules, something that cannot be explained by the binary systems of the Joannes and Susans of the world. When Judith Butler reads Foucault's discussion of the hermaphrodite Herculine, she writes that "the linguistic conventions that produce intelligible gendered selves find their limit in Herculine precisely because she/he occasions a convergence and disorganization of the rules that govern sex/gender/desire. Herculine deploys and redistributes the terms of a binary system, but that very redistribution disrupts and proliferates those terms outside the binary itself."[25] For Butler, who believes that gender is entirely a social and linguistic construct, the existence of the hermaphrodite critiques the "metaphysics of substance" when it comes to gender identification. O'Connor also uses the body of the hermaphrodite to disorganize the rules, to push beyond the limits of our linguistic conventions regarding gender. But she does so not to *eliminate* the categories of male/female but to *subordinate* those categories under the more powerful identification of the body as temple of the Holy Ghost, who encompasses both genders. The move

---

Art and Literature (Princeton: Princeton University Press, 1982) 19–20.

[25] Judith P. Butler, *Gender Trouble* (New York: Routledge, 1990) 23.

does not erase gender difference but displaces any essentialist power it may have claimed as the primary arbiter of identity. So the story echoes Paul that "there is neither Jew nor Greek: there is neither bond nor free: there is neither male nor female. For you are all one in Christ Jesus."[26] By shifting the marginal to the center—which is always the function of the grotesque—the hermaphrodite as Eucharist validates the child's own marginal status as a female who can now choose not to be defined by male desire.[27] It paves the way for her to be defined instead by desire for God.

The child also learns—propelling her far beyond her cousins— that to love God is to love and accept all of creation. He makes no mistakes; freaks are not accidents. She is empowered to claim outsider status if she wants to, confident that "God made me thisaway, and I don't dispute it."[28] Where she had only laughed at the pig-like Alonzo Meyers before, she learns that he too is a temple of the Holy Ghost. The Eucharist opens her to gratitude instead of scorn.[29] So when the

---

[26] Galatians 3:28.

[27] Harpham writes that the grotesque is "embodied in an act of transition, of metonymy becoming metaphor, of the margin swapping places with the center. It is embodied in a transformation of duality into unity, of the meaningless into the meaningful" (*On the Grotesque,* 47).

[28] O'Connor often emphasized that acceptance of one's circumstances is not cowardly, but a heroic act of faith. She wrote to Hester: "About its being cowardly to accept only the nun's embrace: remember that when the nun hugged the child, the crucifix on her belt was mashed into the side of the child's face, so that one accepted embrace was marked with the ultimate all-inclusive symbol of love, and that when the child saw the sun again, it was a red ball, like an elevated Host drenched in blood and it left a line like a red clay road in the sky. Now here the martyrdom that she had thought about in a childish way (which turned into a happy sleeping with the lions) is shown in the final way that it has to be for us all—an acceptance of the Crucifixion, Christ's and our own. As near as I get to saying what purity is in this story is saying that it is an acceptance of what God wills for us, an acceptance of our individual circumstances. Now to accept renunciation, when those are your circumstances, is not cowardly..." (*HB*, 124).

[29] As the catechism of the Catholic church teaches, "the Eucharist is a sacrifice of thanksgiving to the Father, a blessing by which the Church expresses her gratitude to God for all his benefits, for all that he has accomplished through creation, redemption, and sanctification. Eucharist means first of all 'thanksgiving'" (Catholic Church, *Catechism of the Catholic Church* [United States Conference of Catholic Bishops, 2000] 1360).

moon-faced nun (whose embrace she earlier shunned) swoops down on her this time, the nun "nearly smothered her in the black habit, mashing the side of her face into the crucifix hitched onto her belt" (*CW*, 209). The scene is the story in microcosm: the child is marked with and accepts Christ's body through the body of the other. The child is now on her way to the greater joy of this transcendent identification with the body of Christ. It is the joy that had been that of the church's first Perpetua, the historical Christian martyr who went to her death claiming that she was unable to deny Christ because she defined herself to be, in substance, a Christian.[30]

As we watch the child return home in the car, we see that her view has clearly been expanded. When she hears that the police had shut the fair down, "the child's round face was lost in thought. She turned it toward the window and looked out over a stretch of pasture land that rose and fell with a gathering greenness until it touched the dark woods. The sun was a huge red ball like an elevated Host drenched in blood and when it sank out of sight, it left a line in the sky like a red clay road hanging over the trees" (*CW*, 209). The story's closing image is particularly beautiful for its subtlety: when the Host sinks out of sight, saturating the landscape with the blood of Christ, it leaves a line like a red clay road, the same red clay that was on Mr. Cheatam's car (who she had scorned before), and that was the color of his hair and face. The child's mind—a clear parallel to the artist's mind—connects the natural world to the body of Christ; the Incarnation is that which illuminates and validates all of creation as worthy of loving attention. This twelve-year-old girl, poised between childhood and adulthood, embracing both the imagination and the body of the world, finds the Eucharist and thereby fully enters the

---

[30] Perpetua was martyred under the rule of Septimius Severus in the third century. Gonzalez writes that "when Perpetua and her companions were arrested, her father tried to persuade her to save her life by abandoning her faith. She answered that, just as everything has a name and it is useless to try to give it a different name, she had the name of Christian, and this could not be changed" (Justo L. Gonzalez, *The Story of Christianity: The Early Church to the Dawn of the Reformation,* [San Fransisco: HarperCollins, 1984] 83).

sacrament of confirmation.[31] She also thereby opens herself to a Christian vocation not subject to America's limiting categories of "woman." In many ways, this child's story parallels O'Connor's own story: a journal she kept at age twelve reveals her own remarkable vision of a vocation that would lead her to reach far beyond what her era prescribed for its young women.[32] But O'Connor did not believe that to find that vocation was to somehow deny her participation in a separate category of the "female." Because while de Beauvoir argues that the Christian woman's escape from being an "other" to men can come only through denial of her "animality," whereby a woman loses herself to an abstract purity, these two stories argue that such a transcendence can only be reached through the particular individual bodies, male or female, that have been given to each.

---

[31] Twelve is a significant age in Catholic education, for it is a customary age for confirmation at which a baptized child declares her faith in Christ, takes her first communion, and enters more fully into the sacramental mysteries of the church. For more detail, see the *Catechism of the Catholic Church*.

[32] Sally Fitzgerald described this journal to me in a conversation we had in 1996. As of yet, it remains unavailable to scholars.

CHAPTER 5

TRANSCENDING THE TRANSCENDENTALISTS:
BISHOP AS BEAUTY IN
THE VIOLENT BEAR IT AWAY

> *He had no beauty or majesty to attract us to him, and nothing in his appearance that we should desire him.*
>
> —Isaiah 53:2

Flannery O'Connor held fiction—her own and that of others—to the highest artistic standards, and her standards for the novel were especially exacting. A novel, she reflects in a letter to John Hawkes in 1959, should not be written about anything except what is of "gravest concern" to the novelist, and for her "this is always the conflict between an attraction for the Holy and the disbelief in it that we breathe in with the air of the times" (*HB*, 349). It is thus no surprise that her two major works, *Wise Blood* and *The Violent Bear It Away*, tell similar stories. But O'Connor had matured as an artist in the intervening years, and the distinctions she drew between the two reveal how much she intended for *The Violent Bear It Away* to rewrite *Wise Blood*. "It is a more ambitious undertaking," she wrote. "The boy doesn't just get himself saved by the skin of his teeth, he in the end prepares to be a prophet himself…" (*HB*, 350).

Her high ambitions translated into considerable frustration; O'Connor often referred to *The Violent Bear It Away* as her "Opus Nauseous." In an interview given in the same year she wrote Hawkes,

O'Connor explained why it was so challenging: "I think it is easier to come out with something that is negative because it is just nearer fallen nature. You have to strain yourself for the other, strenuously, too."[1] This "other"—the positive—is suggested in *Wise Blood* but not given; Haze "negates himself" back to the cross by instinctively rejecting his own empty philosophy when forced to face it in the form of the corpse of the new jesus. In the end we are left with a Hazel Motes who, like a number of O'Connor's other characters, is redeemed by the skin of his teeth—and dead. In *The Violent Bear It Away*, however, O'Connor consciously strains herself for the positive. Although she keeps her gravest concern intact—the story is about a young prophet who fights against his wise blood and tries to ignore his calling to preach Christ—in the new novel she definitively replaces the concrete center of the story and gives her reluctant prophet something to be drawn to instead of repulsed by. Instead of the dead and perverse incarnation of the new jesus, she gives a complex and living incarnation of the beautiful: the retarded child Bishop.

With this living center, *The Violent Bear It Away* signals, more than any other work, O'Connor's shift in sensibility with regard to the possibilities of the grotesque.[2] Most of the grotesques in her early career signify lack, the absence of something good in characters, the perverse result of the fall. These grotesques can only challenge by repulsion, even when we find that what we are repulsed by is ourselves. But Bishop and the later grotesques signify the presence of Being in being, the divinely created core of humanity that can be seen in spite of our fallen nature. O'Connor called such grotesquerie "the face of good under construction." These grotesques mysteriously attract us even *as* they repel us; they bid us to ask questions, and they suggest beauty of another order entirely. And it is a beauty O'Connor felt her audience could not quite see.

---

[1] Rosemary M. Magee, ed., *Conversations with Flannery O'Connor* (Jackson: University of Mississippi Press, 1987) 26.

[2] Marshall Bruce Gentry also identifies a shift in O'Connor's use of the grotesque from what he calls the "negative grotesque" to the "positive grotesque." See introduction to Marshall Bruce Gentry, *Flannery O' Connor's Religion of the Grotesque* (Jackson: University Press of Mississippi, 1986).

In this novella as in all of O'Connor's fiction, the blindness of her audience and of her characters explains the violence. Because the blind live in worlds of their own making, the prophet/artist must displace those worlds by whatever tools she can find—by distortion, the grotesque, physical pain, and death. In the case of the *via negativa* of *Wise Blood*, O'Connor violently brought the corruption of sin into view by ensuring that readers could see the perversity in the act of Sabbath Hawkes's holding a corpse like a baby. But *The Violent Bear It Away* illustrates that when the artist wants to show the true face of good, she must struggle no less violently and against the same kind of blindness. Because the modern world has violently severed reason from imagination, nature from grace, and judgment from vision, the artist has to push to rejoin them. Under these separations, the modern world believes it determines the nature of the beautiful and the value of every human life. The artist, like the prophet, struggles to show us the high cost of such a determination. While many critics believe *The Violent Bear It Away* dramatizes the struggle for Tarwater's freedom, the story makes more sense as the dramatization of his—and by extension, the artist's—struggle for vision. A wayward prophet, Tarwater would rather not see what he sees and finds plenty of encouragement from the world to keep his prophetic eyes closed.

In "The Nature and the Aim of Fiction," O'Connor wrote that the novelist "intrude[s] upon the timeless" by "the violence of a single-minded respect for the truth" (*MM*, 83). Because of O'Connor's strong commitment to Catholicism and our age's fear of totalitarianism, many critics assume that she meant stories should promote a single-minded *version* of the truth. Such critics naturally read the violence in the stories as the inevitable result of the clash between O'Connor's dominant Catholic worldview and any voice of opposition she unblinkingly levels.[3] But as Robert Brinkmeyer and

---

[3] In *The Question of Flannery O'Connor* Martha Stephens argues that O'Connor was a writer who was "strangely, almost unbelievably, unattuned to the ambiguities, uncertainties, bafflements of life and thought as most of us know and experience them every day. Here was a writer attuned, rather, to the old ways where life rested ultimately on the all-embracing certainty of *the answer*: I am the way, the

others have shown, the fiction cannot be so simply explained. Brinkmeyer argues that O'Connor's vision was sophisticated and resilient enough to accommodate the different points of view she put into conflict with each other, creating a truly dialogic discourse. Though she always remained "within the overarching frame of her Catholic faith," writes Brinkmeyer, she allowed other viewpoints to test that faith. "Such testing for O'Connor was not a sign of weakness, particularly in terms of religious faith; rather it expressed what she believed most modern people lacked—a commitment to make operable in the natural world a faith in the supernatural."[4]

That O'Connor's single-minded respect for the truth does not translate into an unsophisticated version of the truth emerges with special clarity in her essay "Catholic Novelists and Their Readers." In this essay, O'Connor celebrates the Christian artist's freedom to have a holistic vision. While the rest of the world believes Christian dogma limits vision, she argues that "on the contrary, dogma is an instrument for penetrating reality...[it] is about the only thing left in the world that surely guards and respects mystery" (*MM*, 178). Because she believes in the natural and the supernatural, the Christian fiction writer can render without fully explaining, can reveal without abstracting. What appealed to O'Connor about fiction was that everything that could have an explanation had to have it, but that there was always something more. The "residue" of fiction, she writes, "is Mystery with a capital M" (*HB*, 199).

O'Connor insisted that the "fiction writer is an observer, first, last, and always, but he cannot be an adequate observer unless he is free from uncertainty about what he sees" (*MM*, 178). O'Connor knew this would sound suspect to modern ears, and it does. How can certainty unshackle observation? Doesn't it work in exactly the opposite way? O'Connor's answer to that question is that everyone

---

truth, and the life; a writer for whom this answer looms, sometimes suffocatingly close to the immediate action of her stories, sometimes more artfully distanced, over everything she writes..." (Stephens, *The Question of Flannery O'Connor*, Southern Literary Studies [Baton Rouge: Louisiana State University Press, 1973] 105).

[4] Robert H. Brinkmeyer Jr., *The Art & Vision of Flannery O'Connor*, Southern Literary Studies (Baton Rouge: Louisiana State University Press, 1989) 13.

has beliefs and values and that no writer's work operates in some no-man's-land of pure fact. To claim to believe in no absolutes is necessarily no less an absolute claim: "those who have no absolute values cannot let the relative remain merely relative; they are always raising it to the level of the absolute" (*MM*, 178). Stories have focus and perspective; since the writer without faith commitments must speak from *somewhere*, she ends up speaking according to personal whim. So it is, paradoxically, the Catholic fiction writer who is "entirely free to observe" precisely because she has no freedom to invent her own values. Without the burden to remake the world, the committed writer can see it truly. "He feels no call to take on the duties of God or to create a new universe…for him, to 'tidy up reality' is certainly to succumb to the sin of pride" (*MM*, 178).

Most of us resist the paradox that the committed writer can see more than the uncommitted, because we think of the commitment as narrowing one's vision. But O'Connor did not think of it that way: she believed the Catholic writer has to negotiate a double vision because she has two *different* sets of eyes, her own and those of the Church. The novelist is not free to choose between them, but must see through both concurrently, even if it causes tension and struggle—violence. The Christian writer is never left only to his "personal imaginative gift," but has access to a whole history, a whole prophetic vision that he did not make. He has access to "the Church's gift, which, unlike his own, is safeguarded and deals with greater matters" (*MM*, 179). Like T. S. Eliot's appropriation of tradition and Faulkner's use of history, O'Connor's insistence that the novelist look through both her own eyes and the church's eyes suggests that she does not invent the world anew with every work. The Catholic novelist both shapes and is shaped by something larger than her. If she closes her own eyes and expects the church to do the seeing for her, the result will be "another addition to that large body of pious trash for which we have so long been famous" (*MM*, 180).

What many miss in O'Connor's aesthetic is her conviction that these two sets of eyes are often in violent conflict, not easy agreement. The artist succeeds by effectively rendering that conflict, not by overcoming it. [5] "It would be foolish to say there is no conflict between these two sets of eyes. There is a conflict, and it is a conflict which we escape at our peril, one which cannot be settled beforehand by theory or fiat or faith. We think that faith entitles us to avoid it, when in fact, faith prompts us to begin it, and to continue it until, like Jacob, we are marked" (*MM*, 180). The combat does not produce a victor. Neither is it the goal of the artist to produce some new unity between them that alters both, as Eliot argues in "Tradition and the Individual Talent": "the existing order is complete before the new work arrives; for order to persist after the supervention of novelty, the *whole* existing order must be, if ever so slightly, altered; and so the relations, proportions, values of each work of art toward the whole are readjusted; and this is conformity between the old and the new. Whoever has approved this idea of order…will not find it preposterous that the past should be altered by the present as much as the present is directed by the past."[6] Eliot's "idea of order," though more to her liking than Wallace Stevens's, is still too Promethean for O'Connor; she will allow the conflict to stand with much less resolution. Jacob's wrestling match with God is not a record of man's triumph over deity; instead, the battle suggests to her that the artist must refuse two easy solutions: either to insist on her own point of view without listening to outside authority, or unthinkingly to adopt what has been handed down to her as if it was all explained already. In short, there is activity as well as passivity here; the artist must allow herself to be marked by the conflict. It is a messy struggle that always produces grotesques—focal points of contradiction, mystery, displacement. The artist himself could be a casualty because he "like a very doubtful Jacob…confronts what stands in his path and wonders if he will come out of the struggle at all" (*MM*, 183).

---

[5] In his article "Asceticism and Imaginative Vision." Brinkmeyer writes, "only by working with both sets of eyes, by cultivating rather than obliterating the tension between them, could Catholic writers write—and see—with fullness" (Robert H. Brinkmeyer Jr., "Asceticism and Imaginative Vision," in *Flannery O'Connor: New Perspectives* [Athens: University of Georgia Press, 1996] 181).

[6] T. S. Eliot, "Tradition and the Individual Talent," in *Selected Prose of T. S. Eliot*, ed. Frank Kermode (Orlando: *HBJ*, 1975) 38–39.

The Catholic novelist keeps both sets of eyes open by keeping them both mercilessly trained on the concrete. The Catholic novelist should not "shy away from sense experience" because "every mystery that reaches the human mind, except in the final stages of contemplative prayer, does so by way of the senses. Christ didn't redeem us by a direct intellectual act, but became incarnate in human form, and he now speaks to us through the mediation of a visible church. All this may seem a long way from the subject of fiction, but it is not, for the main concern of the fiction writer is with mystery as it is incarnated in human life" (*MM*, 176). In human life the novelist finds the truth that she is never above anything she writes about. O'Connor quotes Baron von Hügel: "the highest realities and deepest responses are experienced by us within, or in contact with, the lower and lowliest" (*MM*, 176). Fiction, like the Incarnation, challenges our view of the lofty, the good, and the beautiful. Jesus is God's grotesque, His insistence that the good is found where we are least likely to look for it. To see Christ as God and man requires that we open both sets of eyes and allow the conflict to remain. Its residue is mystery.

In *The Violent Bear It Away*, Bishop is O'Connor's grotesque. He is the cause of conflict, the generator of violence, the locus of the sacred. Although criticism has tended to minimize Bishop's importance in the novel by treating Tarwater's call as merely the vestiges of the old man's vision, O'Connor's prose illustrates the clear centrality of the character as one that represents the divine mystery with which Tarwater will have to come to terms before he can begin his ministry.[7] He is the ultimate concrete the novelist must look at—with both sets of eyes—in order to see the mystery of being that Christ's Incarnation validates. In Tarwater's struggle against himself to see Bishop's beauty and baptize him, O'Connor insists that

---

[7] Particularly puzzling is Johansen's reading of Bishop—"Young Tarwater also resists the seeds in the blood and flees to the periphery where he confronts an idiot child" (Ruthann Knechel Johansen, *The Narrative Secret of Flannery O'Connor: The Trickster as Interpreter* [Tuscaloosa: University of Alabama Press, 1994] 131)—and Baumgaertner's argument that Bishop is a manifestation of the metaphor of the dead word (Jill P. Baumgaertner, *Flannery O'Connor: A Proper Scaring*, Wheaton Literary Series [Wheaton IL: H. Shaw Publishers, 1988] 148).

the novelist must struggle against this Gnostic age to keep his eyes open to the ontological and transcendental character of beauty, and to see it especially in what is ugliest, weakest, and most useless.

When *The Violent Bear It Away* opens, fourteen-year-old F. M. Tarwater is alone, heady with his new freedom and too drunk to bury his great uncle Tarwater's body. His great uncle had been young Tarwater's guardian and had raised him in the backwoods according to the "ways of prophecy." With old man Tarwater dead, Tarwater must choose between what his great uncle taught him he is—a prophet—and what his uncle Rayber wants him to be—a "normal" child. We soon find that the struggle has been going on for Tarwater's entire life. Old man Tarwater stole him as a baby away from Rayber, his schoolteacher uncle. Although he once believed them, Rayber now considers all the old man's teachings about prophecy to be madness. When Rayber tries to retrieve the baby, the old man shoots his ear off. But with the old man dead, Tarwater, now old enough to decide for himself, rebels against his teaching and the "seeds of the gospel" he planted in his blood. And the drama begins.

O'Connor rightly predicted that readers would see this struggle for the young Tarwater as a struggle between a "reasonable" father figure and his crazy fundamentalist great uncle, and that they would root for the reasonable father figure. Early reviews of the novels bear this out, as do early critical efforts.[8] The impulse persists today: one recent critic describes the novel as a dramatic enactment of the lesson that bad parenting can decimate a young man's psyche.[9] But

---

[8] Josephine Hendin writes that instead of growing up under Rayber's tutelage—an idea Hendin clearly favors—Tarwater plays out a "childhood role for a lifetime" (Hendin, *The World of Flannery O'Connor* [Bloomington: Indiana University Press, 1970] 61).

[9] Suzanne Morrow Paulson in "Apocalypse of Self, Resurrection of the Double: Flannery O'Connor's *The Violent Bear It Away*" argues that O'Connor's "primary aim in this particular novel is to explore the suffering and psychology of a child and those who shaped that child. This suffering was perhaps partly caused by living in the modern world devoid of true faith, but more important, the suffering in this case was caused by parental abuse" (Paulson, "Apocalypse of Self, Resurrection of the Double," in *Flannery O'Connor: New Perspectives* [Athens: University of Georgia Press, 1996] 134).

O'Connor took a kind of impish delight in her support of Tarwater's unconventional upbringing. She wrote that "the modern reader will identify himself with the schoolteacher but it is the old man who speaks for me" (*HB*, 350). In fact, Tarwater and the "normal" Rayber had the same upbringing under the old man, and both have the same instinctive faith in Christ that O'Connor calls "wise blood." Rayber, a kind of secondary protagonist, is like an older Tarwater who has rejected the old man's teachings and now wants to validate his decision by converting and "saving" Tarwater. He wants to win Tarwater over to rationality and self-rule, to free him from the old man's domination.

Rayber, by an act of mental fiat similar to that of Hazel Motes, has dismissed his wise blood. He chalks up any vestiges of his former belief in God as the childish remains of his uncle's manipulation. But Rayber's rational approach to his own childhood struggle comes at a heavy price; he must commit violence against his own personality to arrive at this conclusion. He sees himself as divided into two parts, "a violent and a rational self," and any time the violent self emerges, he controls it by an act of will (*CW*, 417). Rayber's term "violent" is tainted with his view of the old man's extremism. His "violent" self is any part of him, most often uncontrollable, irrational passion, that resonates with the old man's teachings about Christ, prophecy, baptism, etcetera. And this is the part he deliberately shuts down.

There is, of course, good violence and bad violence in this story; violence that would keep a productive tension and usher in the kingdom of heaven, and violence that would destroy that tension. Rayber acts out of the latter. The part of himself he tries to shut down is the part he cannot control—the part that loves fiercely and violently. That there are two types of violence explains why O'Connor wrote that the title of the novel was the most misunderstood but also "the best thing about the book" (*HB*, 387). While readers associate it with Old Testament violence (wherein God is seen in a limited way as vengeful), O'Connor meant with the epigraph to associate it with the words of Jesus: "from the days of John the Baptist until now, the kingdom of heaven suffereth violence, and the violent bear it away."[10] The violence there, O'Connor insists, is a "violence of love, of giving more than the law demands" (*HB*, 382). It is the violence of courage to see more than what the world sees and to act on it.

When Rayber deliberately splits himself between his rational and violent sides and lets his rational side "win," he privileges everything he can understand and process—the law—and demotes everything he cannot—love (or grace). Jacques Maritain blamed Descartes for having "divorced intelligence from mystery" with his "clear ideas."[11] Rayber is an American Descartes who lives out a clean split between what he can know by way of reason and what cannot be known. And like Descartes, Rayber's "mind has become his god; all his psychic efforts are directed toward the rational control of reality."[12] O'Connor pokes fun at Rayber's Cartesian methodism by giving him a hearing aid that he conveniently shuts off when confronted with anything he cannot process. Tarwater, like many children in O'Connor's stories, calls it for what it is: "'What you wired for?' He drawled, 'Does your head light up?'" (*CW*, 395). And later he questions Rayber, "Do you think in the box...or do you think in your head?" (*CW*, 396). Indeed, Rayber's problem is that thinking only in his head causes him to "think in the box" as the saying goes. He puts away everything he cannot explain. His separation of intellect from mystery is so complete that he even says to his nephew Tarwater, "my guts are in my head," which explains why he does not have any.

Rayber cannot fit the old man Tarwater anywhere into his tidy system. True to the rationalist's approach, Rayber tries to explain him away with words. When he interviews the old man for a magazine article and therein labels his behavior as a psychological aberration, Rayber believes the label gives him power and freedom to ignore everything the old man says. When young Tarwater remembers the

---

[10] Matt 11:12.

[11] Jacques Maritain, *Creative Intuition in Art and Poetry* (New York: Pantheon Books, 1953) 162; Maritain continues that "modern science is making us aware of his mistake."

[12] John F. Desmond, *Risen Sons: Flannery O'Connor's Vision of History* (Athens: University of Georgia Press, 1987) 114.

old man's talking about it, he reflects, "The old man had not known when he went there to live that every living thing that passed through the nephew's eyes into his head was turned by his brain into a book or a paper or a chart" (*CW*, 341). When Rayber sees living things with his eyes, he extinguishes the life in them; by straining the mysterious through his brain, he flattens it into a quantifiable chart, book, or set of figures. Thus Rayber treats the inexplicable in the same fashion as does the modern scientist or the analytic philosopher—as a puzzle to solve by manipulating the unknowns into answerable questions. The end result is the elimination—to Rayber's mind anyway—of mystery.[13]

Old man Tarwater is Rayber's foil. He intuitively understands that the words to which Rayber tries to reduce him are stillborn. While the old man had thought Rayber's interest in him indicated a return to the faith of his childhood, he soon discovers that Rayber really intended to explain away the "family madness": "The old man had thought this interest in his forbears would bear fruit, but what it bore, what it bore, stench and shame, were dead words. What it bore was a dry and seedless fruit, incapable even of rotting, dead from the beginning. From time to time, the old man would spit out of his mouth, like gobbets of poison, some of the idiotic sentences from the schoolteacher's piece. Wrath had burned them on his memory, word for word" (*CW*, 341). Christ refers to the kingdom of heaven metaphorically as a seed with great potential for growth and multiplication. Here, Rayber's words are dry and seedless, stillborn. Christ's Incarnation validated the created world and encouraged people to be a part of its continuing creation, growth, and evolution. Here, Rayber works against that life force by trying to reduce the whole of a human person to the sum of his psychological parts, parts that can be described and categorized with abstract words. Rayber's

---

[13] Michael Bishop Foster argues in *Mystery and Philosophy* that "the goal towards which both scientist and philosopher are working is a state in which there will be no more mystery" (Foster, *Mystery and Philosophy* [Westport: Greenwood Press Publishers, 1957] 20). O'Connor would have agreed.

attempt to make flesh into word is so far from being life-giving that it cannot even rot.

As careful as O'Connor is to separate the violent and true love of the kingdom of heaven from a sentimental and false love, it is sometimes difficult to see how the gun-toting, gruff, and abrasive old man *loves* more than Rayber. But like Cordelia who could not speak words of love to Lear, the old man's love is silent (except for the words of prophecy) and unsentimental. It comes in the shape of his expansive vision that the world lives outside of God's purposes for it and needs to be drawn back. Rayber knows this love is "of a different order entirely" and he "always felt with it a rush of longing to have the old man's eyes—insane, fish-coloured, violent with their impossible vision of a world transfigured—turned on him once again. The longing was like an undertow in his blood dragging him backwards to what he knew to be madness" (*CW*, 401). Rayber longs not to see *with* his uncle's eyes, but to have those eyes *on* him again. They are eyes that, having been instructed in the faith, see people whole. They see people as made in God's image, but fallen and in need of redemption.

The difference between each man's capacity to love cannot be seen in their relationship with young Tarwater as much as it can be seen in their views of the insignificant "idiot" child Bishop. Rayber, Bishop's father, sees the child as useless, a mistake of nature. As to the idea of his baptism—what the old man longs for—Bishop is not worthy of the water it would take to spill over him. He wants the old man to forget about his obsession with baptizing the boy. But the old man loves Bishop, as he would any child, without a hint of sentimentality. "That boy cries out for his baptism," the old man says as he tries to get Rayber to move out of the way so that he can perform the ceremony. "Precious in the sight of the Lord even an idiot!" (*CW*, 350). Baptism for the Catholic is not merely an expression of the parents' commitment to raise the child in the Christian tradition. It identifies the child with Christ by giving him a new birth into a new life.[14] It signals a change in ownership; that

---

[14] For a complete description of baptism as O'Connor would have understood

which once belonged to the world and its fallen nature now belongs to Christ. It speaks of the sanctity and value of all created life. But not only does Rayber not believe in Christ or in baptismal regeneration; he also cannot see Bishop's worth as a created being. For him, a person's worth is found only in what he can accomplish. "You'll never lay a hand on him...you could slosh water on him for the rest of his life and he'd still be an idiot. Five years old for all eternity, useless forever...he'll never be baptized—just as a matter of principle, nothing else. As a gesture of human dignity, he'll never be baptized" (*CW*, 351). Rayber plays God by deciding what to value about humanity. To baptize Bishop would be to admit that he may not be a mistake of nature.

Since Rayber cannot see the value of Bishop, he takes his frustrated plans for his own child's development and turns them on the young Tarwater, now free from the old man's care. The old man, he tells Tarwater, "lived a long useless life.... You could have had everything and you've had nothing." He speaks of reforming the young Tarwater as if it were an Enlightenment project: "getting out from under the old man is just like coming out of the darkness into the light. You're going to have a chance now for the first time in your life. A chance to develop into a useful man, a chance to use your talents..." (*CW*, 388–89). In every word Rayber speaks about his plans for Tarwater's usefulness can be seen his disappointment in the "lost cause" of Bishop. A good Cartesian thinker, Rayber focuses on what he can make conform to his abstractions. But Rayber can only believe in his own project to re-create Tarwater into his image of a useful adult when he is not in the room; when Tarwater is present, the project collapses. Rayber cannot wait to get away from the real boy so that he can fix his vision for him into his head again: "Once out of sight of the boy [Rayber] felt a pressure had been lifted from the atmosphere. He eliminated the oppressive presence from his thoughts

---

it, see Walter J. Burghardt, S. J., and William F. Lynch, S. J., *The Idea of Catholicism* [Cleveland: Meridian Books, 1960] 194). This volume was in O'Connor's personal library and is representative of mid-century Catholic ideas.

and retained only those aspects of it that could be abstracted, clean, into the future person he envisioned" (*CW*, 441).

For O'Connor, Rayber's failure to see the beauty of created life just because it *is* is also the failure of the modern novelist who wants to "change the world" by his fiction. Rayber's abstract reform impulse fails for the same reason a new writer's abstractions fail: it arrogantly avoids the limitations of the concrete and real. The writer must learn a healthy sense of her limits. "What the fiction writer will discover, if he discovers anything at all," O'Connor writes, "is that he himself cannot move or mold reality in the interests of abstract truth. The writer learns, perhaps more quickly than the reader, to be humble in the face of what-is" (*CW*, 808). O'Connor describes this pitfall in "The Nature and Aim of Fiction." Her description of the bad novelist sounds remarkably like a description of Rayber.

> But the world of the fiction writer is full of matter, and this is what the beginning fiction writers are very loath to create. They are concerned primarily with unfleshed ideas and emotions. They are apt to be reformers and to want to write because they are possessed not by a story but by the bare bones of some abstract notion. They are conscious of problems, not of people, of questions and issues, not of the texture of existence, of case histories and of everything that has a sociological smack, instead of with all those concrete details of life that make actual the mystery of our position on earth. (*MM*, 67–68)

Like the utopian who believes he can ignore reality to engineer his fantasy, Rayber refuses to see what is around him. In *The Violent Bear It Away* O'Connor mocks Rayber through old man Tarwater, who spots his impotent idealism right away. When Tarwater asks his great uncle why Rayber did not come back for him after the old man kidnapped him, the old man says, "I'll tell you exactly why. It was because he found you a heap of trouble. He wanted it all in his head. You can't change a child's pants in your head" (*CW*, 378). O'Connor adamantly enjoins the fiction writer not to avoid dirty diapers; they are the material of his art. She insists that "the materials of the fiction writer are the humblest. Fiction is about everything human and we are made out of dust, and if you scorn getting yourself dusty, then you shouldn't try to write fiction. It's not a grand enough job for you" (*MM*, 68). Rayber's subjective idealism also heightens the story's irony: while Rayber thinks the old man's calling is only in his head, he fails to recognize that by ignoring the "what-is," Rayber is the one who has created his own reality. He is the true schizophrenic whose delusions come from within.

But try as he might, Rayber cannot ignore Bishop. Rayber's "violent self"—the "insane" love of all life he has inherited from the old man—has a trigger point within the mysterious child. Rayber loves Bishop in spite of himself, and he can make no sense of that love. Accustomed to seeing love only as a tool that can be used to transform psychological "cases" when nothing else works, Rayber recognizes his own love for Bishop as of another order entirely. "It was not the kind that could be used for the child's improvement or his own. It was love without reason, love for something futureless, love that appeared to exist only to be itself, imperious and all demanding, the kind that would cause him to make a fool of himself in an instant" (*CW*, 401).

Rayber thinks of this irrational and overwhelming love as another problem for his mind to solve. But what Bishop represents in his life is precisely that which cannot be reduced to a solvable equation as he attempted to do with the old man. Bishop will not fit into his head. "He had not conquered the problem of Bishop. He had only learned to live with it and had learned too that he could not live without it" (*CW*, 400). He eventually trains himself to think of and to look at Bishop as little as possible. And when Rayber does look at him, he abstracts him in order to keep him at a distance. His "normal way of looking on Bishop was as an x signifying the general hideousness of fate...the little boy was part of a simple equation that required no further solution, except at the moments when with little or no warning he would feel himself overwhelmed by the horrifying love" (*CW*, 401). Although he cannot seem to shake the living child Bishop, he can dismiss the idea of him to the "general hideousness of fate" if he really works at it.

In Bishop the untidy gratuity of life is highlighted. There is no reason for the child to live. Rayber can ignore that grotesque gratuity in Bishop for a little while, but he cannot ignore all of creation that proves to share that same gratuity. Its existence pushes the observer to praise. "Anything he looked at too long could bring it on. Bishop did not have to be around. It could be a stick or a stone, the line of a shadow, the absurd old man's walk of a starling crossing the sidewalk. If, without thinking, he lent himself to it, he would feel suddenly a morbid surge of the love that terrified him—powerful enough to throw him to the ground in an act of idiot praise. It was completely irrational and abnormal" (*CW*, 401). Since the irrational love hits Rayber when he stops thinking and starts looking, Rayber practices a rigid asceticism by not looking at anything too long.

Rayber's love scares him not because it is irrational *per se*, but because it actively overturns conclusions he arrived at through his reason. The love, O'Connor writes, "only began with Bishop and then like an avalanche covered everything his reason hated" (*CW*, 401). When the boundaries his reason affords him dissolve, Rayber's self as he has defined it will be lost. With his detached and intellectualized self in question, he must acquiesce to a definition of his person that comes from without instead of within, that brings together his violent self and his rational self. Bishop, the uncontrollable and inexplicable other in his life, has the power to dislodge Rayber's neat boundaries and to transform his vision.

Bishop's power to transform vision parallels the work of art's potential power to do the same. The artist, like the prophet, points to and values something outside of the self. Both rely upon the power of the other to displace cleanly arranged worlds. But their important difference is that while the prophet speaks truth to transform vision, the artist allows the power of the beautiful to do it. Jacques Maritain, the writer O'Connor claimed to have "cut her aesthetic teeth on," made these parallels and differences explicit. In *Art and Scholasticism*, a volume O'Connor often turned to in order to clarify her own project, Maritain describes the artist's unique vocation in terms of a struggle to lead others to beauty. "Persecuted like the wise man and almost like the saint, the artist will perhaps recognize his brothers at last and discover his true vocation again: for in a way he is not of this world, being, from the moment that he works for beauty, on the path which leads upright souls to God and manifests to them the invisible things by the visible."[15] But when the artist pursues his vocation with care, the very uselessness of the beauty to which he draws attention will stir the contemplator out of himself. Maritain writes, "the beautiful is essentially delightful. This is why, of its very nature and precisely as beautiful, it stirs desire and produces love...love in its turn produces ecstasy, that is to say, it puts the lover outside of himself; ecstasy, of which the soul experiences a diminished form when it is seized by the beauty of the work of art, and the fullness when it is absorbed, like the dew, by the beauty of God."[16] When Rayber feels this love for Bishop, he is tempted to love the world—not for itself, but with a love that will lead him to God.[17]

Rayber, of course, fights that love and all of its expansive potential. By anesthetizing himself to Bishop, he anesthetizes himself to God and keeps his mind firmly in control. Like a man trying to fortify his belief that the earth is flat by converting the undecided, he tries to get Tarwater to see Bishop, and the rite of baptism, just as he sees them. "Just forget Bishop exists," he grits his teeth and tells Tarwater. "He's just a mistake of nature. Try not even to be aware of him" (*CW*, 403). Ironically, Rayber believes that if he can just get Tarwater to look at Bishop, he will see him for what Rayber thinks he is—a meaningless freak of nature—and have the power to resist baptizing him.

But Tarwater has the old man's fish-like eyes, with his violent love of the people of the world, whether they are useless or not. Bishop is his trigger point too, but Tarwater does not want to accept his calling. So he avoids *looking* at him. To look at the idiot child with those eyes will be to see all he represents and to take on the old man's assigned mission to baptize him. Tarwater instinctively knows this. Although he tries to insist that Bishop is just "a hog...he eats like a hog and he don't think no more than a hog and when he dies,

---

[15] Jacques Maritain, *Art and Scholasticism, and the Frontier of Poetry* (New York: Scribner, 1962) 37.

[16] Ibid., 26–27.

[17] It is important to note that his experience of this love is not only through his intellect, but is more accurately an aesthetic experience, a widening of his vision via his imagination as well as his mind.

he'll rot like a hog," he knows differently (*CW*, 403). The child, a walking definition of the grotesque in O'Connor's fiction, forces an expansion of vision. When Tarwater first sees the child after making his way to his uncle's house, "his eyes widened and an inner door in them opened in preparation for some inevitable vision" (*CW*, 388). The inevitable vision is of his own relationship to Bishop, who "stood there, dim and ancient, like a child who had been a child for centuries." Tarwater knows instantly "with a certainty sunk in despair...that he was called to be a prophet and that the ways of his prophecy would not be remarkable" (*CW*, 389).

It is only through Tarwater's eyes that the ways of prophecy are "unremarkable." Like the child in "Temple of the Holy Ghost" who envisioned herself as a martyr, Tarwater wants a glamorous calling. When the old man tells him he will have to baptize Bishop if the old man cannot do it, the boy balks, wanting instead to be a new Moses, Joshua, or Daniel. But in O'Connor's perspective, part of what Tarwater must recognize is that his calling is of the highest because it is of the lowest. This struggle to see Bishop correctly explains why Bishop operates as a kind of Christ figure. He is the lowliest of the low, and it is shocking that God would value him, as shocking as the fact that God would incarnate himself as a human baby. Tarwater's call is to be a John the Baptist prophet for his time, one who would respect the light of the mystery that came before him and say, like John, "this was He of whom I said, 'He who comes after me has a rank higher than I, for He existed before me.'"[18] Tarwater lacks the proper humility at first, and he precisely inverts John the Baptist's declaration, saying to Bishop with indignation, "before you was here, *I* was here" (*CW*, 350). Much later in the novel when he finally does look at Bishop, he ties the child's shoelaces. With this act, Tarwater humbles himself like John the Baptist: "I baptize you in water, but among you stands One whom you do not know. It is He who comes after me, the thong of whose sandal I am not worthy to untie."[19]

---

[18] John 1:15.
[19] John 1:26–27.

Since O'Connor means to dramatize two conflicting views of Bishop, she offers two versions of two of the scenes in which he figures: the city park scene in which Rayber and Tarwater watch Bishop bounding toward the fountain and the Cherokee Lodge scene in which Tarwater murders and baptizes Bishop. She gives each scene through the eyes of Rayber first, and then through the eyes of Tarwater, a structure that parallels the artist's analogical vision: we begin with Rayber's literal view and then move deeper. Through Tarwater's eyes we stare longer and see more.

In *Wise Blood*, O'Connor highlights the new jesus as an aesthetic object by putting him into a glass case in the center of a museum in the center of a park in the center of a town—and all in the central chapter of the novella. Enoch thrusts the *objet d'art* into Haze's face until he knows that this grotesque reification of his new faith should drive him back to the living Christ he set out to reject. In *The Violent Bear It Away*, O'Connor replaces that repellent dead object with a simultaneously attractive and repellent living being: Bishop. The fountain scene clearly emphasizes the replacement. Like the museum scene in *Wise Blood*, this scene also appears in the center of a novel—chapter 6 of 12—and takes place in a small wooded area in the middle of a park. The park is in the middle of the city in an area where Rayber comes to rest on their way to a museum. Just as in *Wise Blood*, the scene's drama comes from the simultaneous attraction and repulsion felt by two characters, each fighting the mystery of the gratuity of life now heightened in a retarded child.

When Rayber pulls Bishop onto his lap, the powerful love overtakes him again. Although Rayber wants to remain purely in his mind, when he takes the pose of a servant and makes physical contact with Bishop's body, Rayber's "forehead became beady with sweat; he looked as if he might have been nailed to the bench" (*CW*, 418). This is a perverted Gethsemane for Rayber. At Gethsemane, Christ surrendered his will to God's as he went willingly to the cross to die for the world. In this scene, God's transforming love is present to Rayber in Bishop, but instead of allowing that love to grow outward to the rest of the world, Rayber fights it. He continues to submerge the "violence" and the "pain" of love by focusing all of it on Bishop, who "contains" it. As Rayber reminisces, we learn that he had once tried to drown the child, only to discover just before he completed the job that he could not bear the thought of life without him. Stirring out of his memory, Rayber leads Tarwater and Bishop "out into the center of the park, [to] a concrete circle with a fountain in the middle of it" (*CW*, 420). Bishop immediately runs and plunges into it.

Here we may recall Bakhtin's observation that "an aesthetic reaction is a reaction to another reaction, and a reaction not to objects and to meaning in themselves, but to objects and to meaning as they are for a given human being, i.e., as correlated with the values of a given human being."[20] In this scene, and by her usual employment of the limited omniscient third person, O'Connor invites the reader to just such a multi-layered aesthetic reaction. She invites us to react to Rayber's reaction to Tarwater's reaction to Bishop. Rayber watches, seemingly unfazed, as the sun comes out to shine brightly on Bishop's white head, but Tarwater's eyes "burned as if he held some terrible compelling vision." Rayber watches Tarwater get pushed and pulled from the child, but he cannot make sense of the scene. "Puzzled and suspicious," he "felt that something was being enacted before him and that if he could understand it, he would have the key to the boy's future" (*CW*, 421). But when Rayber suddenly discovers that Tarwater is about to baptize Bishop, his mind trumps his imagination and he loses sight of the vision and focuses only on preventing the boy from "committing some enormous indignity" by the baptism.

Rayber's failure to understand the scene's significance becomes the main point of comparison between his vision and Tarwater's. When O'Connor retells the scene through Tarwater's eyes—the eyes of the prophet/artist—she invites the reader to see Bishop's significance as a harbinger of mystery. As they walk to the park, Tarwater feels the "approach of mystery" and wants to run, but cannot. Where Rayber had seen only a bright light, Tarwater has this

---

[20] M. M. Bakhtin, *Art and Answerability: Early Philosophical Essays,* ed. Michael Holquist and Vadim Liapunov, trans. Vadim Liapunov (Austin: University of Texas Press, 1990) 222.

view of the scene: "The sun, which had been tacking from cloud to cloud, emerged above the fountain. A blinding brightness fell on the lion's tangled marble head and gilded the stream of water rushing from his mouth. Then the light, falling more gently, rested like a hand on the child's white head. His face might have been a mirror where the sun had stopped to watch its reflection" (*CW*, 432). Since one of Christ's names is "Lion of the tribe of Judah" and the hand is a sign like the dove, the passage evokes John's baptism of Jesus.[21] The Gospel of John, the one that proclaims Christ as the "Word become flesh," emphasizes that John the Baptist came first in order to point to the "light of the world," but that he himself was not that light. Each of the four Gospels gives an account of John as Jesus' baptizer and of how he recognized Jesus: "And John gave testimony, saying: I saw the Spirit coming down, as a dove from heaven; and he remained upon him. And I knew him not: but he who sent me to baptize with water said to me: He upon whom thou shalt see the Spirit descending and remaining upon him, he it is that baptizeth with the Holy Ghost. And I saw: and I gave testimony that this is the Son of God."[22]

In medieval aesthetics, which influenced O'Connor through Jacques Maritain and Etienne Gilson, light plays an indispensable role. The light never emanates solely from within the mind or imagination, but assists it from the outside. It shines on an object to illuminate it. When Aquinas describes at great length the act of grace toward the "illumination of the intellect" that is required for us to see God, he describes it in terms of light and with reference to Jesus' baptism:

Human knowledge is assisted by the revelation of grace. For the intellect's natural light is strengthened by the infusion of gratuitous light, and sometimes also the images in the imagination are divinely formed, so as to express divine things better than do those which we receive naturally from sensible things, as appears in prophetic visions; while sometimes sensible things, or even voices, are divinely formed to express some divine meaning; as in the Baptism, the Holy Ghost was

[21] For additional discussion of the biblical significance of the lion's head and the fountain, see Richard Giannone, *Flannery O'Connor and the Mystery of Love* (Urbana: University of Illinois Press, 1989) 135–37.

[22] John 1:32-34.

seen in the shape of a dove, and the voice of the Father was heard, *This is My beloved Son.*"[23]

O'Connor does not pretend that Bishop is the Christ or even a Christ symbol in a traditional sense. But by evoking the revelation of Christ's divine nature that occurred at his baptism, she does emphasize the role of divine light in prophetic seeing. By making an idiot child the beautiful being Tarwater must learn to see, she also suggests that to see the truly beautiful requires a contemplation of life that may be unnatural to human reason without divine assistance. Here, the sunlight first blinds, but then "falling more gently, rested like a hand on the child's white head" (*CW*, 432). Tarwater can see what Rayber cannot: a sign of the child's created beauty, a hand that points to Bishop as the dove marked out Jesus. Prophets and artists see and show us that light, but they are not that light themselves. O'Connor made the connection between the vision of prophets and the vision of artists explicit on this point. She praised and quoted Boris Pasternak that "all great, genuine art resembles and continues the Revelation of St. John" (*HB*, 305).

O'Connor did not have a mystical view of the artist that led her to go around in search of hands of light descending upon people in Milledgeville. For Aquinas, Maritain, and O'Connor, divine light *assists* human knowledge; it does not bypass it. In the artist's case, vision relies upon *habitus*—a term Maritain borrowed from the ancients. *Habitus* are qualities of the intellect that, when they pertain to "the facilities or powers of the soul," must be acquired "through exercise and use."[24] Art, says Maritain, "is a *habitus* of the practical intellect."[25] Though the artist must have an initial gift and calling, the habit of art is an intellectual virtue that must be developed through discipline. In her essay "Writing Short Stories," O'Connor explains that *habitus* engages the whole personality of the artist: "It is a fact that fiction writing is something in which the whole

---

[23] Saint Thomas Aquinas, *Introduction to Saint Thomas Aquinas*, ed. Anton Pegis (New York: Modern Library, 1948) 95.

[24] Maritain, *Art and Scholasticism*, 10.

[25] Ibid., 12.

personality takes part—the conscious as well as the unconscious mind. Art is the habit of the artist; and habits have to be rooted deep in the whole personality...they have to be cultivated like any other habit, over a long period of time.... I think this is more than just a discipline, although it is that; I think it is a way of looking at the created world and of using the senses so as to make them find as much meaning as possible in things" (*MM*, 101). By exercising the habit of art, the artist finds meaning in things. By looking at the created world both through her eyes and the eyes of the church, she discovers that all being is beautiful, and she designs her work to participate in that beauty, to continue it. In Maritain's words, "in the eyes of God all that exists is beautiful, to the very extent to which it participates in being."[26] Like John the Baptist, the artist and her art decrease as the beauty they portray increases.

O'Connor's incarnational art depends upon a pre-modern idea that all things "participate in being." From Maritain and Aquinas, O'Connor learned that since we are neither angels nor God, we see goodness in the human form because of its participation in being. As Aquinas writes, "every being, as being, is good."[27] The hand of light that rests on Bishop's head indicates his goodness by participation in being, and this goodness is his beauty. It has nothing to do with his behavior or his potential and everything to do with his actual existence as another person. It is life itself, that which the new jesus could only negate.

O'Connor concludes the scene with Bishop: "His face might have been a mirror where the sun had stopped to watch its reflection" (*CW*, 432). In his study of the aesthetics of Thomas Aquinas, Umberto Eco explains Aquinas's notion of *lumen* (light) in its relation to *claritas* (clarity)—one of the three objective features of beauty.[28] Aquinas writes that "the beauty of the heavenly bodies consists mainly in light," and Eco explains that for Aquinas "light is neither a body nor a

---

[26] Maritain, *Creative Intuition*, 163.

[27] Aquinas, *Introduction*, 38.

[28] The other two are "proportion" and "integrity." For a discussion of their metaphysical significance, see Umberto Eco, *The Aesthetics of Thomas Aquinas*, trans. Hugh Bredin (Cambridge: Harvard University Press, 1988) 64–121.

substance, but a quality in a body that is luminous of itself. This quality does not pass over into an opaque body when it is lit up; rather, it generates in the body its own luminosity and color, brings its own intrinsic potency (its 'diaphaneity') into act. In this way, the colors and every kind of brightness are brought into being."[29] When Bishop's face becomes a mirror that reflects the light of the sun, his fullness of being is seen thereby. The light could not be seen without the reflection, and the reflection could not be seen without the light. The same can be said of the medieval appreciation for stained glass—the colors and forms are only brought into being when the light shines through the pane.[30]

Aquinas's notion of beauty as an ontological quality must be separated from the notion of a purely subjective experience of delight and pleasure.[31] In his discourses on art, Maritain returned to Aquinas in order to rescue beauty as a transcendental (a property that is predicable of anything) from the modern definition of it as located only in the spectator's perception.[32] Since the beauty of the object consists in its participation in being, the beauty of the work of art depends upon capturing that participation. Art delights the *intellect*, not just or primarily the emotions. Dissatisfied with modernity's effort to try to remove the intellect from the whole act of aesthetic contemplation—as Rayber tries to sever himself from Bishop—O'Connor turned to Aquinas's definition that art is "reason in the making." She adds that:

---

[29] Eco, *Aesthetics,* 103.

[30] O'Connor perfects the image in "Parker's Back."

[31] This is not to say that Aquinas had no notion of aesthetic pleasure—a point Eco takes pains to make.

[32] For a thorough treatment of this point, see Deal W. Hudson, "The Ecstasy Which Is Creation: The Shape of Maritain's Aesthetics," in *Understanding Maritain* (Macon GA: Mercer University Press, 1987). Hudson writes that Maritain "wanted to disassociate himself from the modern aesthetics, which restricted the consideration of art to the fine arts, and beauty to the spectator's perception of it. Maritain's revival of two ideas—art as a virtue and beauty as a transcendental—from the classical tradition, upon which to erect the foundation of *Art and Scholasticism,* attest to his early antimodernist posture" (237).

This is a very cold and beautiful definition, and if it is unpopular today, this is because reason has lost ground among us. As grace and nature have been separated, so imagination and reason have been separated, and this always means an end to art. This artist uses his reason to discover an answering reason in everything he sees. For him, to be reasonable is to find, in the object, in the situation, in the sequence, the spirit which makes it itself. This is not an easy or simple thing to do. It is to intrude upon the timeless, and that is only done by the violence of a single-minded respect for the truth. (*MM*, 82–83)

The "violence of a single-minded respect for the truth" is the violence of the artist who sees the object, situation, or sequence with his personality whole and intact. The artist must penetrate the concrete with reason *and* his imagination, must see nature *and* grace. When he does, he will find in the object, situation, or sequence "the spirit which makes it itself."

With this kind of vision of the other that goes far beyond mere taste, beauty is truly much more than skin deep. Maritain understood that in this post-Kantian world the Thomist terms for beauty would be confused with a subjective ideal of a beautiful appearance. Though some disagree with his reading of Aquinas,[33] Maritain took pains to separate the object's ontological beauty (its "form") from our ability to see it:

The words *clarity, intelligibility, light,* which we use to characterize the role of "form" at the heart of things, do not necessarily designate something clear and intelligible *for us,* but rather something clear and luminous *in itself,* intelligible *in itself,* and which often remains obscure to our eyes, either because of the matter in which the form in question is buried, or because of the transcendence of the form itself in the things of the spirit. The more substantial and the more profound this secret sense is, the more hidden it is for us; so that, in truth, to say with the Schoolmen that the form is in things the proper principle of *intelligibility,* is to say at the same time that it is the proper principle of *mystery.* (There is in fact no mystery where there is *nothing to know*: mystery exists where there is *more to be known* than is given to our

---

[33] Eco in particular puts much more emphasis on the thing seen that "pleases" as an aesthetic concern.

comprehension.) To define the beautiful by the radiance of the form is in reality to define it by the radiance of a mystery.[34]

When the artist does not do violence to himself by separating judgment from being, reason from emotion—or, as Rayber thinks of it, his violent self from his rational self—he can see this beauty in everything, even in ugly things. He can see it *especially* in ugly things. Thus Maritain writes in a passage O'Connor underlined that "art endeavors to imitate in its own way the condition peculiar to the pure spirits: it draws beauty from ugly things and monsters, it tries to overcome the division between beautiful and ugly by absorbing ugliness in a superior species of beauty, and by transferring us *beyond* the (aesthetic) beautiful and ugly. In other words, art struggles to surmount the distinction between aesthetic beauty and transcendental beauty and to absorb aesthetic beauty in transcendental beauty."[35] Though Maritain uses the term "transcendental" to characterize this kind of beauty, it is not the beauty of the Transcendentalists—not a beauty the artist creates, but one he discovers and tries to show to others. And the artist discovers that the grotesque things, the imperfect things, the unbalanced things are uniquely able to point to the transcendental realm. As Maritain expresses it, "a totally perfect finite thing is untrue to the transcendental nature of beauty. And nothing is more precious than a certain sacred weakness, and *that kind* of imperfection through which infinity wounds the finite."[36]

What O'Connor wants to accomplish with Bishop's imperfection can be further clarified with a look at an article O'Connor read in 1956 in the middle of her most focused work on *The Violent Bear It Away*. In a letter she wrote in December of that year, she writes to Hester ("A"), "Apropos of the Christ image business, the fall issue of Cross Currents has an essay on The Idiot as a Christ symbol by Msgr. Guardini" (*CW*, 1015). The article to which O'Connor refers is Romano Guardini's "Dostoyevsky's Idiot, A Symbol of Christ." In the next paragraph, she writes, "in my novel I have a child—the

---

[34] Maritain, *Art and Scholasticism,* 28.
[35] Maritain, *Creative Intuition,* 165.
[36] Ibid., 167.

school teacher's boy—whom I aim to have a kind of Christ image, though a better way to think of it is probably just as a kind of redemptive figure. None of this may work however; but I have made some progress these last three months or think I have" (*CW*, 1015).

This letter strongly suggests that O'Connor read Guardini's criticism in the formative stages of her development of Bishop. Although O'Connor does not make Bishop a copy of Myshkin, her goal to make him a "redemptive figure" clearly parallels Guardini's description of Dostoevsky's goals. Guardini clarifies that Dostoevsky does not create Myshkin to be some mystically pure or ideal character; Myshkin is, instead, *real*. He has an "authentically human existence" and is a "man with a name," but to that human existence the artist adds "many signs to suggest to us that there is something in it which goes beyond man. Everything here has its own meaning, but at the same time everything reveals something else which is of a decidedly superior order."[37] This "superior order" is the transcendental character of beauty as I have just described it.

Guardini argues that Dostoevsky created Myshkin as an idiot character in order to point to the scandalous character of the Incarnation, the absurd and grotesque act of God's becoming man. Dostoevsky deliberately did not choose a "perfect" being in the world's eyes, but one whose very lowliness would most strenuously point to meaning that lies beyond him. In a passage O'Connor marked in her copy of the article, Guardini writes, "that which is highest in the ladder of being will be feeblest in its external manifestation. The existence of Myshkin would seem to be a direct verification of this axiom: the highest values raised to their maximum, but incarnated in an existence which is incapable of affirming itself in this world."[38]

Myshkin, like Bishop, has been "constituted according to the logic of heaven" and consequently mysteriously draws and repels everyone around him. Myshkin, like Bishop, becomes the center of

---

[37] Romano Guardini, "Dostoyevsky's Idiot, a Symbol of Christ," *Cross Currents* 6/2 (1956): 364.

[38] Ibid.

all glances, the trigger and testing point of one's vision. Guardini explains that Myshkin controverts and confuses all who look at him: "a mysterious presence is there which stirs up mysterious resonances in their deepest recesses, and yet at every moment there falls from their lips the word, 'Idiot!' What is there to say? In a crowd, Myshkin immediately, without in any way seeking it, becomes the center of all glances."[39] The scandal of Christ and Myshkin (and Bishop after them) is that people will reject the holiness present there and their *reasons* will be good ones. Guardini continues that "the fact that Christ is man, is the crux of 'objections' to his divinity. This very gesture of divine love which assumes the form of a slave seems to contradict the essential and personal presence of the Love of God: 'Is he not the son of a carpenter?'"[40] Rayber has reason enough according to the world's logic to think of Bishop as a mistake. In the end, the logic of heaven is designed to cause those who say only "I think, therefore I am" to reject Christ and to leave the children in the lead. Guardini argues that Christ is revealed only to children and to those who "do not listen to logic" because people can always use reason to protect themselves from that which would displace them.[41]

Belief in the Incarnation does not require one to forsake logic. But one can rationalize away belief in order to protect oneself from having to follow Christ into a life of selfless behavior. All the "reasons" the young Tarwater finds for not baptizing Bishop come from the voice of his "friend," who, diabolical or not, appeals to Tarwater's selfishness with an accurate description of the nature of the choice he has to make: "it's Jesus or you." When Tarwater has his vision of Bishop in the fountain, the "friend" is "silent as if in the felt presence, he dared not raise his voice," but soon after he begins to make Tarwater doubt his own eyes: "well, that's your sign, his friend said—the sun coming out from under a cloud and falling on the head of a dimwit. Something that could happen fifty times a day without no one being the wiser" (*CW*, 433). The voice of the self always

[39] Ibid., 372.
[40] Ibid.
[41] Ibid., 373.

argues for self-protection and against displacement. And the voice has no difficulty lumping other members of the human race in with the dimwits; he tells Tarwater to keep his violent love in check the way Rayber has done because "if you baptize once, you'll be doing it the rest of your life. If it's an idiot this time, the next time it's liable to be a nigger. Save yourself while the hour of salvation is at hand" (*CW*, 433).

O'Connor believed incarnational art could defy the modern age's efforts to separate body from mind, imagination from reason, and nature from grace. A character like Bishop epitomizes this effort because we readers, just like Rayber and Tarwater, cannot leave him alone. Indeed, for O'Connor the beauty of the work of art derives from its ability to evoke this kind of response. She accrues detail and compounds signification not to present some esoteric romantic symbol that purposely resists interpretation, but in order to make readers work for the meaning—meaning that must be thought as well as felt; meaning that must be *experienced*. The stories are like parables, as several critics have pointed out, because they preserve the literal sense but also drive the reader into a deeper well of meaning.[42] William Kirkwood explains that Jesus' parables were designed to "provoke acts of self-confrontation" in listeners and that they often "operate beyond (or prior to?) the realm of logical, discursive thought," without trumping their intellectual function.[43]

---

[42] See Sallie McFague, "The Parabolic in Faulkner, O'Connor, and Percy," *Notre Dame English Journal* 40 (1983). In each of these writers, says McFague, "the extraordinary is narrated through the ordinary. This is the way not only of the Bible in general, but of the parables of Jesus in particular" (49).

[43] The first quotation is from William G. Kirkwood, "Parables as Metaphors and Examples," *Quarterly Journal of Speech* 71 (1985): 59, and the second from Kirkwood, "Storytelling and Self-Confrontation: Parables as Communication Strategies," *Quarterly Journal of Speech* 69 (1983): 425. This last article provides particular insight into O'Connor's philosophy of art, because in it Kirkwood refuses to separate the parables as metaphor from the parables as example. They function together, he explains, and to split the two functions is to support a dualism that the vehicle (life) is not as important or sacred as the tenor (the divine reality) (437). O'Connor's work also resists this split.

Like Jesus, O'Connor aimed to give her readers the delight and shock of seeing the world through the emotions *and* the mind. Maritain writes, "the more things given to the intellect, the greater is the possibility of delight. This is why art as ordered to beauty refuses—at least when its object permits it—to stop at forms or colors, or sounds or words grasped in themselves and *as things*...but it grasps them *also* as making known something other than themselves, that is to say, *as signs*...the more the object of art is laden with signification...the greater and richer and higher will be the possibility of delight and beauty."[44]

The Violent Bear It Away's central scene, in which Tarwater accidentally baptizes Bishop as he drowns him, is a triumph for this definition of beauty. The scene's violence puts back together for Tarwater those parts of himself that Rayber fights so hard to keep separate. It avoids the twin problems of the denial of the concrete in abstract rationalism and the ascendancy of emotion over reason in sentimentalism. It accomplishes this the only way possible—by a genuine, dramatic act in space and time. As such, it is one of the most deeply and jarringly sacramental moments in O'Connor's entire *oeuvre.*

When Flannery O'Connor wrote that *The Violent Bear It Away* was her "minor hymn to the Eucharist," she wrote a lot more than most readers with only a cursory understanding of this Catholic doctrine can comprehend. She explained to Ted Spivey that "the water and the bread that Christ is" are the two main symbols Tarwater fights against (*HB*, 387). But O'Connor was adamant that the symbols function literally first. When O'Connor wrote that Emerson's move to eliminate the elements from the Lord's Supper was the beginning of the "vaporization" of religion, she wrote it in the middle of her discussion of the fiction writer, not of religion in America. She was moving toward her point that "the real novelist, the one with an instinct for what he is about, knows that he cannot approach the infinite directly, that he must penetrate the natural human world as it is. The more sacramental his theology, the more encouragement he

---

[44] Maritain, *Art and Scholasticism,* 54–55.

will get from it to do just that" (*MM*, 163). The equation for O'Connor's art is quite clear: the more sacramental the theology, the more effective the novelist.

Tarwater's hunger for the bread must be literal here as well as spiritual—and it is. He cannot hold food down through most of the novel, and yet he feels himself strangely drawn to a loaf of bread he sees in a town bakery. He tries to deny that his hunger in the real world is connected to spiritual hunger, as he insists to the truck driver: "I ain't hungry for the bread of life...I'm hungry for something to eat here and now" (*CW*, 459). He cannot satisfy his actual thirst, either, and when he tries to, he goes for a (revealingly) purple drink. And when he finally accepts his mission, O'Connor expresses the return of his real hunger in a phrase she was fond of: "he could have eaten all the loaves and fishes after they had been multiplied." Jesus fed the masses both physically and spiritually. After satisfying physical appetites, he said, "I am the bread of life." When the body and blood of Jesus are shared in the Eucharist, the partakers remember him as the literal flesh-and-blood man that he was.

The other sacrament in *The Violent Bear It Away* functions equally as literally: baptism. O'Connor knew her challenge was that her audience would see the rite of baptism as having only vague symbolic significance and not actual efficacy. Her well-known discussion of baptism in this novel is one of her most meaningful apologies for the distortion of the grotesque:

> When I write a novel in which the central action is a baptism, I am very well aware that for a majority of my readers, baptism is a meaningless rite, and so in my novel I have to see that this baptism carries enough awe and mystery to jar the reader into some kind of emotional recognition of its significance. To this end I have to bend the whole novel—its language, its structure, its action. I have to make the reader feel, in his bones if nowhere else, that something is going on here that counts. Distortion in this case is an instrument; exaggeration has a purpose, and the whole structure of the story or novel has been made what it is because of belief. This is not the kind of distortion that destroys; it is the kind that reveals, or should reveal. (*MM*, 162)

In Catholic theology the sacraments are never merely ritualistic. But O'Connor knew her readers would feel otherwise, so in *The Violent Bear It Away* she tries to answer the question how, without destroying the natural world as we all experience it, can the writer give the sacraments significance? How can the writer make the reader feel in her bones that something is going on that counts?

Part of O'Connor's answer to that question is to highlight the event of Bishop's baptism as a dramatic act. By bending the entire novel toward this one event and then making the event as extraordinary and memorable as possible, O'Connor refuses to reduce baptism to an abstraction. In other words, she makes the baptism of a particular person the concrete center of the novel, and not the rite of baptism *per se*. In *Toward a Philosophy of the Act*, M. M. Bakhtin insists upon the weight and irreducible nature of what he terms "once-occurrent Being-as-event." A first philosophy, he argues, "can orient itself only with respect to that actually performed act."[45] Being-as-event as seen in the performed act "cannot be transcribed in theoretical terms if it is not to lose the very sense of its being an event, that is, precisely that which the performed act knows answerably and with reference to which it orients itself."[46]

Bakhtin argues that every pre-modern philosophical system acknowledged the "weight" of such events. It is peculiar to modern times to try to bypass the particular and move directly into the abstract. In so doing "the world as object of theoretical cognition seeks to pass itself off as the whole world."[47] What moderns want to do, says Bakhtin, is impossible. After modernity divides thought from "the historical act of its actualization," it then attempts to surmount that divide from *within* theoretical cognition. But it loses answerability in the process. "Inasmuch as we have entered that content, i.e., performed an act of abstraction, we are now controlled by its autonomous laws or, to be exact, we are simply no longer

[45] M. M. Bakhtin, *Toward a Philosophy of the Act*, ed. Michael Holquist and Vadim Liapunov, trans. Kenneth Brostrom (Austin: University of Texas Press, 1993) 28.
[46] Ibid., 30–31.
[47] Ibid., 8.

present in it as individually and answerably active human beings."[48] Abstraction kills the uniqueness of the event and sacrifices moral answerability in the process.

But how are these ideas connected to art? Do we not usually think of art as precisely that which is not life? Bakhtin believed that the work of art—contrary to any view of art for art's sake—is *uniquely* able to enter once-occurrent Being-as-event. He writes that "in its concreteness and its permeatedness with an emotional-volitional tone, this world is closer than any of the abstract cultural worlds (taken in isolation) to the unitary and unique world of the performed act."[49] The unity art effects is not a systematic unity, such as that given by theoretical cognition, but a "unity that is concretely architectonic: the world is arranged around a concrete value-center, which is seen and loved and thought. What constitutes this center is the human being: everything in this world acquires significance, meaning, and value only in correlation with man—as that which is human...everything must be correlated with the human being, must become human."[50] As we react to the character's reaction, the work of art is transferred from the realm of internal cognition into a world where we experience the other. "I partake in it only as a contemplator, but contemplation is the active, effective situatedness of the contemplator *outside* the object contemplated."[51]

When O'Connor bent her entire novel around Bishop's baptism, she built the human concrete architectonic that Bakhtin describes. When Tarwater kills and baptizes Bishop, though he acts in rebellion, he has a clear sense of "I" and "other." "The highest architectonic principle of the actual world of the performed act or deed is the concrete and architectonically valid or operative contraposition of *I* and the *other*."[52] The contraposition of I and other, says Bakhtin, is

---

48 Ibid., 7.
49 Ibid., 61.
50 Ibid.
51 Ibid., 73.
52 Ibid., 74.

"the sense of all Christian morality, and it is the starting point for altruistic morality."[53]

On the other hand, Rayber's theoretical consciousness, his desire to have it all in his head, makes him completely unable to love a being separate from himself. Love requires that the other have value and meaning just because one exists, not because one exists for anything. As Jacques Maritain explains in *The Range of Reason*, rediscovery of being is a rediscovery of God. "I suddenly realize that a given entity, man, mountain, or tree, exists and exercises that sovereign activity to be in its own way, in an independence from *me* which is total, totally self-assertive, and totally implacable."[54] With that "prime intuition" of existence, it is but a step to seeing the necessary existence of "self-subsisting Being, Being existing through itself"—or God.[55] But trapped in the logic of the *cogito*, Rayber refuses this prime intuition. So when he tries to assert himself by drowning Bishop and removing the problem, he finds he cannot act. As Tarwater explains to the truck driver, "my other uncle knows everything…but that don't keep him from being a fool. He can't do nothing. All he can do is figure it out. He's got this wired head" (*CW*, 460).

But Tarwater can act. When Rayber tries to warn him about his "violent half," Tarwater responds, "I ain't worried what my underhead is doing. I know what I think when I do it and when I get ready to do it, I don't talk no words. I do it" (*CW*, 436). Like Hazel Motes, what Tarwater tries to do through much of the novel is "no." When he makes up his mind to kill Bishop, he tells the woman at the lodge "you can't just say NO…. You got to do NO. You got to show it. You got to show you mean it by doing it" (*CW*, 427). The "friend" picks up these words and eggs Tarwater on to drown Bishop and put an end to it.

But the concrete performed act has logic of its own, particularly in O'Connor's sacramental world. Although Tarwater's "friend"

---

[53] Ibid., 75.
[54] Jacques Maritain, *The Range of Reason* (New York: Scribner, 1952) 88.
[55] Ibid., 89.

thinks a violent act of evil will lead Tarwater to abandon his call, when Tarwater actually does it, it has the opposite effect. As Tarwater performs a once-occurrent act, he enters into a concrete and communal relationship with the person he acts toward (even if against). He unwittingly comes out of himself and acknowledges the other. The language O'Connor uses to describe the scene (as re-created in Tarwater's dream) suggests a weirdly passive action: Bishop jumps onto Tarwater's back and "he clung there like a large crab to a twig and the startled boy felt himself sinking backwards into the water as if the whole bank were pulling him down" (*CW*, 462). The physical contact is of utmost importance.[56] When Tarwater pushes Bishop under the water, he *literally* acts out the larger rite of death in Christ; the words of baptism just spill out of him to confirm it. Out of the habit of the act so deeply embedded in Tarwater's soul, the mystery of the sacrament overpowers him. Tarwater acts, but he is also acted upon by the force of the event. Watching from the window, Rayber knows "with an instinct as sure as the dull mechanical beat of his heart that he had baptized the child even as he drowned him, that he was headed for everything the old man had prepared him for, that he moved off now through the black forest toward a violent encounter with his fate" (*CW*, 456).

It is not that O'Connor approves of Tarwater's murder of Bishop. It is that one who acts—even if in violent opposition, as Tarwater does—can be more easily redeemed because of the integrity of his words and actions, his mind and his body, and because of his distinct sense of the interdependency of self and other. The Misfit in "A Good Man Is Hard to Find" is also such a character: he lives his rejection of the reality of Christ with perfect integrity: "If He did what He said, then it's nothing for you to do but thow [*sic*] away everything and follow Him, and if He didn't, then it's nothing for you to do but enjoy the few minutes you got left the best way you can—by killing somebody or burning down his house or doing some other meanness to him" (*CW*, 152). Integrity can also exist at the opposite

---

[56]Tarwater's dream exaggerates the contact, for when we see Tarwater later on, only his pant legs are wet, and not his whole body.

end of the spectrum, among those who perform seemingly mundane acts in the church. O'Connor continually insisted in her letters that interested people "will learn about Catholic belief by studying the sacramental life of the church. The center of this is the Eucharist" (*HB*, 346). She responded to criticism that the sacraments become mere mechanical motions, merely habit to the people who perform them, by writing that "it is better to be held to the Church by habit than not to be held at all.... The Church is mighty realistic about human nature. Further it is not at all possible to tell what's going on inside the person who appears to be going about his obligations mechanically. We don't believe that grace is something you have to feel" (*HB*, 346). The church remains committed to the inexorable connection between mind and body, mystery and manners, habit and belief. The church knows that an act can often penetrate the mind and change it more powerfully than the mind can generate motivation for an act. In a letter to Alfred Corn, a young man who wrote to her of his intellectual doubts, O'Connor recommended that he try to find God in ways other than merely through his intellect. She recounts that when Robert Bridges wrote to Gerard Manley Hopkins asking how Bridges might believe, "Hopkins wrote back, 'Give alms.' He was trying to say to Bridges that God is to be experienced in Charity (in the sense of love for the divine image in human beings). Don't get so entangled with intellectual difficulties that you fail to look for God in this way" (*HB*, 476–77). O'Connor's advice to Corn was not for him to stop thinking (this interpretation of the letter cannot be sustained given the several heady books she recommends later on), but for him to learn that "you can't fit the Almighty into your intellectual categories" (*HB*, 477).

With the conflation of Bishop's murder with his baptism, O'Connor's rewrite of *Wise Blood* is complete. Tarwater knows as he says the words of baptism over Bishop that he can kill Bishop's body, but not his soul. Caught in the power of sacrament, Tarwater's murderous deed works double-time on him: he feels both the overpowering guilt of having murdered an innocent child and the sacramental significance of the literal acting out of a Christian's being buried with Christ in baptism so that he can be raised again. Tarwater begins here to enter that death too, a death to self that he has never before achieved. He begins to open another set of eyes, enabling a violent conflict by which he can see more, not less. So rather than interpreting Tarwater's return to the ways of prophecy as his clinging to or reverting to a "childish or literalistic faith" as Martha Stephens and Josephine Hendin do, we must agree with John Desmond that in Tarwater, O'Connor created a "dramatic portrait of a self-conscious mind that has absorbed contending visions of being, history, and personality, a mind which openly holds these visions in a state of creative tension as possibilities to be enacted in the encounter with reality, a mind developing in such a way that it will paradoxically come to know only through defeat the very limits of mind as a measure of reality."[57]

Tarwater's participation in something bigger than himself explains why he cannot shake the memory of his act, although he certainly wishes he could. He retells it to the truck driver who picks him up, and when he falls asleep in the cab, he re-envisions the entire episode. He has to "deliberately, forcefully" close the inner eye that presents the scene to him again and again (*CW*, 463). When he thinks of the words of the baptism, he tries to convince himself that it was an accident in order not to be affected by the mystery of the act. He does not succeed. He knows something significant has happened, something beyond his understanding.

And so, too, does the reader. Because the violence dramatically centers the baptism, we will not be able to forget it either. To make sense of the story, which is what O'Connor assumed an interested reader would try to do, the reader's vision must operate like Tarwater's, if only for a moment. When we read the story and contemplate the scene, when we consider the levels of meaning woven into it, we share Tarwater's participation in the depth of mystery. Tarwater baptizes Bishop in spite of himself, and we see the mystery operate in spite of ourselves. We are given a glimpse of the anagogical, which O'Connor explains has to do with "the Divine life and our participation in it" (*MM*, 72). And the presence of the

<hr>

[57] Desmond, *Risen Sons,* 114.

anagogical, O'Connor insisted, is the only thing capable of displacing us.

Tarwater's course is now virtually inevitable. Under the pressure of his own participation in the mystery of baptism, and in the face of increasing spiritual hunger, Tarwater has an experience of malevolent evil that finally pushes him to obey his call. The inner voice of the "friend" who had been trying to dissuade him from his vocation is incarnated in the form of a homosexual rapist whose attack reminds him of why he must preach. It turns him back, like Jonah, to the city to which God originally called him. Afterward his scorched eyes "no longer looked hollow or as if they were meant only to guide him forward. They looked as if, touched with a coal like the lips of the prophet, they would never be used for ordinary sights again" (*CW*, 473). With this act of violence against his person, a corollary to his own act of violence against Bishop, Tarwater understands evil as an act against the sanctity of being. Evil is consuming others for the self—using them. Tarwater acknowledges the need for the kind of love his great uncle had demonstrated. When he "threw himself to the ground and with his face against the dirt of the grave, he heard the command. GO WARN THE CHILDREN OF GOD OF THE TERRIBLE SPEED OF MERCY. The words were as silent as seeds opening one at a time in his blood" (*CW*, 478).

Just as the mystery of God's call opens up inside Tarwater's blood, the symbolic layering of the novel opens up inside the reader's mind as the story draws to a close. O'Connor successfully follows her own dictum that "a story really isn't any good unless it successfully resists paraphrase, unless it hangs on and expands in the mind" (*MM*, 108). The story itself constitutes the reader's moment of grace, for when it violently expands in the mind, it also makes room for mystery.

CHAPTER 6

THE ARTIST AT HOME

To call yourself a Georgia writer is certainly to declare a limitation, but one which, like all limitations, is a gateway to reality.

—CW, 844

In O'Connor's fiction, children without mothers struggle spiritually. Forced into an early independence, they instinctively seek real connection but often do not know where to look for it. Sometimes their lack of guidance leads them to their deaths, even as they make true spiritual discoveries. But adult children who live with their mothers—particularly men—choose fates that are far worse in O'Connor's estimation. Caught up in complacent intellectual pride, they take their mothers for granted and look down on them as hopelessly provincial. These sons, exultant in their independence, set out to teach their mothers a lesson and end up learning one instead. Their practical and earthly mothers, though full of faults, possess a kind of wisdom that the son or the writer should not ignore. Their wisdom is the wisdom of limitation and brokenness. With these stories O'Connor controverts the Promethean ideal and establishes significant boundaries for author, narrator, and hero.

Julian in "Everything That Rises Must Converge" is one of these sons. He dreads taking his mother anywhere because he can see nothing good about her—"everything that gave her pleasure was small and depressed him"—and he sees nothing of himself in her. Believing himself to be completely independent, he fails to recognize how much his judgments reflect back on him. So when he sets out to teach his bigoted mother a lesson, the readers know Julian will be the one to learn the deepest lesson. We have seen it happen to Mrs. Shortley, Joy/Hulga, Mr. Head, and numerous other characters who consider themselves above it all. Julian's lesson seems particularly well deserved, for like other well-educated men in O'Connor's fiction, he is arrogant enough to think he can hold his mother's whole world in his head. But when Julian gets his due, we are left with the problem of the authoritative narrator who sized *him* up. How can the narrator escape making the same sorts of judgments he condemns in his characters? Why should the narrator's point of view be privileged, and when will she get her comeuppance?

Critics respond to this dilemma in vastly different ways. Robert Brinkmeyer argues that the narrator's perspective is as monologic, severe, cynical, and demeaning as Julian's and that eventually it "comes undone" under the same forces.[1] Marshall Bruce Gentry argues that the "fact that the narrator's view of the story's events is consistently authoritative limits the story," but he insists that the story "Everything that Rises must Converge" is an exception for O'Connor, and points out that usually her protagonists' unconscious use of the grotesque works in opposition to her narrators' authoritarianism.[2] Anthony Di Renzo argues that the narrator does not judge Julian as much as it would seem because O'Connor has created a "double-minded narrator" by which she blends contempt and longing for the old South that Julian insists is "gone with the wind."[3]

---

[1] Robert H. Brinkmeyer Jr., *The Art & Vision of Flannery O'Connor* (Baton Rouge: Louisiana State University Press, 1989) 71–72. Brinkmeyer writes that "a central irony of the story lies in this mirroring of Julian and the narrator, for because of their close identification, Julian's downfall implicitly signals the narrator's, even if the narrator remains unaware of it."

[2] Marshall Bruce Gentry, *Flannery O' Connor's Religion of the Grotesque* (Jackson: University Press of Mississippi, 1986) 100.

[3] Anthony Di Renzo, *American Gargoyles: Flannery O'Connor and the Medieval Grotesque* (Carbondale: Southern Illinois University Press, 1993) 200. Di Renzo writes that "this compelling blend of contempt and longing that exists in

I think the answer to the problem of narrative judgment must be solved by examining the difference between Julian and the narrator, a difference that hinges on the question of interest and attention. As we have seen, this question is at the center of O'Connor's notion of incarnational art. "Everything That Rises Must Converge" quickly reveals that Julian has no interest in learning and telling his mother's story at all. He sees her only from his disembodied mental bubble, from where he judges her as a tragically thin player in his personal story:

> Behind the newspaper Julian was withdrawing into the inner compartment of his mind where he spent most of his time. This was a kind of mental bubble in which he established himself when he could not bear to be a part of what was going on around him. From it he could see out and judge but in it he was safe from any kind of penetration from without. It was the only place where he felt free of the general idiocy of his fellows. His mother had never entered it but from it he could see her with absolute clarity. (*CW*, 491)

To see his mother as his mother—inexorably connected to him—would be to open himself to "penetration from without." It is much easier and safer to judge her as a one-dimensional example of the "race problem." So to keep their relationship in the realm of the abstract, Julian removes his emotions from it entirely. Without emotional involvement, Julian will never be able to sympathize with either his mother or with the African Americans he claims to be fighting for.[4] They are each only examples of some larger theoretical problem that he is proud to have identified and moved beyond.

As a result, what redeems Julian at the end of the story is simply the recognition that his own story must be told from *inside* his

---

O'Connor's double-minded narrator perfectly expresses the peculiar schizophrenia created by historical change. As time and circumstance in *Everything That Rises Must Converge* destroy the last vestiges of the old white South, we hear a chorus of contradictory voices..." (200–201).

[4] As Richard Giannone writes, Julian "is equipped to wage theoretical war. Emotions must not enter to soften the attack. Though he sees himself as a martyr for an ideal, Julian is an emotional miser. In a conflict of ideas, he need spend no more sympathy on blacks than he squanders on his mother" (Giannone, *Flannery O'Connor and the Mystery of Love* [Urbana: University of Illinois Press, 1989] 163).

mother's story. Julian's jarring self-discovery is at first symbolically
adumbrated when Julian is reflecting on how well he turned out in spite
of his mother's foolish parenting: "Most miraculous of all, instead of
being blinded by love for her as she was for him, he had cut himself
emotionally free of her and could see her with complete objectivity.
He was not dominated by his mother" (*CW*, 492). Just at that moment
the bus stops with a "sudden jerk" that shakes him from his
meditations. A black man enters the bus, and his mother's racist
response infuriates Julian, and he "stared at her, making his eyes the
eyes of a stranger. He felt his tension suddenly lift as if he had openly
declared war on her" (*CW*, 492). Julian's moral problem is thus shown
to be exactly the duplicate of his mother's: he demonizes her as a
complete other to him. He feels "completely detached" from her and
begins to plan ways to teach the lesson. When a black woman enters
the bus wearing the same hat as his mother, Julian is elated that "Fate
had thrust upon his mother such a lesson. He gave a loud chuckle so
that she would look at him and see that he saw. She turned her eyes on
him slowly. The blue in them seemed to have turned a bruised purple"
(*CW*, 496).

Julian can see his mother ironically doubled by the black woman,
but he cannot see how much his own perspective doubles that of his
mother. A plank in his own eye, he grabs at the mote in hers, bruising
her by his lovelessness. His mother sees less and less of the familiar in
him and eventually literally turns away and begins walking in the
opposite direction—back home. "Home"—the connection between
mother and son—is exactly what Julian has been taking away from
her and replacing with cold judgment. She physically collapses, and at
once he recognizes her as "Mamma, Mamma!" But all that is left of
his relationship with her is the distance he has been so violently
cultivating. "One eye, large and staring moved slightly to the left as if
it had become unmoored. The other remained fixed on him, raked his
face again, found nothing and closed" (*CW*, 500). This event finally
draws him out of his mental bubble and into a world where he knows

love for perhaps the first time in his life.[5] Julian sees more, not less, and guilt and sorrow are merely the costs of his spiritual maturity.

Whether or not the narrator of the story falls under the same judgment depends upon how much of what Joyce Carol Oates calls "ultimate irony" we can attribute to the narrator and to O'Connor. For the narrator to follow under the same judgment as Julian, he would have to be seen as effecting the same loveless, ironic distance, to feel no sympathy, and to believe only that Julian got what was coming to him. But O'Connor's rendering of the final event is clearly not ironic for the sake of irony. On the contrary, *"the entire process is divine,"* writes Oates. "There is no ultimate irony in her work, no ultimate despair or pessimism or tragedy, and certainly not a paradoxical sympathy for the devil. ...when the intellectual Julian suffers the real loss of his mother, the real Julian emerges; his self-pitying depression vanishes at once; the faith he had somehow lost 'in the midst of his martyrdom' is restored."[6] The difference is that the narrator cares for the "real Julian." The narrator does not orchestrate or even interpret the events that bring Julian to the redemption that can only come by despair. The events speak for themselves.

In this story, as in many in the collection *Everything That Rises Must Converge*, O'Connor insists that the humble embodiment of the artist as loving, interested other can answer the dilemma the authoritarian narrator initiates. For O'Connor, genuine love—which she preferred to call grace—is unsentimental because it assumes that the truth implicates everyone and is best for everyone. "Parker's Back," the subject of my next chapter, may well be O'Connor's best incarnation of this kind of consummating love for a character. But before she gave us her own artistic success in consummating Parker, she gave us Asbury Fox's failures as an artist. In "The Enduring Chill," Asbury fails to understand that he must see another human

---

[5] Giannone writes that through her death, Julian's mother "succeeds in teaching him to accept spiritual responsibility for another; and in the life of guilt and sorrow, charity, not capital, gauges maturity" (Giannone, *Mystery of Love*, 166).

[6] Joyce Carol Oates, "The Visionary Art of Flannery O'Connor," in *Modern Critical Views: Flannery O'Connor*, ed. Harold Bloom (New York: Chelsea House Publishers, 1986) 49.

from an embodied position, as O'Connor sees Asbury, in order to produce art. Through this story O'Connor both criticizes the modern artist's failure and, in an act of narrative love, gives Asbury an opportunity to escape from the prison of his own making.

Asbury Fox returns to his mother's home from New York City where he has been trying to become a writer. Convinced that he is now terminally ill, he believes he has been plucked out of the glory of his future life as an artist and forced instead to deal with his "literal-minded" mother. He intends to die in a grand, tragic style by which he hopes to teach her a lesson. In the end he discovers that he is not as smart as he thought he was. When he learns that he has only the "undulant fever" instead of a terminal illness, he sees the Holy Ghost descend upon him and his vision widens.

This story, O'Connor's only sustained treatment of a single artist figure, critiques what was for O'Connor philosophical idealism's most monstrous creation: the disembodied modern artist who worships art as his god, claiming that his imagination can and must order the chaotic world around him. Because O'Connor clearly connects Asbury Fox's spiritual problems to his artistic failings, she gives us a unique entrance into her conception of the limits of the incarnational artist, namely, that she must never forget she has a body. From a feminist perspective, what we find in this story and others in the collection might be surprising. For while some critics argue that the most common pose in O'Connor is for God to humiliate intellectual women through men, these stories more often depict arrogant sons who want to "show" their mothers "reality" and in the end are shown their unique physical and emotional dependence upon the mothers. When the sons try to raise themselves out of their own bodies into a view from above, the ultimate "other" penetrates them in an act of eye-opening grace.

When O'Connor was asked for a sentence to introduce "The Enduring Chill," she resisted and then suggested, "'A wretched young man arrives at the point where his artistic delusions come face to face with reality.' What I really mean is *arty* delusions..." (*HB*, 271). Asbury's delusions resemble those described by Jacques Maritain in his book *Creative Intuition in Art and Poetry*. O'Connor annotated chapter 5, "Art and Beauty," in which Maritain clearly attacks a whole tradition of art that begins with Rousseau's *Confessions* and becomes full-blown with the Surrealists.[7] Maritain does not consider all modern art to be equal, and what is bad has an identifiable culprit. The culprit is the "hero writer" who heralds himself as Rousseau did, being more interested in "absolute knowledge" than in the work created. O'Connor marked the following passage, which sounds almost like an outline for her story:

> The initial cause of the trouble heralded by Rousseau—the accidental shift from the creative Self to the self-centered ego—has naturally entailed another shift: from creative emotion as intentional means or vehicle of poetic knowledge, to brute or merely subjective emotion as sheer psychological phenomenon become the matter of the work and a *thing* to be expressed by it. As a result modern literature, in its lower moments, has been invaded by a double disease: emotionalism (that is, search after and communication of brute emotion blurring or replacing the creativity of the intellect and the purity of poetic intuition) and, at the same time, shallow intellectualism (that is, falling back on the empty contrivances of a merely constructive or critical reason estranged from the heart, to make up for the weakening of intuitive reason and of the intellect's genuine creativity stirred by creative emotion and poetic experience).[8]

O'Connor underlined the words *emotionalism* and *shallow intellectualism* in her copy of this book. Asbury Fox, who dramatizes his own death and blames his mother for his failures as an artist, clearly has this "double disease." As the story sets out to show him his means for a cure, it also sets out, as Maritain did, to rescue true poetic knowledge and intuition—which rely upon revelation and a limited, embodied view—from their collapse into the egoism of absolute knowledge.

Perhaps more than any other O'Connor character, Asbury Fox is at the center of his own, self-created universe. His imagination has

---

[7] O'Connor's copy of *Creative Intuition in Art and Poetry* is available in the Flannery O'Connor collection of the Ina Dillard Russell Library at Georgia College.

[8] Jacques Maritain, *Creative Intuition in Art and Poetry* (New York: Pantheon Books, 1953) 195.

become his god, and he creates all the high drama for his own life. As he steps off the train, Asbury "felt that he was about to witness a majestic transformation, that the flat of roofs might at any moment turn into the mounting turrets of some exotic temple for a god he didn't know" (*CW*, 547). His revelation is similar to that of the surrealist poets Maritain berates for having a "pseudoprophetic revelation, bound up with magic and the search for transmuting reality through the power of words."[9] Asbury is pleased that his mother sees "death in his face at once" and that because of him she is finally going to see reality and grow up (*CW*, 547).

Asbury compares his imagination (rather unimaginatively) to a bird his mother has pinioned and domesticated. In New York City he writes a melodramatic letter to her, unburdening this idea: "I came here to escape the slave's atmosphere of home…to find freedom, to liberate my imagination, to take it like a hawk from its cage and set it 'whirling off into the widening gyre' (Yeats) and what did I find? It was incapable of flight. It was some bird you had domesticated, sitting huffy in its pen, refusing to come out!" (*CW*, 554). Asbury misquotes Yeats and reads as an exaltation of personal freedom Yeats's well-known observation of the drifting conditions of modernity in "The Second Coming": "Turning and turning in the widening gyre / The falcon cannot hear the falconer: / Things fall apart; the centre cannot hold; / Mere anarchy is loosed upon the world" (ll. 1–4). Asbury has become one of Yeats's pseudo-intellectual inheritors. The modernist aesthetic of the priestly power of the imagination may be seductive in a genius like Yeats, but it is shown to be an elitist farce when put into the hands of Asbury. Asbury, like Yeats, believes an artist's imagination should be completely liberated and liberating, a force that abstracts meaning out of meaninglessness, a replacement for God in the modern world. His desire for imaginative freedom entails a Gnostic escape from his own body by way of artifice. His life goal parodies the narrator in Yeats's "Sailing to Byzantium" who looks into the world and notices "whatever is begotten, born, and dies" and pleads:

[9] Ibid., 194.

O sages standing in God's holy fire
As in the gold mosaic of a wall,
Come from the holy fire, perne in a gyre,
And be the singing-masters of my soul.
Consume my heart away; sick with desire
And fastened to a dying animal
It knows not what it is; and gather me
Into the artifice of eternity. (17–24)[10]

Asbury also believes his heart is "fastened to a dying animal"—his body, his mother's body, and the farm itself—and that his god, art, can provide an escape into immortality.

Asbury could have committed suicide, of course. But that's not the most glorious of the modernist's responses; Asbury wants instead to aestheticize his own death as a tragic and cosmic event that will transform the world. His early interest in the Jesuit Father Vogle was only because he "appealed to him as a man of the world, someone who would have understood the unique tragedy of his death, a death whose meaning had been far beyond the twittering group around them" (*CW*, 550). Asbury wants to give himself some "last significant culminating experience," made "for himself out of his own intelligence" (*CW*, 568). He thereby becomes the "hero writer" whom Maritain describes as "more interested in constructing his own image as an example, for the generations to come, of a martyr in printed paper."[11] In short, Asbury imagines an ending to his own story of which he views himself the ultimate author. His logic is the reverse of Bakhtin's. For Bakhtin, the one event that exemplifies the need for the embodied other in aesthetic seeing is one's own death. "My death," says Bakhtin, is an event that "occur[s] neither *in* me nor *for*

---

[10] W. B. Yeats, *The Collected Poems of W. B. Yeats*, ed. Richard J. Finnerman (New York: Collier, 1989).

[11] Maritain, *Creative Intuition,* 194.

me. The emotional weight of my own life *taken as a whole* does not exist for me myself."[12]

Asbury's designs for his own death are only part of the story. Asbury believes he will liberate the world by leading the way with his own imagination. In *The Necessary Angel*, Wallace Stevens argues that society has lost the ability to be liberated by the imagination from the pressures of reality. The poet will rescue us from these pressures by "dwelling apart in his imagination" and using it to reorder the world. The poet "will consider that...his own measure as a poet, in spite of all the passions of all the lovers of the truth, is the measure of his power to abstract himself, and to withdraw with him into his abstraction the reality on which the lovers of truth insist. He must be able to abstract himself and also to abstract reality, which he does by placing it in his imagination."[13] This position of abstraction, according to Stevens, enables the poet to see "his imagination become the light in the minds of others." O'Connor renders this notion ridiculous. Asbury believes that the drama of his life will be complete when his mother reads his letter: "He felt that even if she didn't understand at once, the letter would leave her with an enduring chill and perhaps in time lead her to see herself as she was" (*CW*, 555).

Asbury, an untalented disciple of Stevens, believes the poet is a Gnostic priest of the imagination, privy to a special understanding and creative abilities that can ultimately replace belief in the Christian God. Asbury's view can be seen in his conversation with Father Finn, the priest who comes to visit him. When the priest asks him if he prays to Jesus, Asbury responds that the "myth of the dying god has always fascinated me" (*CW*, 565). Asbury has studied away Christianity's claims to reality and has attributed the Christian story to the power of man's myth-making imagination. By calling Christianity a myth, Asbury reduces it to a story that he can stand above and outside of. After all, a poet like him made it up. Like

---

[12] M. M. Bakhtin, *Art and Answerability,* ed. Michael Holquist and Vadim Liapunov, trans. Vadim Liapunov (Austin: University of Texas Press, 1990) 105.

[13] Wallace Stevens, *The Necessary Angel: Essays on Reality and the Imagination* (New York: Vintage Books, 1951) 23.

Emerson who called prayer the "soliloquy of a jubilant soul," Asbury does not believe there is an "other" to give his life meaning or purpose. Meaning comes to us only because there are artists with powerful enough imaginations to generate significant experiences out of their own intelligence. For Asbury, "God is an idea created by man," so "the artist prays by creating" (*CW*, 566).

A self-made priest of the imagination doing battle with a doltish Catholic priest is vintage O'Connor humor. Asbury looks like a slick intellectual compared to the blind-in-one-eye and deaf-in-one-ear Father Finn who cares not a whit that he is unfamiliar with James Joyce. But Finn's bombast, evoking the early fire and brimstone scenes of *Portrait of the Artist as Young Man*, quickly cuts to the difference between where Finn gets his convictions and where Asbury gets his. In short, Finn can afford to be less smart. He unflinchingly stands behind the catechism as that which can explain truths about God and man's relationship with him, while Asbury speaks from his own self-sufficiency and "genius," living up to the Protestant history O'Connor mocks through his name.[14] Eventually the exchange ends with fury, and Asbury blasphemes the Holy Spirit, which is the only unpardonable sin. "'Certainly I've heard of the Holy Ghost,' Asbury said furiously, 'and the Holy Ghost is the last thing I'm looking for!' 'And He may be the last thing you get,' the priest said, his one fierce eye inflamed" (*CW*, 567).

O'Connor does not defend the priest's position intellectually; instead, she refutes Asbury's position dramatically. She makes him completely impotent. Asbury cannot actually *produce* anything, least

---

[14] Francis Asbury helped start the United Methodist Church, in part out of a commitment to personal experience of salvation as opposed to any ecclesiastical authority such as the Catholic church insists upon. By naming her failed artist figure Asbury, O'Connor agrees with Henry Sussman's recent analysis that the Western notion of the artist or the intellectual as "a hypersensitive, hyperbrilliant, singular individual who bridges the gap between normality and sublimity, an idea so well-entrenched as to be naturalized in many cultural quarters today," has as its ultimate precedent the idea of "the individual who struggles directly with God over his own fate in the wake of the Protestant Reformation" (Sussman, *The Aesthetic Contract: Statutes of Art and Intellectual Work in Modernity* [Stanford: Stanford University Press, 1997] 69).

of all his own death. He attempted several stories and plays, all of which he threw away, and the only "work" he plans to leave behind is the two big notebooks that contain the letter to his mother. Although his sister Mary George is also an unhappy intellectual, like the book-throwing girl of "Revelation," she sees the situation for what it is and names it. "You've got to face the facts: Asbury can't write so he gets sick...mark my words...all he's going to be around here for the next fifty years is a decoration" (*CW*, 563). She suggests that they give him shock treatments to "get that artist business out of his head once and for all." Once again O'Connor's humor works for the ring of truth in it: Asbury needs to be brought down to earth, brought back to his body in a real way, shaken of his "arty" delusions for his own life and its self-generated meaning.

For while Asbury blames his literal-minded mother for "pinioning" his imagination, the story proves that Asbury's real problem is just the opposite. What Asbury thinks will make him a great artist—his escape from the realities of the farm—is precisely what makes him fail. When he treats the town, the farm, his mother, and everything local as anathema to him, he eschews the very things O'Connor repeatedly insists are the writer's true materials. Fiction writers' trade is in *techne*—that which is made—and they therefore "engage in the homeliest, and most concrete, and most unromanticizable of all arts" (*CW*, 844). But Asbury does not get it. When he does go into the barn a cow kicks him, scaring him away from the dairy. He refuses to do physical labor, which he considers to be below him. And as he lies on his bed, thinking he is dying, "his mind functioned with a terrible clarity. On the point of death, he found himself existing in a state of illumination that was totally out of keeping with the kind of talk he had to listen to from his mother. This was largely about cows with names like Daisy and Bessie Button and their intimate functions—their mastitis and their screwworms and their abortions" (*CW*, 557). Neither actually on "the point of death" nor "existing in a state of illumination," Asbury cannot see the flesh and blood reality of his mother's world, and he prefers to exalt himself in his own creation of his death, to think of himself at center stage of a play with some romantic ending. As a result, Asbury succeeds only in illuminating the limits of his own mind.

Jacques Maritain describes Asbury's kind of affectation as the corruption of true art. For rather than producing something that "continues in its own way the labor of divine creation," Asbury's kind of artist works instead for the "human subject's omnipotence."[15] Artists in love with their own liberating imagination only replace the true glory of the artist—his work—with this unearned liberty that only *thinks* and cannot *make*. The difference is that true poetic knowledge, according to Maritain, knows in order to produce, not just to know. In true poetic knowledge the artist loses himself in his work and engenders being; but when knowledge yearns only to know it annihilates being. Beauty, an attribute of being, is lost. Maritain writes:

> And the delectation that beauty gives is replaced by the delight of experience of supreme freedom in the night of subjectivity. Are not the first fruits of the future transfiguration to be attained in that state which Breton describes as "an annihilation of being into an internal and blind glittering which is no more the soul of ice than that of fire"? A strange sentence, which in its cryptic way points to the great secret of magical gnosis—that spiritual experience of the blind glitter of nothingness, in which all differences are abolished and all contradictions made one, by virtue of the void, and in which the soul believes it is transferred above everything and enjoys infinite liberty. This is the black mysticism in which poetic knowledge transformed into absolute knowledge finally winds up.[16]

This paragraph has astonishing parallels in "The Enduring Chill." For example, Asbury's pretensions to a liberating art lead him to try to write a play about the "Negro condition." The condescension is apparent in Asbury's speech, and ironically, his openly bigoted mother actually gives the two black workers, Randall and Morgan, more respect than he does: "Those two are not stupid," she tells him, "they know how to look out for themselves" (*CW*, 558). But Asbury,

---

[15] Maritain, *Creative Intuition,* 65.
[16] Ibid., 189.

who sees himself as their artist-redeemer, replies "they need to" and then sets out to "be around them for awhile to see how they really felt about their condition" (*CW*, 558). It is clear that he believes he will be able to use the resultant play (that will likely never be written) for some great social purpose. But Randall and Morgan will not really talk to him. So Asbury tries to buddy up to them by tempting them to break his mother's rules about smoking in the dairy and drinking the unpasteurized milk, creating some kind of significant "scene" in which he plays the part of liberating hero and leader. "We've got to think free if we want to live free!" (*CW*, 559).

O'Connor generates irony by carefully navigating the distance between the narrator and Asbury. "There were no sounds but the steady click of the two milking machines and the occasional slap of a cow's tail against her side. It was one of those moments of communion when the difference between black and white is absorbed into nothing" (*CW*, 558). The narrator looks through Asbury's eyes here: the melting away of the differences between black and white is only in Asbury's earnest imagination, in his creation of the scene. He sins against the true soul of art by bypassing real difference to achieve an abstract unity. It is a unity of mind, not reality. It is Maritain's "magical gnosis...in which all differences are abolished and all contradictions made one, by virtue of the void, and in which the soul believes it is transferred above everything and enjoys infinite liberty."

Asbury's problem becomes clear when seen through Allen Tate's distinction between communication and communion. Tate argues that modernism's elevation of individual freedom has led individuals to simply repeat a "plotless drama of withdrawal."[17] When the artist glorifies and participates in this kind of freedom, he will stand above his subject communicating instead of being involved in his subject in communion. Tate fully intends the sacramental resonance to the word "communion." We *participate* in communion through love in a particular place and time, whereas we only *use* communication to trumpet our discoveries from some placeless place. By definition

---

[17] Allen Tate, *The Forlorn Demon: Didactic and Critical Essays* (Chicago: Regnery, 1953) 9.

literature gives whole experiences, experiences we share. "Literature has never communicated...it cannot *communicate*: from this point of view we see the work of literature as a participation in communion. Participation leads naturally to the idea of the common experience. Perhaps it is not too grandiose a conception to suggest that works of literature, from the short lyric to the long epic, are the recurrent discovery of the human communion *as experience*, in a definite place and at a definite time."[18] What keeps literature in communion is precisely its link with a definite place and a definite time. It is about being embodied in a community, not floating above it.

For O'Connor, the force of fiction comes by those links between definite places and times. In "The Artificial Nigger," the black woman's body and the plaster statue are Nelson and Mr. Head's point of communion with their own community's sins and with the black community they thought they were above. Their concrete encounter with the black community and with the force of their own sin leads them to a greater understanding that does not abolish difference in the movement. Because Nelson and Mr. Head's experiences are sunk in the body, Tate could choose no more appropriate word than "communion" to describe how experience operates. When the Eucharist is shared, the community of believers must be present bodily in order to participate. In "The Enduring Chill," Asbury's "arty delusions" prevent genuine communion with the black servants who do not even recognize his body: "When they said anything to him, it was as if they were speaking to an invisible body located to the right or left of where he actually was..." (*CW*, 558). Trying to attain an isolated bodilessness, Asbury replaces the true body and blood of Christ in communion with tobacco and unpasteurized milk. Not surprisingly, when he denies community and the traditional authority of the former (in which he would be one of many participants) to promote the independent and rebellious attitude of the latter (in which he leads others to his own way), his attempts at communication fail miserably.

---

[18] Ibid., 12.

O'Connor describes the artist Asbury's failures in her essay "The Catholic Novelist in the Protestant South." She argues that communication only makes sense within a community; it is "talking inside a community of which one is a part" (*CW*, 856). The true Southern writer understands that "when one Southern character speaks, regardless of his station in life, an echo of all Southern life is heard. This helps to keep Southern fiction from being a fiction of purely private experience" (*CW*, 855). The true Southern writer is not alienated from society, and she "feels the need of expatriation less than other writers in this country" (*CW*, 856). When Asbury leaves the South and isolates his imagination, he follows the modern road and kills his art. O'Connor writes that "the isolated imagination is easily corrupted by theory. Alienation was once a diagnosis, but in much of the fiction of our time it has become an ideal. The modern hero is the outsider. His experience is rootless. He can go anywhere. He belongs nowhere." Belonging nowhere is a problem that always ends in failure because "being alien to nothing, he ends up being alienated from any kind of community based on common tastes and interests. The borders of his country are the sides of his skull" (*CW*, 856).

O'Connor's criticism of modernism's pretensions in "The Enduring Chill" suggests an interesting connection to feminism denied to her by most critics. Donna Haraway's essay on the science question in feminism is just one of many I could invoke here, but it is particularly useful in discussing O'Connor, who was equally suspicious of scientific pretensions to be all-knowing and all-seeing and to communicate truths from a disembodied position.

Haraway indicts all pretense to complete objectivity in vision, a pretense she calls the "god trick." While science is most prone to the error, no one claiming to see all with "ultimate clarity" is immune to the charge. In response to this all-seeing eye, feminism offers "situated knowledges" and insists on the "embodied nature of all vision."[19] It refuses the unmarked, disembodied "transparent eyeball"

---

[19] Donna Haraway, "The Science Question in Feminism and the Privilege of Partial Perspective," *Feminist Studies* 14/3 (1988): 581.

of the romantic poet and his modern inheritor. Haraway argues that such a position actually prevents clear vision of the world: "knowledge from the point of view of the unmarked is truly fantastic, distorted, and irrational. The only position from which objectivity could not possibly be practiced and honored is the standpoint of the master, the Man, the One God, whose Eye produces, appropriates, and orders all difference...the god trick is self-identical, and we have mistaken that for creativity and knowledge, omniscience even."[20]

At first glance, Haraway's insistence on partial knowledge resembles any number of postmodern critiques of phallocentricism, notably our discovery of the absent center, that the Truth is not available to us and never will be. But from the standpoint of O'Connor's poetics, what interests me about Haraway's essay is her equally strong indictment of relativism, an indictment she delivers on the *same terms*. In fact, Haraway's main aim in her essay is to recover some notion of objectivity by denying a mutually exclusive dichotomy of "master theory vs. webbed accounts," "world system vs. local knowledges," and "common language vs. heteroglossia."[21] Complete relativism commits the same error as any totalizing consciousness in that it claims to "see all from nowhere."[22] "Relativism is a way of being nowhere while claiming to be everywhere equally. The 'equality' of positioning is a denial of responsibility and critical inquiry. Relativism is the perfect mirror twin of totalization in the ideologies of objectivity: both deny the stakes in location, embodiment, and partial perspective; both make it impossible to see well."[23] Haraway's clear interest is not just in limitations of vision but also in "seeing well." Her essay pleads that it is no solution to the problem of subjectivity to claim that nothing can be seen or known at all.

Not surprisingly, Haraway's solution involves a community of partial viewers. "We seek [the knowledges] ruled by partial sight and

---

[20] Ibid., 587.
[21] Ibid., 688.
[22] Ibid., 584.
[23] Ibid.

limited voice—not partiality for its own sake, but rather, for the sake of the connections and unexpected opening situated knowledges make possible. *Situated knowledges are about communities, not about isolated individuals. The only way to find a larger vision is to be somewhere in particular*"[24] (emphasis mine). Anyone familiar with O'Connor's fiction and her occasional prose can see that O'Connor could have written that last sentence. It is one she *did* write with every misfit, backwoods preacher, and buck-toothed teenaged girl she brought into being. Her discussions of the unique vision of Southern literature are saturated with the importance of being somewhere in particular. For O'Connor, it is only by an honest, local, particular, and bodied descent into one's region that a larger vision will be found:

> As far as the creation of a body of fiction is concerned, the social is superior to the purely personal. Somewhere is better than anywhere. And traditional manners, however unbalanced, are better than no manners at all. The discovery of having his senses respond to a particular society and a particular history, to particular sounds and a particular idiom, is for the Southern writer the beginning of a recognition that first puts his work in real human perspective for him. He discovers that the imagination is *not* free, but bound. The energy of the South is so strong in him that it is a force which has to be encountered and engaged, and it is when this is a true engagement that its meaning will lead outward to universal human interest. (*CW*, 856-7)

Art is not about the "god trick"; it should not claim to see everything as one without a body might. It does not exalt freedom of the imagination above all else; instead, it accepts its limitations as the truest "gateway to reality."

The individual artist is not only limited by her embodiment in a community. She is also limited by art's own boundaries. Since art is a virtue of the practical intellect, engaged always in *making*, the artist is bound to her material and does not ascend above it. O'Connor wrote to Hester that "I have no notion that the artist should be above the common people...I even dislike the concept *artist* when it sets you above, all it is is working in a certain kind of medium to make

---

[24] Ibid., 590.

something right. The material is no more exalted than any other kind of material and the idea of making it right is what should be applied to all making. St. Thomas said the artist is concerned with the good of that which is made, that art is a good-in-itself" (*CW*, 1028–29).

Because art is always that which is made out of the particular, it has a kind of built-in epistemological humility, even for someone as driven by her spiritual convictions as O'Connor was. For all her talk about the theological basis for her fiction, O'Connor takes pains to separate the artist's responsibility from the church's. The artist should be held accountable to the art, and the church to souls. When a Catholic leader read this in one of O'Connor's essays and apparently wanted to modify it, O'Connor wrote to Hester about her disapproval: "I don't by any means think he is a small or mean man, I think he just sees this as an abstract theoretical problem and from a great distance. Whereas the writer himself is traveling the rocky road, and feels every individual bump" (*CW*, 1028). Even to see the goals of an artist from above is to abstract them into a theoretical problem instead of to tackle them as a practical problem. The writer, living in the material, feels all the bumps.

O'Connor writes that "the artist has his hands full and does his duty if he attends to his art. He can safely leave evangelizing to the evangelists. He must first of all be aware of his limitations as an artist—for art transcends its limitations only by staying within them" (*MM*, 171). The language O'Connor chooses indicates her position: the artist has his "hands full" and "does his duty" by remembering his own limits, one of which is the limit of his own body. When the word "morality" enters into O'Connor's discourse about her own work, it is only to clarify that the writer's moral sense must coincide with his dramatic sense—that he must tell a story and tell it accurately. To do that is to see the world accurately. "I suppose when I say that the moral basis of Poetry is the accurate naming of the things of God, I mean about the same thing that Conrad meant when he said that his aim as an artist was to render the highest possible justice to the visible universe" (*HB*, 128).

Asbury's failures as an artist come into sharper focus now. He is the aesthete, the artist as dandy, the one who doesn't want to get his hands dirty in the material of his art. He cannot understand O'Connor's insistence that "the materials of the fiction writer are the humblest. Fiction is about everything human and we are made out of dust, and if you scorn getting yourself dusty, then you shouldn't try to write fiction. It's not a grand enough job for you" (*MM*, 68). He also wants to play the god trick by rising above his own life, aestheticizing his death as a lesson to everyone else. But ultimately, of course, Asbury has neither the view nor the control to which he aspires. Instead, the common and simple expression of Doctor Block that "blood don't lie" carries the day. Asbury's own body, dependent and weak, betrays him; he has only undulant fever, not a terminal illness. The fever came simply and unromantically because he drank unpasteurized milk.

O'Connor's irony knocks Asbury down with two swift punches. First, his pretense to disembodiment is radically mocked when Dr. Block compares his condition to that of a farm animal: "'undulant fever ain't so bad, Azzberry,' he murmured. 'It's the same as Bang's in a cow'" (*CW*, 572). In his dramatic delusions of his illness Asbury had insisted that "what is wrong with me is way beyond Block," but now Asbury can do nothing but moan and stay quiet, left to recognize that he is physically not that far from the same cows and their "intimate functions" his mother spoke about.[25] As O'Connor clarified in a letter to Ted Spivey, "it's the knowledge that he has no high and tragic mortal illness but only a cow's disease that brings the shock of self-knowledge that clears the way for the Holy Ghost" (*CW*, 1076).

Second, Asbury's pretensions toward ultimate liberty are shamed by the justification of his mother's rules, which turn out to have pragmatic viability. Drinking the unpasteurized milk was, according to the farm hands, "*the* thing she don't 'low" (*CW*, 559). His mother forbade it not because, as Asbury thought, she did not want whites to drink after blacks or because the farm would lose money, but because

---

[25] As David Eggenschwiler puts it "no matter how much the intellectual defies himself, there is always a cow with Bang's ready to prove kinship" (Eggenschwiler, *The Christian Humanism of Flannery O'Connor* [Detroit: Wayne State University Press, 1972] 60).

of the inevitable physical consequences. No one, not even the artist, can ever be above his own body and the rules of nature. Lying on his bed Asbury recognizes his real, physical embodiment and his dependence upon a woman. He needs her authority, her outside view of his body. The most dramatic event of his life comes from the laws of the earth, not his mind, and the laws of the earth are the provinces of his mother and of the farm hands who know better than he does. The irony, of course, is the same irony that applies to storytelling in O'Connor's conception: if Asbury had stayed within the farm's true limits he would have been literally free instead of now "frail, racked, but enduring" for the rest of his days (*CW*, 572).

This picture of Asbury silenced by the earthly authority of his mother should lead us to reexamine the characteristic approach feminist scholars have taken toward O'Connor's work. Louise Westling, for example, argues that the most common picture O'Connor gives is of a woman who is chastised by satanic male agents of God, agents who demand allegiance and submission. Westling argues that O'Connor "aligns herself with this punishing father" and that "sons are granted the power of action, for maternal dominance is seen as unnatural and debilitating."[26] She reads "Everything That Rises Must Converge," "The Comforts of Home," and "Greenleaf" as particularly strong examples of a "mother's pride smashed by male force."[27]

The claim that O'Connor uses men to silence these women is shortsighted at best. Although Thomas does kill his mother in "The Comforts of Home," Westling errs when she equates his action with any real or enviable power.[28] In fact, Thomas shoots his mother

---

[26] Louise Hutchings Westling, "Fathers and Daughters in Welty and O'Connor," in *The Female Tradition in Southern Literature*, ed. Carol S. Manning (Urbana and Chicago: University of Illinois Press, 1993) 117–18.

[27] Louise Hutchings Westling, *Sacred Groves and Ravaged Gardens: The Fiction of Eudora Welty, Carson Mccullers, and Flannery O'Connor* (Athens: University of Georgia Press, 1985) 145.

[28] Westling argues that the "mother's power is so great that it must be crushed again and again" and that "sons are granted the power of action, for maternal dominance is seen as unnatural and debilitating" (Westling, "Fathers and

accidentally because he cannot escape the voice of his father, who equated manhood with ruling with an iron fist and who "never let anything grow under his feet. Particularly nothing a woman planted" (*CW*, 590). Thomas shoots his mother because he does not want anything to disturb the peace of perfect order—*his* idea of order. Thomas is shown to be arrogant, intractable, and weak. Like a lot of intellectual men in O'Connor, and contrary to what Westling argues, he has a problem taking simple, right action. The mothers, connected to life on the particular and embodied level, are almost always able to do so, although the action is small and seemingly insignificant. The truly powerful figure in "The Comforts of Home" is the mother, who could love and take into her home a girl who needed a second chance. O'Connor was careful to subject males and females alike to the *deus ex machina* that broadens their vision by showing them their limits. The "god trick" is a spiritual problem to which no one is immune. But far from advancing a patriarchal vision of the world, when O'Connor uses her power as a storyteller to shatter characters with scientific, Enlightenment-driven pretenses to order and objective seeing, the characters are usually men—and usually sons.

As we have seen, Asbury is just such a son, and what he learns about his embodied dependence upon others prepares him for his final vision. Indeed, Asbury's vision of the Holy Ghost's descent upon him, bringing new life, is impossible without this preparation. Man's dependence upon others is one of the favorite themes of Baron von Hügel. In his chapter "Responsibility in Religious Belief," Von Hügel argues that "religion is a profoundly social force, which operates from one contemporary man to other contemporaries and on from generation to generation," and that only if a man were to "walk this planet without a body" could he escape the "great human association—the Family, the Guild, the State, the Church."[29] Von Hügel continues, "indeed the paradox is, meanwhile, really true, that

---

Daughters," 118). Once again, Westling mistakes ill-fated action for the genuine power to act, a power given as often to women as to men in O'Connor's fiction.

[29] Baron Friedrick von Hügel, *Essays and Addresses on the Philosophy of Religion: First Series* (New York: E. P. Dutton, 1928) 13, 14.

the more utterly independent a man thinks himself of all traditions and institutions, the more excessively, unwisely dependent he is usually, in reality, upon some tradition or institution...."[30] No one can escape history and institutions. Only by trusting in wiser teachers and trainers has "any such man any chance of escaping from, possibly life-long, self-imprisonment."[31] O'Connor makes it clear in "The Enduring Chill" that Asbury believes himself to be imprisoned by family (his feelings about his mother) and out of the purview of the church (his view in the catechism conversation). So when Asbury's vision of the Holy Ghost does come, it is fitting that it should be by the animation of "the fierce bird which through the years of his childhood and the days of his illness had been poised over his head" (*CW*, 572). The bird—like region, history, and one's own family—is a constant, humbling, and revelatory "other."

O'Connor deliberately transforms the bird from a symbol of the imagination to a symbol of the Holy Ghost. Countless modern artists from Kate Chopin to Constantin Brancusi have used birds to symbolize the freedom of the imagination or to depict its struggle to be free. Almost without exception, birds in modern literature do not descend unless they have been injured or pinioned by others or unless they make "ambiguous undulations" as do the pigeons that sink to darkness in Wallace Stevens's "Sunday Morning." But instead of soaring to the heights to gain an otherworldly view, O'Connor's bird descends deliberately to humble such pretensions in Asbury. Actually O'Connor reclaims the symbol, for the bird as other rather than self is a much older image. John Milton pleads to the Holy Spirit as a bird in *Paradise Lost*:

> And chiefly thou O Spirit, that dost prefer
> Before all temples th' upright heart and pure,
> Instruct me, for thou know'st; thou from the first
> Wast present, and with mighty wings outspread
> Dove-like sat'st brooding on the vast abyss

---

[30] Ibid., 14.
[31] Ibid.

And mad'st it pregnant. (17–22)[32]

Whatever pretense Milton may have had about his ability to "justify the ways of God to men," this passage suggests that the poet is not an isolated mind hovering over the waters of chaos, seeing all, and ordering it. The poet instead pleads the Spirit to instruct him because the Spirit was before him and knows more than he does. "What in me is dark / Illumine, what is low raise and support" (22–23).[33]

O'Connor also takes pains to separate Asbury's final vision of the bird's descent from his previous imaginative efforts. For while Asbury easily invents the dramatics of his own death and of the communion scene with the black men, he hits a wall when he tries to understand the leak on the ceiling. While he sees the leak as a "fierce bird" that "had been there since his childhood and had always irritated him and sometimes had frightened him" (*CW*, 555), the illusion of its descending movement has never made any sense to him. While he stares at the bird, he "felt that it was there for some purpose that he could not divine" (*CW*, 568). And that is the point: Asbury cannot divine it on his own. Only when his eyes are "shocked clean" at the end does the vision descend upon him. Like many of O'Connor's characters, his vision comes only when he reaches the end of his earthly resources. At the end of his own artistic capability, Asbury must now accept revelation.

By viewing this final scene as the modern artist's humbling by a vision he did not generate, I am not suggesting that O'Connor viewed the artist as a passive recipient of some message from above, as if he or she were a writer of divinely inspired scripture or engaged in some mysterious "automatic writing." Instead, the scene dramatizes the unique interaction of human reason with divine grace that O'Connor believed characterized all true knowledge of one's self and God. Aquinas argued that human knowledge of the sensible world through natural reason has a limit, but it is a limit that leads one to accept the existence of God and to understand the need for revelation. O'Connor

---

[32] John Milton, *Paradise Lost*, ed. Scott Elledge (New York: Norton, 1975).
[33] Ibid.

underlined the indicated portion of the following paragraph in her copy of the writings of Aquinas:

> Our natural knowledge begins from sense. Hence our natural knowledge can go as far as it can be led by sensible things. But our intellect cannot be led by sense so far as to see the essence of God; *because sensible creatures are effects of God which do not equal the power of God, their cause.* Hence from the knowledge of sensible things the whole power of God cannot be known; nor therefore can His essence be seen. But because they are His effects and depend on their cause, we can be led from them so far as to know of God *whether He exists,* and to know of Him what must necessarily belong to Him, as the first cause of all things, exceeding all things caused by Him. (93–94)[34]

Asbury's vision of God as over him is made possible by the light of grace, but it was prepared for by his discovery of his limited, embodied vision. The scene is duplicated in Ruby's experience in "Revelation": the vision of the bridge of souls heading toward heaven comes to her only after she can see herself among the hogs, see that she can be "a hog and me both" (*CW*, 652). It is a unique combination of the rational project of self-knowledge combined with divine revelation of the ultimate Other. In Aquinas's epistemology, each contributes to the other.

Asbury's self-knowledge might save him as an artist, too, though we are not privy to that story.[35] He has to be purified of his "double disease" that sees his own personality as supreme in order to be able to dirty himself in the true project of fiction. This purification is something O'Connor thought about a great deal; her struggles with point of view were in part struggles to write honestly about what she knew (herself) without seeing the world entirely through her own vision. As O'Connor wrote to Hester:

> to have sympathy for any character you have to put a good deal of yourself in him. But to say that any complete denudation of the writer occurs in the successful work is, according to me, a romantic

---

[34] The italicized section is what O'Connor marked, which can be seen in her copy held at the Ina Dillard Russell library at Georgia College.

[35] O'Connor had tentative plans to continue with Asbury as a character in a novel (*CW* 1076–77), but she ran out of time before she could return to him.

exaggeration. A great part of the art of it is precisely in seeing that this does not happen. Maritain says that to produce a work of art requires the "constant attention of the purified mind," and the business of the purified mind in this case is to see that those elements of the personality that don't bear on the subject at hand are excluded. Stories don't lie when left to themselves. Everything has to be subordinated to a whole which is not you. Any story I reveal myself completely in will be a bad story. (*CW*, 957)

Both Maritain and O'Connor discuss the writer's role in a way similar to Christ's teaching that one must "lose oneself in order to find oneself." Maritain emphasizes that the writer *produces* something other to him, so that the writer's "creative self dies to itself in order to live in the work."[36] O'Connor wrote that "I never completely forget myself except when I am writing and I am never more completely myself than when I am writing. It is the same with Christian self-abandonment" (*HB*, 458).[37]

The distance between the artist as romantic hero and the artist as self-sacrificing craftsperson is the same as that between the terms "individual" and "person" as O'Connor understood them, having learned the terminology from Emmanuel Mounier. Mounier writes that God "no longer makes the world a unity through the abstraction of the idea, but by an infinite capacity for the indefinite multiplication of these separate acts of love."[38] Personalism denies the Cartesian fantasy of self-birth. While the independent mind of the *individual* may live in the isolation of the *cogito*, the *person* exists only in relation to others. The "thou" precedes the "I." Personalism teaches that the human subject cannot be nourished by "auto-digestion"; instead it must go out of itself to a real other. "Real love is creative of distinction; it is a gratitude and a will towards another

[36] Jacques Maritain, *Creative Intuition in Art and Poetry* (New York: Pantheon Books, 1953) 144.

[37] For additional discussion of this issue, see Robert H. Brinkmeyer Jr., "Asceticism and Imaginative Vision," in *Flannery O'Connor: New Perspectives* (Athens: University of Georgia Press, 1996).

[38] Emmanuel Mounier, *Personalism*, trans. Philip Mairet (New York: Grove Press, 1952) xii.

because he is other than oneself."[39] Part of Asbury's problem is that he is an individual; he defines himself by what Maritain calls "the narrowness of ego, and separation from others," instead of by a loving recognition of the distinct personhood of those around him.[40] The artist in particular must be a person who recognizes people; she can only be in an "act of spiritual communication" if she remains other to the character and the stories so that they are "a whole which is not you." Left to themselves, as O'Connor insisted, the stories do not lie. The thing is to leave them to themselves—and to do this, the writer must lose herself; but if writing is her vocation, the work she believe herself to be uniquely created to do, the writer is also never more herself than while doing it.

The theological importance of point of view, along with the sheer difficulty of navigating it, explains O'Connor's evident frustration. "Point of view runs me nuts," she once wrote. When a novelist's subject is the interior lives of the characters, the course is treacherous, with two losing positions. If the novelist chooses a completely distanced, third person point of view and cannot render the interior lives of her characters, then the story of their changes is not told, and the artist fails. But if the author slides completely into the characters and tells only her own story, she sacrifices the condition of true art: the embodiment of the other.

To navigate these difficult waters, O'Connor took her lead from Percy Lubbock's slim and influential work *The Craft of Fiction*. She read this volume early in her career, and the copy held in the Ina Dillard Russell Library shows her fine, penciled marginalia over large sections throughout the book. She mentions the book often in her letters and always with respect. "This sounds like a how-to-do-it book but it is not; it's a very profound study of point of view" (*HB*, 192). For Lubbock, mastering point of view is essential to the craft of fiction. He particularly emphasizes that storytellers require a "choice and disciplined method" to get the most drama out of a story, to present it whole. He argues that the writer's discipline is both to

---

[39] Ibid., 23.
[40] Maritain, *Creative Intuition,* 142.

remain separate from the character, and to see through his eyes at the same time: "Nobody notices," Lubbock writes, "but in fact there are now two brains behind that eye; and one of them is the author's, who adopts and shares the position of his creature, and at the same time supplements his wit."[41] Analysis of the story teaches the reader that what is presented is not just the view of the person described, but that "someone else is looking over his shoulder," seeing more.

Lubbock's word choice should ring bells for O'Connor readers. The method of point of view requires *discipline*—the discipline of staying within the limits of the author and hero as separate beings, of keeping a separate shoulder for the author to look over, even as she looks through the character's eyes. Lubbock discusses Flaubert and James as the masters of seeing from within and from without, but with "no blurring of the focus by a double point of view." Lubbock clearly favors the dramatic third person point of view; for him, the first person point of view restricts the liberty of the novelist to "edge away" from his character and supersede his or her vision by irony. Flaubert's genius lies in his ability to show us, without betraying Emma's consciousness, that she is a foolish woman. The irony "is in his tone—never in his words, which invariably respect her own estimate of herself."[42]

The result, for Lubbock and for O'Connor, is the dramatic. Henry James, who Lubbock says is "the only real *scholar* in the art," succeeded because he was able to "render objectively the world of consciousness."[43] If he found himself too much in the character, if he lost the exterior view and became his characters, he would lose the very vision that defines art. Lubbock admired *The Wings of the Dove* in particular because "the author has encompassed the struggle that is proceeding within [Milly], and has lifted it bodily into the understanding of the reader."[44] This gives "solidity, weight, a third dimension." It is, in short, an incarnation. The strength of the novel

---

[41] Percy Lubbock, *The Craft of Fiction* (New York: The Viking Press, 1957) 258.
[42] Ibid., 89.
[43] Ibid., 187.
[44] Ibid., 178.

lies in how little narration it contains and how the silent drama is played out before us where we can "see its actual movement." This method uniquely assigns the point of view to the reader because the process of thinking and seeing is exposed to the view of the reader, and we have "the vision *of* a vision."[45] The kind of view Lubbock describes here is a trademark of O'Connor's fiction. That she wrote many stories and never once employed the first person point of view indicates that she always felt the importance of maintaining an embodied distance from her characters, even when she entered their consciousness.

If all this seems like elementary teaching about the novel, that is precisely the point. For O'Connor, the very rules of fiction as she saw them have some theological content. For as "The Enduring Chill" thematically works out Asbury's dependence upon the other, its existence as one person's story—assumed to be worth the telling—demonstrates, in the words of Bakhtin, a "human being's absolute need for the other, for the other's seeing, remembering, gathering, and unifying self-activity—the only self-activity capable of producing his outwardly finished personality. This outward personality could not exist, if the other did not create it: aesthetic memory is *productive*—it gives birth, for the first time, to the *outward* human being on a new plane of being."[46] Nowhere does O'Connor more convincingly tell this story of humanity's birth at the hands of an artist than in "Parker's Back."

---

[45] Ibid., 186.
[46] Bakhtin, *Art and Answerability,* 35–36.

CHAPTER 7

MARY ANN'S FACE AND PARKER'S BACK: THE GROTESQUE BODY UNDER CONSTRUCTION

> *By virtue of the Creation and, still more, of the Incarnation,* nothing *here below is profane for those who know how to see.*

—Pierre Teilhard de Chardin

At the height of Flannery O'Connor's career, and not long before her death, a group of nuns asked her to write the story of the life and death of a little girl with a cancerous facial tumor, Mary Ann. The girl had apparently left a deep impression on the Sisters at Our Lady of Perpetual Help Free Cancer home in Atlanta, and they wanted to inspire others with her story. The Sisters wrote to O'Connor that "after one meeting one never was conscious of her physical defect but recognized only the brave spirit and felt the joy of such contact. Now Mary Ann's story should be written but who to write it?" With characteristic wit, O'Connor later described her answer: "Not me, I said to myself" (*CW*, 822). But they pressed, and O'Connor eventually persuaded the Sisters to write a factual account themselves, which she agreed to help prepare and edit. She then bet the Sisters two of her peahens that nobody would ever publish it.

Mary Ann's account was eventually published, and O'Connor wrote its introduction. Like the essay "The King of the Birds," her "Introduction to a Memoir of Mary Ann" is an odd and often ignored piece, but one that illuminates O'Connor's work as a whole.[1] In 1961, as she finished *The Violent Bear It Away* and began to work on her final stories, she wrote to Elizabeth Hester ("A") that "in the future, anybody who writes anything about me is going to have to read everything I have written in order to make legitimate criticism, even and particularly the Mary Ann piece" (*HB*, 442).

Why *particularly* the Mary Ann piece? The answer to this question underscores the ultimate importance of the Incarnation in O'Connor's aesthetic and illustrates her final move toward the displacing power of the positive grotesque that would culminate in "Parker's Back." In "Introduction to a Memoir of Mary Ann," O'Connor celebrates a community of women and their care for a child whom society would consider useless. In so doing, she illustrates the aim of her own grotesques, which serve to champion the same end. As she suggests in this introduction and would fully develop in "Parker's Back," it is only through the aestheticizing vision of the other—the artist and the community—that our grotesque bodies, characterized by weakness and limitation, can reveal the "face of Christ under construction." O'Connor's fiction insists that the true potential for good is found in the oddest of places. It is the artist's job to show it.

The comparison between her own grotesques and the way the Sisters reared Mary Ann first became clear to O'Connor as a matter of vocation. When the Sisters visited her, one of them asked why she wrote about grotesques, why the grotesque was, "of all things," her vocation. O'Connor writes:

> I was struggling to get off the hook she had me on when another of our guests supplied the one answer that would make it immediately plain to all of them. "It's your vocation too," he said to her.

> This opened up for me also a new perspective on the grotesque. Most of us have learned to be dispassionate about evil, to look it in the face and find, as often as not, our own grinning reflections with which we do

---

[1] Marshall Bruce Gentry, for instance, gives an insightful reading of O'Connor's move from the negative to the positive grotesque, but he makes only one reference to this essay (Marshall Bruce Gentry, *Flannery O'Connor's Religion of the Grotesque* [Jackson: University Press of Mississippi, 1986] 14).

not argue, but good is another matter. Few have stared at that long enough to accept the fact that its face too is grotesque, that in us the good is something under construction. The modes of evil usually receive worthy expression. The modes of good have to be satisfied with a cliché or a smoothing down that will soften their real look. When we look into the face of good, we are liable to see a face like Mary Ann's, full of promise. (*CW*, 829–30)

O'Connor is exaggerating about her discovery at the meeting; this "new perspective" on the grotesque had been increasingly apparent in her work since *The Violent Bear It Away*. But the comparison of these two seemingly disparate vocations provides us with new insights into O'Connor's goals for the grotesque. She explains that the cancer home is a community of women who are not afraid of the "real look" of good. Pure evil can be easily categorized, unified, and fought against, as O'Connor's one-armed Mr. Shiftlet in "The Life You Save May Be Your Own" demonstrates. O'Connor often wrote about how much easier it was to depict evil than to depict good. But what the Sisters discovered—and what feminist critics are increasingly interested in—is that what we call ugly or untidy might actually be where the good resides, however unrecognizable. In "Introduction to a Memoir of Mary Ann" O'Connor insists that when we truly look into the face of good we are not going to see the purified intellect and a refined abstraction, but a *face*. And it will be an unfinished face, a "face like Mary Ann's, full of promise."

To truly understand the epistemological weight O'Connor attributes to Mary Ann's body, we must follow O'Connor as she traces the history of the Our Lady of Perpetual Help Cancer Home, the home in which the Sisters reared Mary Ann. O'Connor first points out that the home had been founded by Rose Hawthorne, Nathaniel Hawthorne's daughter. With this bit of history in mind, she picked up Mary Ann's picture, stared at it, and found that she could not put it down. "I continued to gaze at the picture long after I had thought to be finished with it," she writes. "The child's picture had brought to mind [Hawthorne's] story, *The Birthmark*" (*CW*, 823). O'Connor could not have drawn a more telling parallel. In Hawthorne's story, Alymer, the quintessential modern scientist, tries to use his "art" to rid his wife Georgiana of a small birthmark on her face, and his obsession with her perfection eventually leads to her death. Although conventional criticism of the story sees the birthmark as a symbol of original sin that Alymer tries to circumvent, O'Connor reads the story more widely. Alymer is a modern scientist who, under the influence of pure Cartesian categories, tries to use science to eliminate anything he considers to be impure and mysterious in human existence. He wants to do the kind of "tidying up" that can only lead to marginalization and exclusion of real bodies.[2] On the face of a woman, the mark carries even more significance as "impure," for a birthmark there signifies humanity's reproduction through grotesque means, its ever-changing state, and its march toward death. To hate the birthmark is to hate what is truly human, and to hate the way the body, particularly the female body, always reminds us of it.[3] O'Connor quotes the discussion in which Georgiana first becomes aware of Alymer's dislike of her birthmark, which she had been accustomed to view as a charm: "Ah, upon another face perhaps it might," replied her husband, "but never on yours. No, dearest Georgiana, you came so nearly perfect from the hand of Nature that this slightest defect, which we hesitate to term a defect or a beauty, shocks me, as being the visible mark of earthly imperfection" (*CW*, 823). Alymer cannot love that which reminds him of his earthiness.

In O'Connor's appropriation of Hawthorne's story, the little hand is a minor version of Mary Ann's deformed face. Not merely an imperfection, to O'Connor (and to Hawthorne in her reading), the

---

[2] For a full explanation, see Rosi Braidotti, "Mothers, Monsters, and Machines," in *Writing on the Body: Female Embodiment and Feminist Theory* (New York: Columbia University Press, 1997).

[3] "The Birthmark" illustrates Simone de Beauvoir's argument that men tend to associate women with immanence and death, locking them into simultaneous repulsion and desire. "Thus what man cherishes and detests first of all in woman—loved one or mother—is the fixed image of his animal destiny; it is the life that is necessary to his existence but that condemns him to the finite and to death. From the day of his birth man begins to die: this is the truth incarnated in the Mother" (De Beauvoir, *Second Sex*, rev. ed. [London: Everyman's Library, 1993] 174).

hand is a reminder of our bodies as distinct, unique, personally created, and mysterious. Like the mark of Cain, the birthmark symbolizes God's ownership even as it represents man's sin.[4] But Alymer, the Gnostic scientist, can only view Georgiana's birthmark with more and more disgust, for to him the body is a trap, a link with the earth and death, and with that which is out of his control: "It was the fatal flaw of humanity which Nature, in one shape or another, stamps ineffaceably on all her productions, either to imply that they are temporary and finite, or that their perfection must be wrought by toil and pain... the spectral hand... wrote mortality where he would fain have worshipped."[5] The little birthmark wrecks Alymer's worship of the perfectibility of humanity, of the scientific mind's ability to escape what it deems to be messy. Alymer possesses the scientist's version of what Allen Tate would later call the "angelic imagination," that imagination which "tries to disintegrate or to circumvent the image in the illusory pursuit of essence... divine love becomes so rarefied that it loses its human paradigm, and is dissolved in the worship of intellectual power, the surrogate of divinity that worships itself."[6]

Of course, Hawthorne's story moves on to its tragic and inevitable end: Alymer finds out the hard way that a human being is a whole, body and mind together, and that by trying to erase the untidy aspects, he can only kill. A large part of the tragedy of the story results from Georgiana's trust in Alymer and her complicity in the project; she "exults" in his "pure and lofty" love. She "felt how much more precious was such a sentiment than that meaner kind which would have borne with the imperfection for her sake, and have been

---

[4] It is often assumed that the Bible treats the mark of Cain as a mark of God's disdain, when in fact the mark was meant for Cain's protection: "And the Lord said to him, 'therefore, whoever kills Cain, vengeance shall be taken on him sevenfold.' And the Lord set a mark on Cain, lest anyone finding him should kill him" (Gen 4:15, NKJV).

[5] Nathaniel Hawthorne, *Nathaniel Hawthorne's Tales: A Norton Critical Edition*, ed. James McIntosh (New York: Norton, 1987) 120.

[6] Allen Tate, *The Forlorn Demon: Didactic and Critical Essays* (Chicago: Regnery, 1953) 37.

guilty of treason to holy love by degrading its perfect idea to the level of the actual; and with her whole spirit she prayed that for a single moment, she might satisfy his highest and deepest conception."[7] A few moments after Alymer's science has achieved his "highest and deepest conception" of beauty, Georgiana dies, apparently too pure to remain human.

O'Connor brings this story into her essay because the Sisters in the cancer home promote an agenda that controverts Alymer's on every point. They teach patients to be content with their "earthier natures." They teach that the actual, far from degrading, is the only pathway to God. "The Birthmark" is thus a powerful way for O'Connor to introduce the Sisters' memoir. But O'Connor does not stop there; she takes a step further into Hawthorne's own life, to describe the original impetus for this story. O'Connor recalls a scene from *Our Old Home* in which Hawthorne describes a man who visited a workhouse in Liverpool and who was followed by, in O'Connor's terms, "a wretched and rheumy child, so awful-looking that he could not decide what sex it was" (*CW*, 824). After a long pause, the man stops to pick it up, upon which Hawthorne comments, and O'Connor quotes, "it could be no easy thing for him to do, he being a person burdened with more than an Englishman's customary reserve, shy of actual contact with human beings, afflicted with a peculiar distaste for whatever was ugly, and, furthermore, accustomed to that habit of observation from an insulated standpoint which is said (but I hope erroneously) to have the tendency of putting ice into the blood" (*CW*, 824).

What interests O'Connor here is that the story of the man in Liverpool is not purely fictional. It is Hawthorne's own. He was the one in the workhouse who, tempted by Alymer's perspective, was "shy of actual contact" and who would have preferred to "observe from an insulated standpoint." Hawthorne knew that the writer's habit of observation can be too readily influenced by Alymer's hubris of scientism. The "mind over matter" road that modern thought has taken is a cold and bitter road indeed. As O'Connor continues to peel

---

[7] Hawthorne, *Tales,* 128.

away the layers beneath Hawthorne's story, she finds triumph not in something Hawthorne learned from the experience *per se*, but in the single act that brought him to self-discovery. In his personal journal, which Hawthorne's wife later published, Hawthorne tells of his encounter with an "underwitted" child, of the same description as in the fictional account, who followed him around until he finally picked it up. "I should never have forgiven myself if I had repelled its advances," he later wrote (*CW*, 825). O'Connor wants her readers to notice that the story we have in "The Birthmark" came out of Hawthorne's triumph over Alymer's spirit in himself.

But what has Hawthorne's triumph to do with Mary Ann? And what has Mary Ann to do with O'Connor's fiction? A great deal, if we read carefully. O'Connor is primarily interested in Hawthorne's account of his experience for its effect on Rose Hawthorne, his daughter. Out of admiration for her father's action—which she learned about only through his account—she began the work that would become Servants of Relief for Incurable Cancer. O'Connor considers Rose Hawthorne's work to be a completion of what her father began. "She discovered much that he sought, and fulfilled in a practical way the hidden desires of his life. The ice in the blood which he feared, and which this very fear preserved him from, was turned by her into a warmth which initiated action. If he observed, fearfully but truthfully; if he acted, reluctantly but firmly, she charged ahead, secure in the path his truthfulness had outlined for her" (*CW*, 826). When Hawthorne felt repulsed but picked up the grotesque child anyway, he let the truly human touch him physically and emotionally—not just intellectually. He had a whole experience; his imagination encountered but did not transcend or purify. He rescued his intellect from the clutches of Cartesianism: he did not see what he *willed* to see. Writing about it in his journal and in his stories (however indirectly), he imparted that victory to readers. One reader, his daughter, charged ahead to build a community of women who do nothing but make life easier for those who are dying.

O'Connor writes that there is a "direct line" from Hawthorne's act in the workhouse to Mary Ann and to the work of the Sisters that she stands for. "Their work is the tree sprung from Hawthorne's small act of Christlikeness and Mary Ann is its flower" (*CW*, 831). It may seem in this organic progression that Hawthorne's literary contribution has been displaced by the Sisters' charitable actions, as if O'Connor clearly privileges practical life over an accounting of it. But this oversimplification misses O'Connor's sophisticated point. Hawthorne's "small act of Christlikeness" was not just to pick up the child, but to write the truth about his experience in fictional and in nonfictional accounts. O'Connor supported the Sisters in their desire to tell Mary Ann's story because in the act of telling, they foreground what others want to marginalize or ignore.

What we most want to ignore is the grotesque body, the part of each of us that is quirky, embarrassing, nonsensical, and apparently accidental. But the Sisters, though untalented writers themselves, privilege it as the starting point of creativity. With attention placed on what cannot be easily explained, the writer fades away and the mystery of a life made by God remains. To emphasize this, O'Connor describes her first encounter with the Sisters' manuscript: "there was everything about the writing to make the professional writer groan...yet when I had finished reading, I remained for some time, the imperfections of the writing forgotten, thinking about the mystery of Mary Ann. They had managed to convey it" (*CW*, 828). This response does not invalidate the importance O'Connor ascribed to literary craft. But her view of the artist's craft has a medieval root: the purpose of excellence in form is not to draw attention to the skill of the writer, but to the beauty inherent in the subject.[8] That beauty requires more than pure intellect to see. But O'Connor wrote for an audience she knew to be far removed from the medieval sensibility. She was keenly aware that the modern audience does not take for granted that God created and subsequently values all human life. We no longer live in Dante's age, O'Connor writes in an earlier essay on the grotesque, "we live now in an age which doubts both fact and

---

[8] C. S. Lewis in *The Discarded Image* writes that medieval art is the art of people who "have a complete confidence in the intrinsic value of their matter. The telling is for the tale...it is not a transforming imagination but a realising imagination" (Lewis, *The Discarded Image* [Cambridge: Cambridge University Press, 1964] 205–206).

value, which is swept this way and that by momentary convictions. Instead of reflecting a balance from the world around him, the novelist now has to achieve one from a felt balance inside himself. There are ages when it is possible to woo the reader; there are others when something more drastic is necessary" (*CW*, 820). Because a little girl with a cancerous tumor on her face does not make sense to the modern world, the community of the Sisters must work to impart significance to her life and death in a way that will teach new values. So viewed, the Sisters' involvement in Mary Ann's life is itself a continuing act of "drastic" creativity. By teaching Mary Ann what to make of her own death, they invite the readers to do the same. As O'Connor continues, "The story was as unfinished as the child's face. Both seemed to have been left, like creation on the seventh day, to be finished by others. The reader would have to make something of the story as Mary Ann had made something of her face. She and the Sisters who had taught her had fashioned from her unfinished face the material of her death. The creative action of the Christian's life is to prepare his death in Christ. It is a continuous action in which this world's goods are utilized to the fullest..." (*CW*, 828).

When O'Connor writes that a story is left "like creation on the seventh day, to be finished by others," she opens a world of theological and aesthetic import. O'Connor believed writers participated in the continuing creation of the world by imparting significance to the particular beings they create in a way parallel to (but not in imitation of) God's creation. What is different here is that she brings in the community of readers as the final link to the production of meaning. She invites us to the grotesque—to stare long enough at that which naturally repels us. In defiance of modern categories, O'Connor has privileged both the body and a tradition of valuing that body.

O'Connor inherited the idea that the community values and participates in the grotesque body from the medieval grotesque.[9] In *Rabelais and his World*, M. M. Bakhtin explores the changing nature of the grotesque in literature. In the medieval era, argues Bakhtin, grotesque realism celebrated the body as "deeply positive." The body

---

[9] See Di Renzo for a full treatment of this issue.

is not a private but a universal body, a body that belongs to the community. By its emphasis on bodily processes (reproduction, eating, birth, death, etc.), the grotesque illustrates that humanity is incomplete, always in process. It characterizes not stable perfection but "a people who are continually growing and renewed."[10] Death is decidedly not something to fear, for in the grotesque "the world is destroyed in order to be regenerated and renewed. While dying it gives birth."[11] The humor of the grotesque is its spirit of acceptance of all aspects of human experience.

But in the romantic tradition, Bakhtin explains, the body lost its corporate status and became individualized. At the same moment, the grotesque lost its humor; it became dark, gothic, alien, and terrifying.[12] The body became, paradoxically, "other" to us. Because of the violent dichotomizing of the *cogito*, reason, in an effort to overcome skepticism, became estranged from the body, and the body became the dumping point for everything we do not understand and everything we fear because we do not understand. The consequences are portentous.

Bakhtin's conception of the shift in the grotesque from the corporate to the individual body has roots in some of his earlier work. In *Art and Answerability*, Bakhtin defines aesthetic activity broadly, as any productive view we can have of another person. Aesthetic activity exists because we have bodies we cannot see on our own. As a result, with its emphasis on self-directed mind, neo-Platonism (and Cartesianism by extension) nearly destroyed the possibility for art. In these philosophies, "the aesthetic value of the body becomes almost extinct"; our living, actual birth is replaced by the birth of "I-for-myself" that makes us think we can do without the other.[13] We cannot possibly live that way, because "only the other is *embodied*

---

[10] M. M. Bakhtin, *Rabelais and His World*, trans. Helene Iswolsky (Cambridge: M.I.T. Press, 1968) 19.

[11] Ibid., 48.

[12] Ibid., 38.

[13] M. M. Bakhtin, *Art and Answerability: Early Philosophical Essays,* ed. Michael Holquist and Vadim Liapunov, trans. (Austin: University of Texas Press, 1990) 54.

for me axiologically and aesthetically. In this respect, the body is not
something self-sufficient: it needs the *other*, needs his recognition and
his form-giving activity."[14]

The best example we have of "form-giving activity," Bakhtin
continues, is verbal art. When Mary Ann and the Sisters who taught
her had "fashioned from her unfinished face the material of her
death," the community performed a genuine aesthetic act for Mary
Ann. They performed what she could not do by herself—particularly
because Mary Ann could not see her own death from inside her life.
By anticipating, surviving, and then writing about her death, they
could view and present her life as a whole. This is what Bakhtin calls
aesthetic *consummation*. We find forms of justification for another
person's life, "forms of justification that he is in principle incapable
of finding from his own place."[15]

As we have seen, for Bakhtin aesthetic consummation is not the
result of the artist's genius, his power to pick and choose what to
remember, to make some new whole out of other lives and out of the
raw material of reality. It is precisely the opposite. In Bakhtin's
terms, the true aesthetic act privileges being in its "givenness" over
any meaning we can ascribe to it. In an aesthetic act, we face honestly
the grotesque and untidy state in which we find ourselves; we face the
fact that we all go down to death, to that state Alymer could never
face in humanity. But we inheritors of the modern tradition must
relearn that we cannot do it for ourselves; the work can only be done
through the aesthetic project, through memory that is embodied. As
Bakhtin writes, "my *memory* of the other and of the other's life
differs radically from my contemplating and remembering my own
life. Memory sees a life and its content in a different way formally:
only memory is aesthetically productive."[16] And "aesthetically
productive" is exactly what the Sisters' "Memoir of Mary Ann" is. It

---

[14] Ibid., 51.
[15] Ibid., 130. For Bakhtin, an autobiography can never truly succeed in giving
value to the writer's life, because a life cannot be consummated by the self from
within that life (147).
[16] Bakhtin, *Art and Answerability*, 107.

is a literary product that values the existence of—without explaining the "reason for"—a seemingly meaningless life.

When the Sisters did publish the account, O'Connor had to persuade them to abandon the sentimental titles they wanted such as "The Crooked Smile," "The Bridegroom Cometh," and "Scarred Angel" (*CW*, 1139). O'Connor pushed for a factual account with the title "A Memoir of Mary Ann" because she viewed the sentimental as one more roadblock to acceptance of the real. "If other ages felt less, they saw more, even though they saw with the blind, prophetical, unsentimental eye of acceptance, which is to say, of faith. In the absence of this faith now, we govern by tenderness. It is a tenderness which, long since cut off from the person of Christ, is wrapped in theory. When tenderness is detached from the source of tenderness, its logical outcome is terror" (*CW*, 830). The terror O'Connor describes here is the kind of terror that comes when human beings seize the power to determine the value of any given life. "It ends in forced labor camps and in the fumes of the gas chamber," O'Connor concludes (*CW*, 831). When the Bishop preached Mary Ann's funeral sermon, he said the world would ask why Mary Ann should die. O'Connor has a better grasp on the values of the modern world, and she writes, "The Bishop was speaking to her family and friends. He could not have been thinking of that world, much farther removed yet everywhere, which would not ask why Mary Ann should die, but why she should be born in the first place" (*CW*, 830).

Writing in 1960, O'Connor certainly had Hitler in mind. But these words have a new salience today because we live in a world that will soon realize science's search for genetic perfection—a brave new world into which children like Mary Ann might never be allowed to be born.[17] O'Connor warns that the Cartesian legacy of "clear and

---

[17] Mary Ann is genuinely ill, but as science determines human value, the definition of "ill" can only widen, as Appleyard argues: "Of course, we might now say, But you are not sick if you tend to get angry. But what sickness is or is not tends to be defined by the prevailing wisdom. Just as genetics may come to teach us that somebody with a predisposition to heart disease later in life is sick now, so it may come to convince us that certain personality traits are sicknesses and should be treated as such. Look at the way surgery is now widely used for cosmetic purposes.

distinct ideas," cold scientific objectivity, and the desire to triumph over nature causes us to miss out on redemption because redemption is possible only through recognition of human weakness and dependency. Instead of corporate laughter at our condition, there is individual terror as we try, by our own "arts," to fix it. O'Connor writes that "the Alymers whom Hawthorne saw as a menace have multiplied. Busy cutting down human imperfection, they are making headway also on the raw material of good" (*CW*, 830).

By this we have come back around again to the role of fiction for O'Connor. Although it is an art made up completely of "lies," its highest value is honesty. It starts with the body as it is; it does not aim to transmute it to the realm of spirit. O'Connor's conception of art inverts, for example, Percy Shelley's neo-Platonic claim that poetry "transmutes all it touches, and every form moving within the radiance of its presence is changed by wondrous sympathy to an incarnation of the spirit which it breathes; its secret alchemy turns to potable gold the poisonous waters which flow from death through life; it strips the veil of familiarity from the world, and lays bare the naked and sleeping beauty which is the spirit of its forms."[18] While O'Connor's grotesques are manipulations—she called them

---

Yet do we regard ugliness as a sickness? Many people, both doctors and patients alike, now act as though it is. The possibility of changing any human condition immediately transfers that condition into the medical realm—a place dominated by the simple polarity of sickness versus health" (Bryan Appleyard, *Brave New Worlds: Staying Human in the Genetic Future* [New York: Viking, 1998] 20).

[18] Percy Bysshe Shelley, *Shelley's Poetry and Prose: A Norton Critical Edition*, ed. Sharon B. Powers and Donald H. Reiman (New York: Norton, 1977) 505. I do not mean to suggest that genre distinctions are not important; Shelley is talking about poetry, and he considered storytelling to be something entirely different. "The story of particular facts is as a mirror which obscures and distorts that which should be beautiful: Poetry is a mirror which makes beautiful that which is distorted" (485). What interests me here is how Shelley clearly privileges poetry, and with it, promotes a theory of the imagination that opposes O'Connor's views. The genre distinctions enter Bakhtin's treatment of the novel in *The Dialogic Imagination: Four Essays*, ed. Michael Holquist, trans. Caryl Emerson and Michael Holquist (Austin: University of Texas Press, 1981). For a thorough discussion of novelistic dialogism in O'Connor, see Robert H. Brinkmeyer Jr., *The Art & Vision of Flannery O'Connor* (Baton Rouge: Louisiana State University Press, 1989).

distortions—their aim is always to "use the concrete in a more drastic way" so that the reader can see what is actually there, good and bad. Shelley's poetry, in love with the human imagination, is always going to be exalted and serious; O'Connor says the look of her fiction is "going to be wild...it is almost of necessity going to be violent and comic" (*CW*, 816). As for the violent, the Catholic writer, says O'Connor, "will feel life from the standpoint of the central Christian mystery: that it has, for all its horror, been found by God to be worth dying for" (*CW*, 808). As for the comic, O'Connor would agree with William Lynch who argues that comedy's "whole function is to be a perpetual and funny, if disconcerting, reminder that it is the limited concrete which is the path to insight and salvation. Its whole art is to be an art of anamnesis, or memory, of the bloody human (in the sense in which the English use that adjective) as a path to God, or to any form of the great."[19]

O'Connor invites the reader to participate in the work of the Sisters that teaches us to deal honestly with our own lives and our own deaths. As Bakhtin describes it, the relationship between author and reader is a kind of community that bestows "aesthetic grace...a lovingly merciful justification of its being that is impossible from within the soul itself."[20] This relationship explains how art is communion, not communication, as we have seen. The artist shares his vision within a community of which he is inexorably a part. He is not the isolated genius, the unacknowledged legislator of the world who has come to save us from the failures of our unenlightened imaginations. Instead, the artist participates in the self-effacing action of charity: the "direct line" from Hawthorne's experience to his art to Mary Ann's life and to her memoir is formed through invisible acts of love within community. "This action by which charity grows invisibly among us, entwining the living and the dead, is called by the Church the Communion of Saints. It is a communion created upon human imperfection, created from what we make of our grotesque state. Of

---

[19] William F. Lynch, S. J., *The Image Industries* (New York: Sheed and Ward, 1959) 96–97.

[20] Bakhtin, *Art and Answerability,* 67.

hers Mary Ann made what, like all good things, would have escaped notice had not the Sisters and many others been affected by it and wished it written down" (*CW*, 831). What this "Communion of Saints" depends upon, in every sense of the word, is the fact of the Incarnation.

"Parker's Back" tells this story of the communion of imperfection. It is, therefore, O'Connor's most mature expression of the grotesque beauty of art driven by the Incarnation and of the human body as validated by it. It is at once her most salient revelation of the discordant face of the divine in the human and a dramatization of art's unique role in that revelation. And it gives laughter, as Bakhtin said of Cervantes, as a corrective to the narrow-minded seriousness of spiritual pretense.[21] O'Connor marked none of her characters more than she marked Obadiah Elihue Parker; through his body, O'Connor bids us to help each other stare long enough at the good to realize that "its face too is grotesque, that in us the good is something under construction."

Parker is a drifter who suddenly finds himself married to Sarah Ruth Cates, a fundamentalist interested in little more than nagging Parker and disapproving of everything around her. Parker's search for meaning leads him to get one tattoo after another until his entire body is covered, except for his back. None of his tattoos satisfy him, but in a final effort to appeal to his wife, he gets one more tattoo: the Byzantine Christ. He returns to his wife, thinking she will finally be pleased with the "looks of God" on his back, but he finds her angrier than ever. She swats him with a broom, kicks him out of the house, and leaves him crying under a tree.

Among the many critics who write about "Parker's Back," few understand the nature of its humor better than Anthony Di Renzo. Through his treatment of comedy and the carnivalesque body, he reminds us to make sure we get the joke. "Tender-minded critics believe that O'Connor's Christ can be separated from her grotesques when in fact her grotesques are her Christ. That is the central joke of her fiction, a joke that she has inherited from medieval

---

[21] Bakhtin, *Rabelais*, 22.

scholasticism."[22] Although the story is funny, it also offers a serious illustration of O'Connor's sacramental aesthetic. Parker's body is O'Connor's most apropos canvas; here she finds an image that perfectly replaces the aesthetic function of the "new jesus" in *Wise Blood*. In that novella, a dead body was the *objet d'art* that Haze needed to see; in "Parker's Back," art is incarnated on Parker's ugly, mottled back, and it is there for *us* to see. The tattoo of Jesus does more than symbolize that the Incarnation has become real for Parker, more than illustrate how Parker comes to understand that the "stern eyes," now permanently drawn on his back, are "eyes to be obeyed." The tattooed Christ marks Parker as a unique character in O'Connor's world. By focusing everyone's eyes on Parker's body and making his value a question of seeing it properly, O'Connor emphasizes what Bakhtin identifies as the specific character of verbal art: "in aesthetic seeing you love a human being not because he is good, but, rather, a human being is good because you love him."[23] Through Parker's back, O'Connor transforms artistic activity into an act of love.

To talk about O'Connor's love for her characters is to enter a critical battle. Readers often struggle to see the good in stories that feature a grandmother shot to death, a woman gored by a bull, a boy raped by a homosexual, and a retarded daughter abandoned in a restaurant. Casual readers wrote O'Connor letters that accused her of not "uplifting" them enough. John Hawkes is O'Connor's most infamous early reader; his argument that O'Connor cooperates with the devil in her treatment of characters has legendary status in O'Connor criticism.[24] One critic writes that the strength of

---

[22] Anthony Di Renzo, *American Gargoyles: Flannery O'Connor and the Medieval Grotesque* (Carbondale: Southern Illinois University Press, 1993) 57.

[23] M. M. Bakhtin, *Toward a Philosophy of the Act*, ed. Michael Holquist and Vadim Liapunov, trans. Kenneth Brostrom (Austin: University of Texas Press, 1993) 62.

[24] Hawkes writes "within her almost luridly bright pastoral world—usually created as meaningless or indifferent or corrupted—the characters of Flannery O'Connor are judged, victimized, made to appear only as absurd entities of the flesh" (John Hawkes, "Flannery O'Connor's Devil," in *Modern Critical Views: Flannery O'Connor*, ed. Harold Bloom [New York: Chelsea House, 1986] 12).

O'Connor's fiction springs from rage and that her characters are "soulless."[25] Richard Giannone wrote *Flannery O'Connor and the Mystery of Love* in part to counter these depictions of O'Connor as a misanthrope, but the theme continually reemerges, especially in feminist treatments.[26] One recent critic even suggests that O'Connor's literary technique subverts her Catholic views about God's love for his creation.[27]

"Parker's Back" answers these accusations in an exemplary way, and not just because O'Connor leaves Parker blubbering at the end of the story instead of dead. In a 1960 letter to Andrew Lytle, O'Connor wrote, "I have got to the point now where I keep thinking more and more about the presentation of love and charity, or better call it grace, as love suggests tenderness, whereas grace can be violent or would have to be to compete with the kind of evil I can make concrete" (*CW*, 1121). Grace is never cheap in O'Connor's world, and love that is mere compassion or sentiment is no love at all. Love, wanting what is best for the loved one, hurts before it heals. As C. S. Lewis wrote in *The Four Loves*, "of all arguments against love none makes so strong an appeal to my nature as 'Careful! This might lead

---

[25] Josephine Hendin writes that the characters "have no inner life. Nor, in a sense, do they have a character. Living soullessly and deadly by the frontal lines and masses, they exist on the surface of reality, anchoring themselves with things...or with *pictures* of loving hearts" (Hendin, *The World of Flannery O'Connor* [Bloomington: Indiana University Press, 1970] 155).

[26] For example, Louise Westling argues that O'Connor struggles against womankind (and the feminine in herself) by having her intellectual female characters destroyed. She applies Virginia Woolf's description of Charlotte Bronte to O'Connor: "One sees that she will never get her genius expressed whole and entire. Her books will be deformed and twisted.... She will write of herself where she should write of her characters. She is at war with her lot" (Louise Hutchings Westling, "Fathers and Daughters in Welty and O'Connor," in *The Female Tradition in Southern Literature*, ed. Carol S. Manning [Urbana and Chicago: University of Illinois Press, 1993] 5).

[27] Joanne Halleran McMullen writes that "O'Connor's linguistic choices infuse and even overtake her message creating a narrative detachment from her characters so thoroughly pervasive that the resulting fictional product works against any conviction she may have that souls are worth saving, that God's creatures may freely choose or reject his grace, or that her God is one of love or compassion" (McMullen, *Writing Against God* [Macon GA: Mercer University Press, 1996] 36).

you to suffering.'"[28] Bakhtin's discussion of the relations between author and hero in *Art and Answerability*, and Teilhard de Chardin's discussion of the Incarnation, which profoundly influenced O'Connor's later work, permit us a more nuanced idea of grace as O'Connor worked it out in the lives of her characters. By them we can gain a new sense of O'Connor's vision for fiction as an aesthetics of love.

The joke of "Parker's Back" is the divine joke of the seemingly limitless human mind placed in an obviously limited human body. Our bodies serve as constant reminders that we are no better positioned to make sense of our lives as a whole than we are to see our own backs. This is the condition in which we find Parker at the beginning of the story. Sitting on the front step, he tries to figure out the life he is in the middle of living. He cannot explain why he is with his wife Sarah Ruth, a dogmatic, judgmental fundamentalist of whom he had a suspicion that she "actually liked everything she said she didn't." Her actions nonetheless make sense to Parker even while his own do not, for, as the narrator tells us, "he could account for her one way or another; it was himself he could not understand" (*CW*, 655). Through narrative flashbacks, we follow Parker in his instinctive search for meaning and connection—he joins the navy, covers his body with tattoos, marries Sarah Ruth. At no stage can Parker make sense of himself as an individual in any way connected to his actions or his existence. Especially significant, he even hates his given name, "Obadiah Elihue," and threatens Sarah Ruth that "If you call me that aloud, I'll bust your head open" (*CW*, 662).

Of all the ways Parker tries to give himself that significance, the tattoos best reveal his motives and his problems. At age fourteen he saw a tattooed man at the fair, and the man's tattoos came together for Parker as a "single intricate design of brilliant color" (*CW*, 657). It was a high aesthetic moment for him; when he saw the whole body of another person, grotesque but somehow beautiful, it gave him his first inkling of hope. Until he had seen this man "it did not enter his head that there was anything out of the ordinary about the fact that he

---

[28] C. S. Lewis, *The Four Loves* (New York: Harcourt, Brace & Co., 1960) 120.

existed" (*CW*, 658). Trying to achieve that beautiful effect, he gets one tattoo after another, thinking each one will be the final one needed to give him the "arabesque of colors and lines" he noticed on the man. But he hates each tattoo he gets more than the last, for as he strives to see them in the mirror, they effect not an intricate arabesque of colors but "something haphazard and botched" (*CW*, 659). Parker's problem is aesthetic. In love with his body for himself, his tattoos are for his own pleasure, evidenced by the fact that he will not get any on his back. Parker had "no desire for one anywhere he could not readily see it himself" (*CW*, 659).

Parker unwittingly falls prey to the modern world's notion that we generate meaning in our lives by constructing them as we choose without needing anyone else. Parker forgets that he saw the man at the fair from "near the back of the tent, standing on a bench" (*CW*, 657). While willing to take a whole look at another man, Parker does not want anyone else to freeze his body in a "long view." Views are important in O'Connor's fiction. The narrator describes how Parker pictures his world: "The view from the porch stretched off across a long incline studded with iron weed and across the highway to a vast vista of hills and one small mountain. Long views depressed Parker. You look out into space like that and you begin to feel as if someone were after you, the navy or the government or religion" (*CW*, 661). Parker lacks the perspective to see himself whole, but he does not want to give anyone else the right or power to do it. Like many moderns, Parker believes that being a part of a community would only control him, not free him to be himself. When the tattoo artist mocks his choice of the Christ tattoo by asking, "Have you gone and got religion? Are you saved?" Parker replies, "I ain't got no use for none of that. A man can't save his self from whatever it is he don't deserve none of my sympathy" (*CW*, 669).

But Parker cannot save himself. He cannot give his own body the beauty he saw at the fair. Our inability to see or truly value our own bodies is Bakhtin's starting point in "The Author and Hero in Aesthetic Activity." For Bakhtin, our embodiment makes what he calls "aesthetic seeing"—and indeed the whole project of art—both possible and necessary. He writes that "my own exterior (that is, all of the expressive features of my body, without exception) is experienced by me from *within* myself. It is only in the form of scattered fragments, scraps, dangling on the string of my inner sensation of myself, that my own exterior enters the field of my outer senses, and, first of all, the sense of vision."[29]

Although Parker consciously resists this logic, he operates according to it. Like many of O'Connor's wayward saints, his instincts are redemptive. His first encounter with Sarah Ruth physically jolts him out of isolation: as he curses over his car, she swats him with a broom. When she takes the hand he claims to have hurt, "Parker felt himself jolted back to life by her touch" (*CW*, 657). Sensing that the body of another is life giving, Parker now uses his body and bodily appetites to court Sarah Ruth. He brings her penurious family apples and other fruit to eat; he grabs at her; he flirts by suggesting she look at his tattoos in "other places." And to her question as to whether he is saved or not, he responds, "I'd be saved enough if you was to kiss me" (*CW*, 663).

Sarah Ruth's problems with the body, as numerous critics have pointed out, are severe. She needs Parker's body to escape from her rigid fundamentalism. But few critics focus on the necessary role Sarah Ruth plays in Parker's redemption.[30] It is out of desire to please her that he goes for another tattoo, and when he does, he comes to his real bodily limitations. Because there is literally no more fleshly canvas left, Parker must get his final tattoo on the one place he cannot enjoy it himself: his back. With this tattoo, Parker is even more like a dog chasing his own tail or like a cockroach who flails his legs but cannot turn himself over. His need for her is now clear. Although Sarah Ruth disapproves of Parker, she *sees* him, and her vision keeps his existence from the realm of absurdity. For Parker "to see a tattoo on his own back he would have to get two mirrors and stand between them in just the correct position and this seemed to Parker a good way to make an idiot of himself" (*CW*, 663). Although

---

[29] Bakhtin, *Art and Answerability,* 27–28.

[30] Gentry's thesis that O'Connor characters drive themselves toward their own redemption runs into particular problems with this story.

he consciously resists Sarah Ruth because he does not want to be enframed into fatherhood, he instinctively returns to her. He needs her to give his life meaning, to be the "other" to complete the arabesque of colors, to take an aestheticizing peek at his body. Thus, the story's title as possessive explains the title as declarative: Parker's back is why Parker is always back.

Because of our inability to see ourselves, Bakhtin argues that the outside view of aesthetic seeing is a "grace gift" of which we are nearly completely passive recipients. In spite of Parker's attempts to be proactive, his real growth comes from passivity. For example, just as Parker begins to contemplate which tattoo to put on his back, he has his vision in the field: "The sun, the size of a golf ball, began to switch regularly from in front to behind him, but he appeared to see in both places as if he had eyes in the back of his head. All at once he saw the tree reaching out to grasp him. A ferocious thud propelled him into the air, and he heard himself yelling in an unbelievably loud voice, 'GOD ABOVE!'" (*CW*, 665). Everything that happens to Parker here happens to him from an outside agent. By none of his own doing, Parker's vision expands. He sees the sun both in front and behind him, as if he had eyes in the back of his head. The landscape is active, Parker, passive; the tree reaches out for him and a thud propels him into the air. He even hears his own voice as other to him, reminding him of the perspective of the ultimate seeing other: "God above." He falls flat on his back, a position of utter helplessness, and the tree catches flame. "The first thing Parker saw were his shoes, quickly being eaten by the fire; one was caught under the tractor, the other was some distance away, burning by itself. He was not in them. He could feel the hot breath of the burning tree on his face" (*CW*, 665). The narrator deliberately emphasizes bodily distances and bodily sensations: Parker's shoes are burning from afar, without him in them, and the heat of the tree affects his face.

The biblical symbolism reinforces what happens physically to Parker. The burning tree evokes the burning bush of Exodus, and the burning shoes God's command to Moses to remove his sandals because he is standing on holy ground. But what Parker must learn from it is not that he has been called to any particular duty, as Moses is called to free the Israelites, but to learn what Moses learned about himself and the Israelites in relation to God. In Exodus 3, after seeing the bush and hearing God's voice and command to lead the Israelites to freedom, Moses doubts himself and questions God: "'Suppose I go to the Israelites and say to them, "The God of your fathers has sent me to you," and they ask of me, "What is his name?" Then what shall I tell them?' God said to Moses, 'I AM WHO I AM. This is what you are to say to the Israelites: "I AM has sent me to you.""'[31] Moses' self-doubt is answered by God's ontological reality: he is the I AM, separate from them, above them and watching them, giving them both their significance and their physical deliverance.

Parker knows something has happened to him that he did not effect himself; consequently, when he goes to get the tattoo on his back, the action is already loaded with significance. Parker could not put this tattoo on himself even if he wanted to. His choice of the tattoo of the Byzantine Christ with the "all-demanding eyes" further emphasizes his bodily-based instinct that only someone with a penetrating view from elsewhere will give him the significance he seeks. It is the artist's vision; the artist does not freeze the character in a portrait but suggests, in the act of inscribing on the body, that another set of eyes is needed to truly value that body. As Bakhtin writes, the author's position outside the hero enables him to collect and complete the hero to "the point where he forms a *whole* by supplying all those moments which are inaccessible to the hero himself from within himself (such as a full outward image, an exterior, a background behind his back, his relation to the event of death and the absolute future, etc.)...to justify and to consummate the hero independently of the meaning, the achievements, the outcome and success of the hero's own forward-directed life."[32] In other words, the artist consummates and directs his hero, but the hero is also uniquely his own. For the artist's notion of beauty, the character's *existence* is far more important than what he *does*.

---

[31] Exodus 3:13–14.
[32] Bakhtin, *Art and Answerability,* 14.

Parker's significance in spite of himself and what he does is O'Connor's best apologetic for her own grotesque art. Consider the parallels between the scene of the tattoo artist's revelation of his work to Parker, the barroom scene, and Parker's later revelation of his back to Sarah Ruth. When the tattoo artist finishes the project, Parker does not want to look at it. The artist, not wanting his work to be ignored, insists. Finally "Parker looked, turned white and moved away. The eyes in the reflected face continued to look at him—still, straight, all-demanding, enclosed in silence" (*CW*, 670). It is difficult to overstate the importance of this moment. The all-demanding eyes are on Parker's own back; they are a part of him now. Parker sees that his own body animates the body of Christ. Parker's body is now a grotesque participant in the Incarnation, and Parker's understanding is sacramental, not verbal. He has been literally clothed with Christ, baptized in Christ.[33] With the eyes permanently secured on his back he can never escape the connection between his body and Christ's body that has been drawn—quite literally—for him.[34]

With Christ now animated on his back, Parker unwittingly draws an audience. When he goes to a bar to try to drink away his new knowledge, the community of men teases him about his new tattoo. When they pull up his shirt, "Parker felt all the hands drop away instantly and his shirt fell again like a veil over the face" (*CW*, 671). The apostle Paul taught that whereas Moses needed to veil his face after speaking with God "so that the children of Israel could not steadfastly behold the face of Moses, for the glory of his countenance," with the coming of Christ the veil is taken away.[35] Because of the Incarnation and the ascension, there is now no veil

---

[33] In the New Testament, the Greek word *baptizo* means change of identification, such as when one dyes a cloth a different color. Parker no longer belongs to himself.

[34] Consistent with O'Connor's aesthetic, the tattoo artist himself does not fully know the mystery he has participated in communicating. He takes no responsibility for how his work has affected Parker: "it was your idea, remember," he says, as if he knew it would speak deeply to Parker in a way he could not now avoid. "I would have advised something else" (*CW*, 670).

[35] 1 Corinthians 3:7, 14.

between God and his people, for believers now manifest God's glory in their own bodies. Christ is in them *for* them. This is what Paul emphasizes in the first part of this chapter: "Being manifested, that you are the epistle of Christ, ministered by us, and written: not with ink but with the Spirit of the living God: not in tables of stone but in the fleshly tables of the heart."[36]

When the community lifts the veil of Parker's shirt, they see Christ. The tattoo artist's grotesque creation has conveyed the mystery of the divine as it intersects with the human, Christ as he chooses the lowliest human forms to display his glory. Parker is a "little Christ" in the making. His grotesquerie is, like Mary Ann's, the face of good under construction. And as in Mary Ann's case, the community must be taught to see Christ in Parker's body in order to value it. Paul argues that we witness the transformation of our own bodies and other bodies into the image of Christ: "we all, with unveiled face beholding as in a mirror the glory of the Lord, are being transformed into the same image from glory to glory, just as from the Lord, the Spirit."[37] But the group in the bar does not want to see or participate in such a transformation; they drop the veil over Parker's back and over their spiritual eyes at the same moment.

Parker is not ready for the job anyway. He provokes a fight in the bar, and when the men throw him out the door, "a calm descended on the pool hall as nerve shattering as if the long barn-like room were the ship from which Jonah had been cast into the sea" (*CW*, 672). Critics have pointed out how Parker as reluctant prophet parallels Jonah's resistance to preach to the Ninevites, but the comparison between the two scenes is even richer. In the scriptural account, the men cast Jonah from the ship because he admits to them that the storm they are experiencing is his fault: he has disobeyed the Lord, and the Lord is punishing him. The sailors throw Jonah overboard to save themselves, but not before they get a picture of God's power, negatively but powerfully manifested in Jonah simply because God

---

[36] 1 Corinthians 3:3.
[37] 1 Corinthians 3:18, NAS.

chose him to manifest it. Likewise, Parker is a walking picture of God in spite of himself. All anyone need do is look at him.

Look at him is precisely what Parker tries to get Sarah Ruth to do. He thinks a tattoo with a religious subject will finally "bring her to heel," which for Parker means only that it would bring her to accept him, to value his body. When he returns home with the face of Christ on his back, he does not speak; he just removes the "veil." Sarah refuses to look, saying "another picture...I might have known you was off after putting some more trash on yourself." But Parker insists in the same manner the artist had: "Parker's knees went hollow under him. He wheeled around and cried 'Look at it! Don't just say that! *Look* at it!'" (*CW*, 674). Parker has a strong implicit faith that if Sarah Ruth would just stare until she could see, it would fix what he rightly senses is wrong with her. But Sarah Ruth, of course, will not look. She will not open her eyes, will not follow the lead of the artist. It is all idolatry to her.

O'Connor links Sarah Ruth's failure to understand art with her failure to see Parker's human potential, to see his body as good, as validated by the Incarnation. Her kind of Gnosticism, which O'Connor described as "the notion that you can worship in pure spirit" (*CW*, 1218), is the worst threat to both a sacramental theology and a sacramental aesthetic. Since Sarah Ruth closes her eyes to the physical world, she also closes them to the only way of salvation. She refuses to see what this living art can uniquely illustrate—that Parker, "as ordinary as a loaf of bread," is, like the Eucharist, the actual body and blood of Christ. He is the church, a temple of the Holy Ghost, not to be worshiped himself, but by his redeemed existence to lead others to God. In "Catholic Novelists and Their Readers," O'Connor describes what this has to do with fiction: "Christ didn't redeem us by a direct intellectual act, but became incarnate in human form, and he speaks to us now through the mediation of a visible Church. All this may seem a long way from the subject of fiction, but it is not, for the main concern of the fiction writer is with mystery as it is incarnated in human life" (*MM*, 176).

Late in O'Connor's career, one thinker in particular—Pierre Teilhard de Chardin—impacted her sense of how the writer is concerned with mystery as it is incarnated in human life.[38] Although O'Connor clearly did not accept all of Teilhard's ideas in their scientific application, his picture of creation as the continuation of the Incarnation of Christ appealed to her sensibilities as a novelist.[39] Teilhard was convinced, as O'Connor was even before she read him, that the Incarnation validated the ongoing creation of distinct people. God would not have taken on a human form if that form were inherently corrupted or irredeemable. Teilhard's work extends the "metaphysics of individuation" that Claude Tresmontant originally fleshed out in his *Study of Hebrew Thought*. But where Tresmontant made primarily metaphysical and linguistic claims, Teilhard makes scientific ones. In his vast work *The Phenomenon of Man* he attempts, in the words of one reviewer, to "transpose Christian revelation into a new, scientific key." Teilhard compares species variety in the natural world to the increasing differentiation of human people as the population grows. In order to name this process of growth by differentiation, he coined the word *cosmogenesis*. In *cosmogenesis*, each new birth is a particular added to the entire universe, a universe that, by God's design, brings the actual body of Christ into completion here. Each new person is valued and kept, for the universe "goes on building itself above our heads in the inverse direction of matter which vanishes. The universe is a collector and conservator, not of mechanical energy, as we supposed, but of persons."[40]

In 1961 when O'Connor reviewed Teilhard's second book, *The Divine Milieu*, she wrote in admiration of his abilities to bring the

---

[38] For a discussion of this influence, see Karl-Heinz Westarp, "Teilhard de Chardin's Impact on Flannery O'Connor: A Reading of 'Parker's Back,'" *The Flannery O'Connor Bulletin* 12 (1983). Westarp traces the progression of Parker's tattoos as they parallel Teilhard's discussion of humanity's progression toward the Omega Point: Christ.

[39] In a letter in 1961, O'Connor wrote, "I'm much taken...with 'Pere' Teilhard. I don't understand the scientific end of it or the philosophical but even when you don't know those things, the man comes through. He was alive to everything there is to be alive to and in the right way" (*HB*, 449).

[40] Pierre Teilhard de Chardin, *The Phenomenon of Man* (New York: Harper & Row, 1959) 272.

importance of the Incarnation to readers' minds. *The Phenomenon of Man*, she writes, "is scientific and traces the development of man through the chemical, biological and reflective stages of life. This second volume is religious and puts the first in proper focus. They should be read together for the first volume is liable to seem heretical without the second and the second insubstantial without the first."[41] In *The Divine Milieu*, Teilhard explains how each person's activities and passivities work together to complete the Incarnation within himself and within the world. It is a completion based on a fundamental unity between body and soul, spirit and matter. "Owing to the interrelation between matter, soul and Christ, we bring part of the being which he desires back to God *in whatever we do*. With each one of our *works*, we labour—in individual separation, but no less really—to build the Plemora; that is to say, we bring to Christ a little fulfillment."[42]

It may seem that Teilhard's system places less and less importance on the individual since "everything that rises must converge" under the new unity that is Christ. But Teilhard actually argues that Christianity is the only religion that promotes a unity in which no particularities are lost. Pantheism is his example of a "seduction" that emphasizes unity at the expense of particularity: "If it were true, it would give us only fusion and unconsciousness; for, at the end of the evolution it claims to reveal, the elements of the world vanish in the God they create or by which they are absorbed."[43] When God became incarnate on earth in a particular person and ascended into heaven in a recognizable human body, he valued particularity once and for all. He showed himself to be a God who "pushes to its furthest possible limit the differentiation among the creatures he concentrates within himself."[44]

---

[41] Leo J. Zuber, comp., *The Presence of Grace and Other Book Reviews by Flannery O'Connor*, ed. Carter W. Martin (Athens: University of Georgia Press, 1983) 108.

[42] Pierre Teilhard de Chardin, *The Divine Milieu* (New York: Harper & Row, 1960) 62.

[43] Ibid., 116.

[44] Ibid.

The particular differences are not only preserved, they are essential, for the body of Christ is constructed here on earth from the interrelations between the pieces as the light of God illuminates them. Whereas an individual is defined in isolation, a person is defined only in community. Teilhard again argues this point from the natural world: "The egocentric idea of a future reserved for those who have managed to attain egoistically the extremity of 'everyone for himself' is false and against nature. No element could move and grow except with and by all the others with itself."[45] When we look into nature, he says, we "are confounded by the interdependence of its parts. Each element of the cosmos is positively woven from all the others...here is no repetition of the same theme on a different scale. The order and design do not appear except in the whole. The mesh of the universe is the universe itself."[46]

The paradoxical notion that increased individuation is supported by and essential to interconnection provides the drama of "Parker's Back." By returning to Sarah Ruth, Parker instinctively admits he need the "Thou" of Sarah Ruth and his relationship to her to make sense of his "I" as a separate and distinct being. So he returns and stands outside her door, begging to be let in. "'It's O.E.,' he says, bamming the door two or three more times. 'O.E. Parker. You know me'" (*CW*, 673). Sarah Ruth responds that she does not know any O.E., and when she says, "Who's there?" O'Connor writes, "Parker turned his head as if he expected someone behind him to give him the answer. The sky had lightened slightly and there were two or three streaks of yellow floating above the horizon. Then as he stood there, a tree of light burst over the skyline. Parker fell back against the door as if he had been pinned there by a lance" (*CW*, 673). Parker's turn to the "someone behind him" for the answer to his identity is the turn that enables his enlightenment. When Sarah Ruth asks for the fourth time, "Who's there, I ast you?" Parker "bent down and put his mouth near the stuffed keyhole. 'Obadiah,' he whispered and all at once he felt the light pouring through him, turning his spider web soul into a

---

[45] Teilhard, *Phenomenon of Man,* 244.
[46] Ibid., 44–45.

perfect arabesque of colors, a garden of trees and birds and beasts. 'Obadiah Elihue!' he whispered" (*CW*, 673).

This scene is critical because Parker presents himself to Sarah Ruth by his given name for the first time. In a passage O'Connor marked in her copy of *A Study of Hebrew Thought*, Tresmontant explains that "each individual is created for his own sake. The Hebrew metaphysics of individuation is illustrated by the significance of the proper name in the Bible. 'I have known you by your name.' God speaks to Jeremiah as to the particular being that he is: 'before I formed you in the belly I knew you; and before you came forth out of the womb I sanctified you,' for particular beings are willed and created for their own sake. Each one's name, each one's essence is unique and irreplaceable. Each being is, in the words of Laberthonniere, *apax legomenon*."[47] When Parker gives Sarah Ruth the right to use his given name, he also assents to his given uniqueness.

The scene also outlines the role of art and aesthetic vision in the process of self-acceptance. When Parker stands at the door, he sees a tree of light burst over the skyline, and the light moves him back against the door as if pinned by a lance. When he says his name, the light pours though him, creating the arabesque of colors for which he had longed. Like the medievals, Teilhard uses the idea of light to emphasize our ability to see the interrelated nature of the parts that make up the "divine milieu." The relations have always been there—what changes is our ability to see them. Like a stained-glass window, only when each individual part is fully illuminated by light does the whole emerge. "The more fulfilled, according to their nature, are the beings in whom it comes to play, the closer and more sensible this radiance appears; and the more sensible it becomes, the more the objects which it bathes become distinct in contour...."[48]

Teilhard's ideas were of interest to O'Connor for the same reason that Maritain's and Gilson's were: he reanimated and clarified the best part of medieval philosophy. While the medieval worldview has been soundly criticized for its "totalizing" hierarchies, its

---

[47] Trestmontant, *Study of Hebrew Thought,* 98.

[48] Teilhard, *Divine Milieu,* 130–31.

"Model," according to C. S. Lewis, was recognized by its constructors as provisional. In other words, the Model had a "modest epistemological status" because new facts could disrupt it at any time.[49] While O'Connor was not interested in the medieval Model *per se*, her fiction illustrates that she was interested in the medieval conception of light in the revelation of spiritual truth, and in how that translates into art. In his book *Art and Beauty in the Middle Ages*, Umberto Eco argues that for medievals, aesthetic vision involves a "swift but complex interaction between the multiplicity of objective properties available to perception and the activity of the subject in comparing and relating them."[50] Stained glass is the best example of the medieval aesthetic moment; our ability to see it is dependent upon outside light—*lumen*—that illuminates an object and reveals its color. This idea enters "Parker's Back" directly. Only by an outside light can Parker feel the arabesque of colors coming together on his body. Jesus' eyes had seen through him before, had made him feel "as transparent as the wing of a fly," but now the light makes him beautiful.

But as I mentioned before, Parker's body has no aesthetic value without the other, so he tries to show Sarah Ruth his body under a glowing lamp. Sarah Ruth's response is to thrash him on the back with a broom. But her acceptance or rejection of Parker at the end of his story is largely a moot point.[51] While Sarah Ruth *verbally* denies Parker's body as a visible Incarnation of Christ, complaining that the image on his back is idolatrous, when she hits Parker on the back, she *actually* acknowledges him as a physical other and sets the groundwork, at least, for reconciliation between them. What is important is the communion of whole, embodied people, not the communication between mere minds. The welts that form on the

---

[49] C. S. Lewis, *The Discarded Image* (Cambridge: Cambridge University Press, 1964) 16.

[50] Umberto Eco, *Art and Beauty in the Middle Ages*, trans. Hugh Bredin (New Haven: Yale University Press, 1986) 69.

[51] The basic message of the biblical book of Obadiah is that God's purposes for his named nation, Israel, will prevail in spite of opposition. Sarah Ruth will be brought down from on high and "grounded."

image of Christ's face show Parker's identification with Christ's physical reality through his real, bodily sufferings. Teilhard argues that these "passive diminishments" contribute to the process of an individual completing the Incarnation in his or her own body. For Sarah Ruth, Parker's body, always "back," might be the starting point of her possible escape from the strictures of her fundamentalism.[52]

The automatic, instinctual drive Parker has toward Sarah Ruth's body is a source of humor for O'Connor, but it is also a serious theological point. Teilhard argues that when one loves Christ, one moves closer to loving others, and vice-versa. "Hence automatically, by a sort of living determinism, the individual divine *milieux*, in proportion as they establish themselves, tend to fuse one with another; and in this association they find a boundless increase of their ardor. This inevitable conjunction of forces has always been manifested, in the interior lives of the saints, by an overflowing love for everything that, in creatures, carries in itself a germ of eternal life."[53] Sobbing like a baby, Parker has achieved the new birth; he has identified himself with Christ. But he has also been bereaved; once again, Sarah Ruth fails to understand the nature of the connection between them.

While this may seem a far cry from Mary Ann's story, it is not. In both, the aestheticizing view of another body gives value to the grotesque body. By championing a girl with a cancerous facial tumor and a shiftless man covered with tattoos, O'Connor projects a world that, like a medieval stained-glass pane, is beautiful because nothing is lost. From the beginning to the end of her career, O'Connor used the grotesque to draw attention to something she felt needed to be seen. Here, she draws Christ on a man's body in order to illustrate the value God places on even the most ridiculous of people. Even if O'Connor were to believe that life on earth was completely meaningless, she

---

[52] As in a number of O'Connor stories, whether she will embrace her moment of grace or not is left for the reader to ponder. But if she does find God, it will be through Parker's body, as Anthony Di Renzo explains: "finally there is no other place for her, or for the reader, to find God in this story other than Parker's body. Conventional religion is the last place God is" (*American Gargoyles*, 55).

[53] Teilhard, *Divine Milieu*, 144.

would still give meaning to Parker's existence simply by choosing to tell his story. O'Connor's defense of Parker stands out against Sarah Ruth's condemnation: "at the judgment seat of God, Jesus is going to say to you, 'What you been doing all your life besides have pictures drawn all over you?'" (*CW*, 663–64). Sarah Ruth has no understanding of the grace that accepts a person's existence simply for his existence.

This, ultimately, is why "Parker's Back" concerns the artist's unique role in helping us to see ourselves as created, embodied beings. When the artist incarnates a particular character and asks us to value his life for what it can reveal, she also begs us to consider that outside eyes might also give our lives value that we cannot possibly construe from our own embodied position. Art, by its very nature, kills the idea of enlightened self-sufficiency. O'Connor does not claim a disembodied, transcendental genius role for the artist, but one who can see more than Parker can see because she is other to him. The story's title is the same as the canvas on which the tattoo artist unites an image of Christ because Parker's back is the body of the text, the only body on which his story can be seen. It is not that the artist insists that it be interpreted one way, that we make of it one grand narrative, that we find the one meaning she intended it to have. Instead, the fact that O'Connor *did render Parker at all* gives value to the narrative of his life. Even in this contemporary world that questions the existence of meaning, when we paint a canvas, mold a sculpture, or tell a story, we do not do so without purpose. Art that does not ask for some interpretation, some narrowing in of the viewer's vision, is not art at all. O'Connor bids us to look over the artist's shoulder and see Parker's back and Mary Ann's face with new eyes and a new spirit. We might be surprised—even displaced. What had been only repulsive to us might be pointing to that for which we have so long searched.

EPILOGUE

I began this study by arguing that Flannery O'Connor saw herself as a prophet called to push violently against the spirit of the age. She believed that our religious and philosophical thinkers alike have become secular and Gnostic. They are helping us only to take increasingly large strides away from a healthy view of the self—the conviction that we are created beings, made in the image of God, but limited and dependent—toward an unhealthy belief that we are cosmic accidents whose only hope is to remake ourselves into whatever image fits our fancy.

O'Connor's prophetic insistence that we are embodied, particular beings in need of redemption has never seemed more timely and relevant. We are rapidly becoming posthuman, where posthuman can be defined by the technological achievement of a disembodied autonomy that the liberal subject has always desired.[1] We are on the verge of genetically engineering our children, of literally giving them made-to-order bodies—and, we're convinced, the made-to-order lives that we assume will make them happy. But O'Connor knew that this is not an assumption we can ever afford to make. She also knew that science, with its idealistic goal to control nature and perfect humanity, has never been able to question whether we *should* do something just because we *can*. Writers must take on the role of the prophet and open our eyes to those questions.

---

[1] For a discussion of the continuity between liberal humanism and the posthuman, see N. Katherine Hayles, *How We Became Posthuman: Virtual Bodies in Cybernetics, Literature, and Informatics* (Chicago: University of Chicago Press, 1999).

One of the many contemporary writers trying to come to terms with our seemingly unlimited technological future is Lauren Slater in her essay "Dr. Daedalus." Slater's piece focuses on Joe Rosen, a plastic surgeon at the Dartmouth-Hitchcock Medical Center who dreams of giving human beings wings, fins, and other performance-enhancing implants. Rosen sees himself as an artist, and he takes his artistic vision into medical-ethics conventions where he encourages students to see plastic surgery as an avenue to a new and limitless world. Rosen asks, "Why are plastic surgeons dedicated only to restoring our current notions of the conventional, as opposed to letting people explore, if they want, what the possibilities are?"[2]

That Rosen's fascination with the possibilities of the posthuman is frighteningly myopic is apparent from his reading of Mary Shelley's *Frankenstein*. According to Slater, Rosen uses the book to teach students to see the beauty of hybrids and chimeras. While he correctly reads Shelley's concern for humanity in the way that the community mistreats Frankenstein's monster, Rosen somehow misses all of Shelley's other, more salient, warnings. It is the unchecked and irresponsible Dr. Frankenstein who is the monster here: his hubris, his isolated individualism, his grasping after ultimate power. If Dr. Frankenstein can be seen as an artist figure, he is not one that we are meant to emulate.

Rosen's posthuman fantasy makes Slater feel uneasy, too, though she has difficulties identifying why. After all, what really is the difference between fixing a man's face after he's been in a brutal car accident and giving a forked tongue to someone who wants to become an iguana? Among other concerns, Slater links her uneasiness to the problem of the modern fixation on Proteus, the mythological shape-shifting character. We are in love with our abilities to remake ourselves, she argues, and the prospect of new enhancements is certainly thrilling. But the problem is that to be all potential and future is to be nothing actual and authentic. Slater argues that "there

---

[2] Lauren Slater, "Dr. Daedalus" 4. *The Best American Science Writing 2002* (New York: HarperCollins, 2002). Edited by Matt Ridley. Series editor Jesse Cohen. pp. 1-20.

is no psychic stability, no substantive self, nothing really meaty and authentic. We sense this about ourselves. We know we are superficial, all breadth and no depth. Rosen's work embodies this tendency, literally. He desires to make incarnate the identity diffusion so common to our culture. Rosen is in our face making us face up to the fact that the inner and outer connections have crumbled. In our ability to be everything, are we also nothing?"[3]

O'Connor's fiction can help us to navigate this incredible cultural moment. Her fiction insists that there is a crucial difference between *reforming* the self and *redeeming* it—a difference essential to our view of the role of God, the artist, and human imagination. O'Connor's characters, like most Americans, either strive to reform (remake) themselves by their own power, or they feel that they are already perfect and others need to be reformed. She wants her fiction to teach us that our efforts to remake ourselves are meaningless when they deny our need for redemption. *Reformation*, as I am using the term here, is a self-generated activity. It is a desire to transcend human pain and limitations, to enter a perfect world that we construct, an Eden of our own design. But what we refuse to learn is that because this striving is always already fantastical, by definition a step beyond us, it paradoxically shuts down our potential rather than releasing it. This striving is writ large in our American culture. And instead of truly inspiring us, it renders us increasingly unable to accept our particular selves and our true particular potential.

But for O'Connor, redemption begins and ends in a different place. It begins with human limitation and ends with the *Imago Dei*—and it is the artist's job to remind us of that. The artist is not like God in that she emulates his act of creation. The artist is like God only in that she shares God's affirming vision of creation. He looks on creation with a loving eye and calls it good, without denying that it is also fallen and broken. The incarnational artist tell us that yes, creation needs to be redeemed—but also tells us that we should never forget that it is worthy of it. The artist is not the god-like plastic surgeon who promises a life without pain. That dream is actually a

---

[3] Ibid., 15.

disguised hatred of the inescapable fact of our embodiment. Instead, for O'Connor the artist is the one who returns us fully to ourselves by helping us to see the image of the Christ that is lovingly inscribed onto all of our backs, waiting to be uncovered, revealed.

BIBLIOGRAPHY

Abrams, M. H. *The Mirror and the Lamp: Romantic Theory and the Critical Tradition*. New York: Norton, 1958.

Appleyard, Bryan. *Brave New Worlds: Staying Human in the Genetic Future*. New York: Viking, 1998.

Aquinas, Saint Thomas. *Introduction to Saint Thomas Aquinas*. Edited by Anton Pegis. New York: Modern Library, 1948.

Asals, Frederick. *Flannery O'Connor: The Imagination of Extremity*. Athens: University of Georgia Press, 1982.

Bakhtin, M. M. *Art and Answerability: Early Philosophical Essays*. Edited by Michael Holquist and Vadim Liapunov. Translated by Vadim Liapunov. University of Texas Slavic Series 9. Austin: University of Texas Press, 1990.

———. *The Dialogic Imagination: Four Essays by M. M. Bakhtin*. Edited by Michael Holquist. Translated by Carl Emerson and Michael Holquist. University of Texas Slavic Series 10. Austin: University of Texas Press, 1981.

———. *Rabelais and His World*. Cambridge: MIT Press, 1968.

———. *Toward a Philosophy of the Act*. Edited by Michael Holquist. Translated by Vadim Liapunov. Austin: University of Texas Press, 1993.

Barge, Laura. "René Girard's Categories of Scapegoats and Literature of the South." *Christianity and Literature* 50/2 (2001): 247–68.

Baumgaertner, Jill P. *Flannery O'Connor: A Proper Scaring*. Wheaton IL: Harold Shaw Publishers, 1988.

Bloom, Harold. *The American Religion: The Emergence of the Post-Christian Nation*. New York: Simon & Schuster, 1992.

———. Introduction to *Modern Critical Views: Flannery O'Connor*. Edited by Harold Bloom. New York: Chelsea House Publishers, 1986.

Bordo, Susan. *The Flight to Objectivity: Essays on Cartesianism and Culture*. Albany: State University of New York Press, 1987.

Braidotti, Rosi. "Mothers, Monsters, and Machines." *Writing on the Body: Female Embodiment and Feminist Theory.* Edited by Katie Conboy, Nadia Medina, and Sarah Stanbury. New York: Columbia University Press, 1997.

Brinkmeyer, Robert H., Jr. *The Art and Vision of Flannery O'Connor.* Baton Rouge: Louisiana State University Press, 1989.

———. "Asceticism and Imaginative Vision." *Flannery O'Connor: New Perspectives.* Athens: University of Georgia Press, 1996.

———. "'Jesus Stab Me in the Heart!': *Wise Blood*, Wounding, and Sacramental Aesthetics." *New Essays on "Wise Blood."* Edited by Michael Kreyling. Cambridge: Cambridge University Press, 1995.

Burghardt, Walter J., S. J., and William F. Lynch, S. J. *The Idea of Catholicism: An Introduction to the Thought and Worship of the Church.* Cleveland: Meridian Books, 1960.

Butler, Judith P. *Gender Trouble: Feminism and the Subversion of Identity, Thinking Gender.* New York: Routledge, 1990.

Carritt, E. F., editor. *Philosophies of Beauty: From Socrates to Robert Bridges, Being the Sources of Aesthetic Theory.* Foreword by D. W. Prall. New York: Oxford University Press, 1931.

Catholic Church. *Catechism of the Catholic Church.* United States Conference of Catholic Bishops, 2000.

Chesterton, Gilbert K. *Orthodoxy.* New York: Doubleday, 1990.

Coffey, Warren. "Flannery O'Connor." *Commentary* 40/5 (1965): 96.

Dawson, David. *Literary Theory.* Guides to Theological Inquiry Series. Minneapolis: Fortress Press, 1995.

De Beauvoir, Simone. *Second Sex.* Revised edition. London: Everyman's Library, 1993.

Desmond, John F. *Risen Sons: Flannery O'Connor's Vision of History.* Athens: University of Georgia Press, 1987.

Di Renzo, Anthony. *American Gargoyles: Flannery O'Connor and the Medieval Grotesque.* Carbondale and Edwardsville: Southern Illinois University Press, 1993.

Eco, Umberto. *Art and Beauty in the Middle Ages.* Translated by Hugh Bredin. New Haven: Yale University Press, 1986.

———. *The Aesthetics of Thomas Aquinas.* Translated by Hugh Bredin. Cambridge: Harvard University Press, 1988.

Eggenschwiler, David. *The Christian Humanism of Flannery O'Connor.* Detroit: Wayne State University Press, 1972.

Emerson, Ralph Waldo. *Selected Essays.* Edited by Larzer Ziff. New York: Penguin Books, 1982.

Eliade, Mircea. *Patterns in Comparative Religion.* Translated by Rosemary Sheed. New York: Sheed and Ward, 1958.

Eliot, T. S. "Tradition and the Individual Talent." *Selected Prose of T. S. Eliot*. Edited by Frank Kermode. Orlando: *HBJ*, 1975.

Feeley, Kathleen. *Flannery O'Connor: Voice of the Peacock*. New York: Fordham University Press, 1982.

Fisher, Philip. *Still the New World: American Literature in a Culture of Creative Destruction*. Cambridge: Harvard University Press, 1999.

Fitzgerald, Robert. "The Countryside and the True Country." *Modern Critical Views: Flannery O'Connor*. Edited by Harold Bloom. New York: Chelsea House Publishers, 1986.

Fitzgerald, Sally. "Flannery O'Connor: Patterns of Friendship, Patterns of Love." *Georgia Review* 52/3 (Fall 1998): 407–25.

Foster, Michael Bishop. *Mystery and Philosophy*. Westport: Greenwood Press Publishers, 1957.

Frederic, Sister M. Catherine, O.S.F. *The Handbook of Catholic Practices*. New York: Hawthorn Books, 1964.

Friedan, Betty. *The Feminine Mystique*. 20th anniversary edition. New York: Dell Publishing Co., 1984.

Friedman, Maurice S. "Healing Through Meeting: Martin Buber and Psychotherapy." *Cross Currents* 5/4 (Fall 1955): 297–310.

Gentry, Marshall Bruce. *Flannery O'Connor's Religion of the Grotesque*. Jackson: University Press of Mississippi, 1986.

Gianonne, Richard. *Flannery O'Connor and the Mystery of Love*. Urbana: University of Illinois Press, 1989.

———. *Flannery O'Connor: Hermit Novelist*. Urbana: University of Illinois Press, 2000.

Gigante, Denise. "The Monster in the Rainbow: Keats and the Science of Life." *PMLA* 117/3 (2002): 433–48.

Gilson, Etienne. *History of Christian Philosophy in the Middle Ages*. New York: Random House, 1955.

———. *Reason and Revelation in the Middle Ages*. New York: Charles Scribner and Sons, 1938.

———. *The Unity of Philosophical Experience*. London: Sheed and Ward, 1955.

Girard, René. *Violence and the Sacred*. Translated by Patrick Gregory. Baltimore: Johns Hopkins University Press, 1977.

Gonzalez, Justo L. *The Story of Christianity: The Early Church to the Dawn of the Reformation*. Volume 1. San Francisco: HarperCollins, 1984.

Gordon, Sarah. *Flannery O'Connor: The Obedient Imagination*. Athens: University of Georgia Press, 2000.

Guardini, Romano. "Dostoyevsky's Idiot, A Symbol of Christ." *Cross Currents* 6/2 (Fall 1956): 359–82.

Haddox, Thomas F. "Contextualizing Flannery O'Connor: Allen Tate, Caroline Gordon, and the Catholic Turn in Southern Literature." *The Southern Quarterly* 38/1 (1999): 173–90.

Haraway, Donna. "The Science Question in Feminism and the Privilege of Partial Perspective." *Feminist Studies* 14/3 (Fall 1988): 575–99.

Harding, Sandra. "From Feminist Empiricism to Feminist Standpoint Epistemologies." *From Modernism to Postmodernism: An Anthology.* Edited by Lawrence E. Cahoone. Cambridge: Blackwell, 1996.

Harpham, Geoffrey Galt. *On the Grotesque: Strategies of Contradiction in Art and Literature.* Princeton: Princeton University Press, 1982.

Hawkes, John. "Flannery O'Connor's Devil." *Modern Critical Views: Flannery O'Connor.* Edited by Harold Bloom. New York: Chelsea House, 1986.

Hawthorne, Nathaniel. *Nathaniel Hawthorne's Tales: A Norton Critical Edition.* Edited by James McIntosh. New York: Norton, 1987.

Hayles, N. Katherine. *How We Became Posthuman: Virtual Bodies in Cybernetics, Literature, and Informatics.* Chicago: University of Chicago Press, 1999.

Hendin, Josephine. *The World of Flannery O'Connor.* Bloomington: Indiana University Press, 1970.

Hudson, Deal W. "'The Ecstasy Which is Creation': The Shape of Maritain's Aesthetics." *Understanding Maritain: Philosopher and Friend.* Macon GA: Mercer University Press, 1987.

Ingraffia, Brian D. *Postmodern Theory and Biblical Theology: Vanquishing God's Shadow.* Cambridge: Cambridge University Press, 1995.

Johansen, Ruthann Knechel. *The Narrative Secret of Flannery O'Connor: The Trickster as Interpreter.* Tuscaloosa: University of Alabama Press, 1994.

Joyce, James. *A Portrait of the Artist as a Young Man.* New York: Penguin, 1991.

Jung, Carl G. *Modern Man in Search of a Soul.* New York: Harvest Books, Harcourt Brace, 1933.

Kahane, Claire. "Flannery O'Connor's Rage of Vision." *Critical Essays on Flannery O'Connor.* Edited by Melvin J. Friedman and Beverly Lyon Clark. Boston: G. K. Hall & Co., 1985.

Kinney, Arthur F. *Flannery O'Connor's Library: Resources of Being.* Athens: University of Georgia Press, 1985.

Kirkwood, William G. "Parables as Metaphors and Examples." *Quarterly Journal of Speech* 71 (1985): 422–40.

———. "Storytelling and Self-Confrontation: Parables as Communication Strategies." *Quarterly Journal of Speech* 69 (1983): 58–74.

Kittel, Gerhard. *Theological Dictionary of the New Testament.* Volume 4. Grand Rapids: William B. Eerdmans, 1967.

Klug, M. A. "Flannery O'Connor and the Manichean Spirit of Modernism." *Southern Humanities Review* 17/4 (Fall 1983): 303–13.

Kristeva, Julia. *Desire in Language: A Semiotic Approach to Literature and Art*. Edited by Leon S. Roudiez. Translated by Thomas Gora, Alice Jardine, and Leon S. Roudiez. New York: Columbia University Press, 1980.

Leiva-Merikakis, Erasmo. *Fire of Mercy, Heart of the Word: Meditations on the Gospel According to St. Matthew*. Volume 1. San Francisco: Ignatius Press, 1996.

Lewis, C. S. *The Discarded Image*. Cambridge: Cambridge University Press, 1964.

———. *The Four Loves*. New York: Harcourt, Brace & Co., 1960.

Lubbock, Percy. *The Craft of Fiction*. New York: The Viking Press, 1957.

Lundin, Roger. *The Culture of Interpretation: Christian Faith and the Postmodern World*. Grand Rapids: William B. Eerdmans, 1993.

Lynch, William F., S. J. *Christ and Apollo: The Dimensions of the Literary Imagination*. New York: Sheed and Ward, 1960.

———. *The Image Industries*. New York: Sheed and Ward, 1959.

MacIntyre, Alasdair C. *Dependent Rational Animals: Why Human Beings Need the Virtues*. Chicago: Open Court, 1999.

Magee, Rosemary M., editor. *Conversations with Flannery O'Connor*. Jackson: University of Mississippi Press, 1987.

Marcel, Gabriel. *The Mystery of Being*. London: The Harvill Press, 1950.

Maritain, Jacques. *Approaches to God*. Translated by Peter O'Reilly. New York: Harper, 1954.

———. *Art and Scholasticism and the Frontiers of Poetry*. Translated by Joseph W. Evans. New York: Charles Scribner's Sons, 1962.

———. *Creative Intuition in Art and Poetry*. New York: Pantheon Books, 1953.

———. *The Range of Reason*. New York: Charles Scribner's Sons, 1952.

Martin, Carter W. *The True Country: Themes in the Fiction of Flannery O'Connor*. Nashville: Vanderbilt University Press, 1968.

May, John R. *The Pruning Word: The Parables of Flannery O'Connor*. Notre Dame: University of Notre Dame Press, 1976.

McCarthy, Cormac. *The Crossing*. New York: Alfred A. Knopf, 1994.

McFague, Sallie. "The Parabolic in Faulkner, O'Connor, and Percy." *Notre Dame English Journal* 40 (Spring 1983): 49–66.

McMullen, Joanne Halleran. *Writing Against God: Language as Message in the Literature of Flannery O'Connor*. Macon GA: Mercer University Press, 1996.

Mellard, James M. "Framed in the Gaze: Haze, *Wise Blood*, and Lacanian Reading." *New Essays on "Wise Blood."* Edited by Michael Kreyling. Cambridge: Cambridge University Press, 1995.

Miles, Margaret. "Carnal Abominations: The Female Body as Grotesque." *The Grotesque in Art and Literature: Theological Reflections*. Edited by James Luther Adams and Wilson Yates. Grand Rapids: Eerdmans, 1997.

Milton, John. *Paradise Lost*. Edited by Scott Elledge. New York: Norton, 1975.

Mounier, Emmanuel. *Personalism*. Translated by Philip Mairet. New York: The Grove Press, 1952.

Oates, Joyce Carol. "The Visionary Art of Flannery O'Connor." *Modern Critical Views: Flannery O'Connor*. Edited by Harold Bloom. New York: Chelsea House Publishers, 1986.

O'Connor, Flannery. *Collected Works*. Edited by Sally Fitzgerald. New York: Library of America, 1988.

———. *The Habit of Being: Letters of Flannery O'Connor*. Edited by Sally Fitzgerald. New York: Farrar, Straus and Giroux, 1979.

———. *Mystery and Manners: Occasional Prose*. Edited by Sally Fitzgerald and Robert Fitzgerald. New York: Farrar, Straus and Giroux, 1969.

Paulson, Suzanne Morrow. "Apocalypse of Self, Resurrection of the Double: Flannery O'Connor's *The Violent Bear It Away*." *Flannery O'Connor: New Perspectives*. Athens: University of Georgia Press, 1996.

Pegis, Anton C., editor. *Introduction to St. Thomas Aquinas*. New York: The Modern Library, 1948.

Poe, Edgar Allan. *Selected Writings of Edgar Allan Poe*. Edited by Edward H. Davidson. Boston: Houghton Mifflin, 1956.

Prown, Katherine Hemple. *Revising Flannery O'Connor: Southern Literary Culture and the Problem of Female Authorship*. Charlottesville: University Press of Virginia, 2001.

Ragen, Brian Abel. *A Wreck on the Road to Damascus: Innocence, Guilt, & Conversion in Flannery O'Connor*. Chicago: Loyola University Press, 1989.

Ransom, John Crowe. *The World's Body*. New York: Charles Scribner's Sons, 1938.

Rorty, Richard. *Philosophy and the Mirror of Nature*. Princeton: Princeton University Press, 1979.

Seel, Cynthia. *Ritual Performance in the Fiction of Flannery O'Connor: Studies in American Literature and Culture*. Rochester NY: Camden House, 2001.

Shaw, Mary Neff. "'The Artificial Nigger': A Dialogical Narrative." *Flannery O'Connor: New Perspectives*. Athens: University of Georgia Press, 1996.

Shelley, Percy Bysshe. *Shelley's Poetry and Prose: A Norton Critical Edition*. Edited by Sharon B. Powers and Donald H. Reiman. New York: Norton, 1977.

Shloss, Carol. "Epiphany." *Modern Critical Views: Flannery O'Connor*. Edited by Harold Bloom. New York: Chelsea House Publishers, 1986.

Slater, Lauren. "Dr. Daedalus" 4. *The Best American Science Writing 2002* (New York: HarperCollins, 2002). Edited by Matt Ridley. Series editor Jesse Cohen. pp. 1-20.

Stephens, Martha. *The Question of Flannery O'Connor*. Baton Rouge: Louisiana State University Press, 1973.

Stevens, Wallace. *The Necessary Angel: Essays on Reality and the Imagination*. New York: Vintage, 1951.

Stevens, Wallace. *Opus Posthumous*. Edited by Milton J. Bates. New York: Vintage, 1990.

Stevens, Wallace. "Notes Toward a Supreme Fiction." *The Palm at the End of the Mind.* Edited by Holly Stevens. Vintage Books edition. New York: Knopf, 1989.

Sussman, Henry. *The Aesthetic Contract: Statutes of Art and Intellectual Work in Modernity*. Stanford: Stanford University Press, 1997.

Tanner, Stephen L. "Flannery O'Connor and Gabriel Marcel." *Literature and Belief* 17/1–2 (1997): 149–57.

Tate, Allen. *The Forlorn Demon: Didactic and Critical Essays*. Chicago: Regnery, 1953.

Teilhard de Chardin, Pierre. *The Divine Milieu*. New York: Harper & Row, 1960.

———. *The Phenomenon of Man*. New York: Harper & Row, 1959.

Tocqueville, Alexis de. *Democracy in America*. Edited by Richard D. Heffner. New York: New American Library, 1956.

Tresmontant, Claude. *A Study of Hebrew Thought*. Translated by Michael Francis Gibson. New York: Desclee Company, 1960.

Verderame, Carla L. "A Retreat Home: Flannery O'Connor's Disempowered Daughters." *The Flannery O'Connor Bulletin* 26–27 (1998–2000): 139–53.

Von Hügel, Baron Friedrick. *Essays and Addresses on the Philosophy of Religion: First Series*. New York: E. Press. Dutton, 1928.

———. *Essays and Addresses on the Philosophy of Religion: Second Series*. New York: E. P. Dutton, 1930.

Westarp, Karl-Heinz. "Teilhard de Chardin's Impact on Flannery O'Connor: A Reading of 'Parker's Back.'" *The Flannery O'Connor Bulletin* 12 (1983): 93–113.

Westling, Louise. *Sacred Groves and Ravaged Gardens: The Fiction of Eudora Welty, Carson McCullers, and Flannery O'Connor*. Athens: University of Georgia Press, 1985.

———. "Fathers and Daughter in Welty and O'Connor." *The Female Tradition in Southern Literature*. Edited by Carol S. Manning. Urbana and Chicago: University of Illinois Press, 1993.

Wood, Ralph C. "From Fashionable Tolerance to Unfashionable Redemption." *Modern Critical Views: Flannery O'Connor*. Edited by Harold Bloom. New York: Chelsea House Publishers, 1986.

Yaeger, Patricia Smith. *Dirt and Desire: Reconstructing Southern Women's Writing, 1930–1990*. Chicago: University of Chicago Press, 2000.

Yeats, W. B. *The Collected Poems of W. B. Yeats*. Edited by Richard J. Finneran. New York: Collier, 1989.

Zuber, Leo J., compiler. *The Presence of Grace and Other Book Reviews by Flannery O'Connor*. Edited by Carter W. Martin. Athens: University of Georgia Press, 1983.

INDEX